IMAGES
of Rail

THE ANN ARBOR RAILROAD

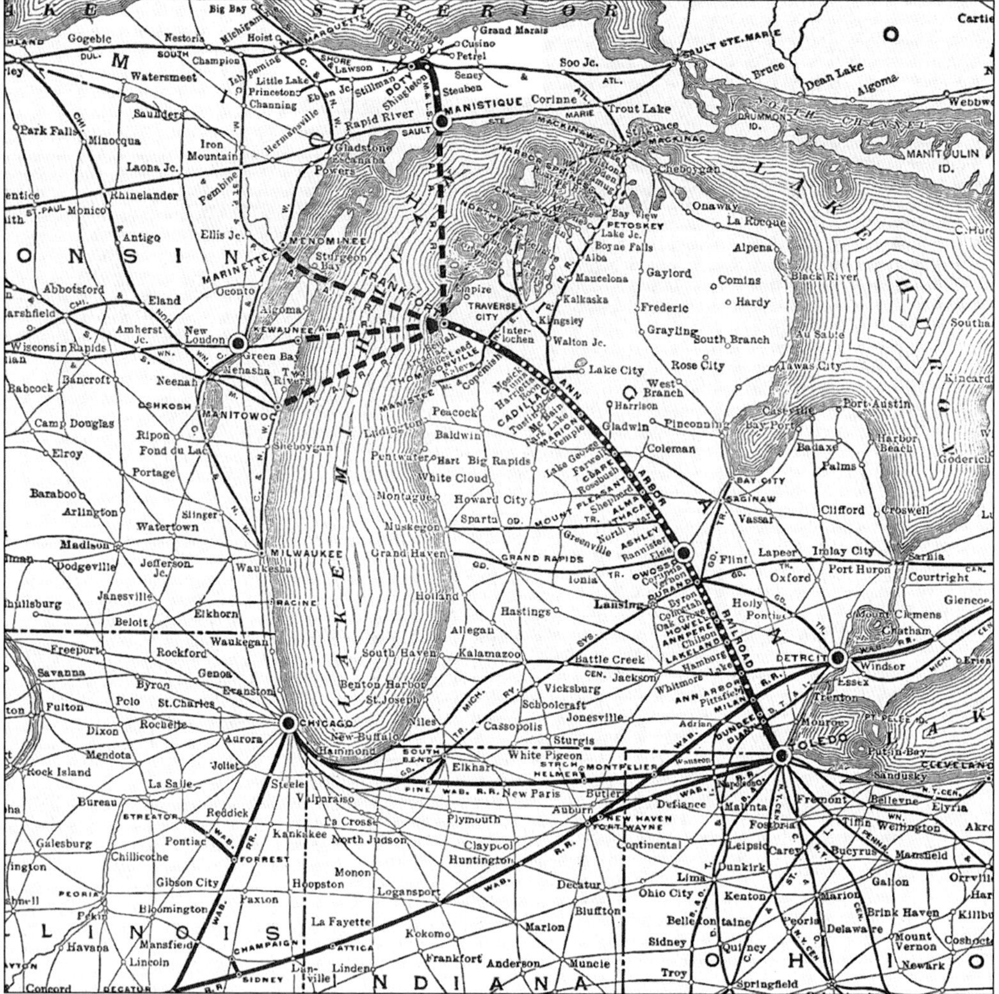

SPANS THE STATE. This map shows the route of the Ann Arbor Railroad and its four steamship lines, as they existed in 1943. The connecting lines of the Wabash Railroad, which controlled the Ann Arbor from 1925 to 1963, are also shown. (Collection of D. C. Jesse Burkhardt.)

Cover: The Ann Arbor Railroad's Boat Landing Yard in Elberta, Michigan, is pictured *c.* 1938. (Courtesy of the Claude T. Stoner Collection, Bentley Historical Library, University of Michigan.)

IMAGES
of Rail

THE ANN ARBOR RAILROAD

D. C. Jesse Burkhardt

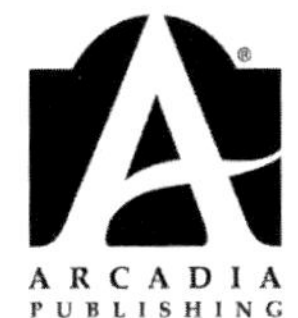

ISBN 978-0-7385-3429-9

Published by Arcadia Publishing
Charleston, South Carolina

Printed in the United States of America

Library of Congress Catalog Card Number: 2005927495

For all general information contact Arcadia Publishing at:
Telephone 843-853-2070
Fax 843-853-0044
E-mail sales@arcadiapublishing.com
For customer service and orders:
Toll-Free 1-888-313-2665

Visit us on the Internet at www.arcadiapublishing.com

*For the mariners of the Great Lakes region . . .
and for all the crews who brought trains
over the Ann Arbor line.*

Contents

Foreword

In 1964, shortly after the Detroit, Toledo & Ironton gained control of the Ann Arbor Railroad, the Ann Arbor obtained 10 new road locomotives in exchange for its fleet of aging Alco FAs. In a stark departure from the classic blue-gray scheme that had graced the rails under Wabash ownership, the new GP35 diesels arrived in bright orange paint with giant black billboard lettering spelling out "Ann Arbor" on the sides. To further put a DT&I stamp on the new power, the locomotives entered service with a compass herald placed just below the cab windows, along with the phrase: *We Have the Connections*. While this was actually just a simple extension of the existing DT&I marketing effort to promote its own rail system, the slogan applied to the new Ann Arbor diesels turned out to have a much deeper meaning. As history demonstrates, it seems almost certain that no more appropriate words have ever been stenciled on a locomotive.

My connection with the boats and trains of the Ann Arbor Railroad began in the early 1970s, when visits to my grandparents' summer home on Lake Michigan would invariably include a detour to Frankfort. After a quick stop at the downtown bakery for a bag of fresh doughnuts, we would drive around Betsie Bay to park along M-168 in Elberta. Then, in the moment I had been anticipating for the entire trip, my dad would boost me up to the roof of the car. And it was there on top of the family Pontiac, bathed in the light of a perfect northern Michigan dawn, that I fell in love with the marvelous machines working along the harbor.

During the same time period, and quite possibly on many of the same mornings, D. C. Jesse Burkhardt—who was then living in Ann Arbor—began exploring this classic Midwestern shortline from an entirely different perspective. Being older, and not under the eye of a watchful parent, Jesse experienced a much more personal connection with the railroad. Over the years, he was motivated enough to hike along the entire line, and to occasionally travel on the carferries. Fortunately, he sometimes carried a camera on these adventures.

Thirty years later, Jesse's photographs led to our friendship and collaboration. In the process of collecting a broad variety of memorabilia from this great railroad, I purchased an old "bad order" card from Jesse. When the package arrived, I found he had included pictures he'd taken from a variety of locations along the Ann Arbor line. Our subsequent conversations led to the discovery that we both had a passion for the Ann Arbor Railroad.

Why is it that somehow, for reasons beyond our understanding, this particular railroad made such a connection in our souls? How could words painted on the side of a locomotive evoke so much feeling? What magic was contained in two lengths of steel spiked to a bed of ties spread across northern Ohio and the Lower Peninsula of Michigan? Was it the way the track stretched to both horizons, connecting the here and now with far away places and times? Was it the mysterious way flanges would sing softly along the rails as a slow-moving train eased through a sharp curve and faded quietly into the north woods? Or was it perhaps the lasting memory of a ferry apron at dusk, silhouetted against Lake Michigan with the last glimmer of a late summer sunset reflecting from rails that reached out to the unseen Wisconsin shore?

For those who loved this railroad, it was not just ties and rails or ballast and right of way. It was not just back-to-back sets of locomotives pulling a long train with a traditional red caboose up the grade to Cadillac, nor was it ferries doing battle against waves and wind on the great lake. It was all of this, but it was much more—it was a living entity that connected people, places, and machines with a legacy of unspoken, time-honored tradition. It was a deep-rooted community that spanned geography and generations. It was a way of life.

It was the aura of progress you could feel at the turn of the 20th century as the railroad spurred the growth of sawmills and icehouses and grand hotels. It was the promise of new prosperity, attainable through the hard work and dedication of marine and rail workers and their families, who settled and developed the towns along the line.

It was the smell of Manitowoc, Wisconsin, in the 1930s: the air thick with coal smoke from carferries and steam locomotives working in choreographed harmony to carefully sort and load freight cars for the 80-mile journey across Lake Michigan to the Ann Arbor's home port at Elberta.

It was the sound of Boat Landing Yard in the 1950s, as burbling Alco diesel switchers shoved strings of hoppers and boxcars to clank and clatter along the tracks. It was the gentle slapping of waves along the seawall, and the soft creaking of a wooden apron as a ferry was being loaded at a weather-beaten slip. It was the signature blast of the carferry whistles that for decades provided an exquisite accompaniment to the entire scene, as the unmistakable echoes reverberated off the lush green hills and across the water of Betsie Bay.

It was the sight of boxcars lined up in Ferry Yard behind Michigan Stadium during the 1970s: loaded with auto parts visible through half-open doors, patiently waiting to be delivered to the Ford plant in Saline, or perhaps to be interchanged with Penn Central in the shadow of the classic girder bridges spanning Main Street and the Huron River. For almost a century, you could feel the connections.

But now the tracks at Ferry Yard in Ann Arbor are empty and overgrown with weeds, and the wind blows gently through the cast-iron handles of switches that will be thrown no more. There are trees growing through the rails on the old Ann Arbor-Penn Central interchange, and the Main Street crossing has long since been paved over. The loading aprons on the south shore of Betsie Bay are bare, the counterweights hang askew, and the coal tower leans like an ever-vigilant ghostly sentinel over the remains of the turntable and the abandoned roundhouse. But there are no engines left to turn, and only in the imagination will the Ann Arbor's orange diesels ever be seen again toiling along the shore, framed against the colorful foliage of a cool, crisp autumn morning.

Yet while many of the physical connections are gone, the legacy of the Ann Arbor Railroad lives on. It lives in childhood memories of sitting on top of a car parked along the hill above the bay, and in the sights and sounds from docks that will in my mind forever be alive with the magical movement of boats and trains.

It lives in the photos taken by a young man as he was out on the breakwater or hiking along the line. It lives in the priceless recollection of carferry rides, and in pictures snapped to ensure that history was being adequately recorded as an era moved toward its end. It lives in the hearts and souls of all who were privileged enough to experience this amazing railroad, and it lives in the pages of this book.

It has now been more than 40 years since the Ann Arbor Railroad's new diesels received their famous slogan. As I conclude this foreword, my faithful dog "Annie" lies patiently at my feet, and there is a photo on my desktop of the *Viking* being loaded in the west slip at Boat Landing. I still feel the connections.

Kristian N. Foondle
Saline, Michigan
February 28, 2005

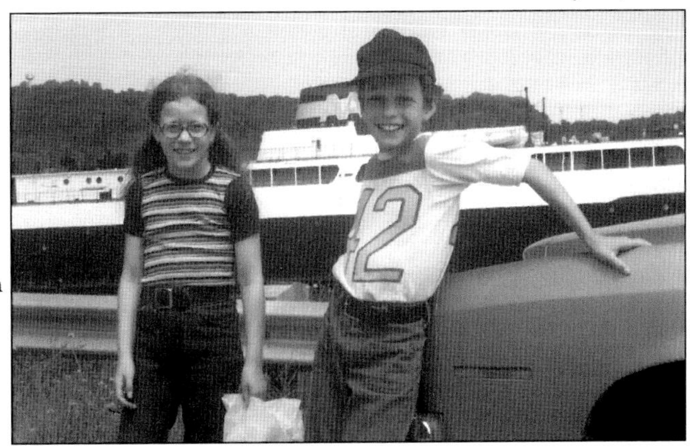

LASTING CONNECTIONS. Kristian Foondle and his sister Lissa are pictured at Elberta, Michigan, in 1974. In the background is the Ann Arbor's *Arthur K. Atkinson*. (Photo by James A. Foondle.)

ACKNOWLEDGMENTS

The author appreciates the assistance of the following individuals and organizations for their valuable contributions to this book: Geoff Holmes, John Pearson, Maura Brown, and all of the Arcadia Publishing team, for recognizing the value of celebrating history and keeping alive vital images from our past; Kristian N. Foondle of Saline, Michigan, a dedicated professional with the Michigan Department of Transportation, who writes so eloquently about his appreciation for the Ann Arbor Railroad; Leslie and Clare Burkhardt, always and for everything—including understanding and supporting my many trips to my home state of Michigan; Robert and Lois Burkhardt, for choosing a house so close to the tracks when I was growing up in Jackson, Michigan, my birthplace; Grover and Ruth Sparling, for introducing me to the magic of Frankfort in the summer of 1969; Scott Sparling of Lake Oswego, Oregon, for providing some great photos—and for our many travels on the carferries in the height of the free summers; Thomas Lacinski of Maple City, Michigan, for sharing the remarkable voyage on the *Chief Wawatam* in 1977, and for the trips to Thompsonville and Clare and Boon and elsewhere in northern Michigan to witness the changes over the years; Harold K. Vollrath of Kansas City, Missouri, for maintaining a great collection of historical photos and offering to share them in this book; Dennis Schmidt of Alma, Michigan, for providing a treasure of images spanning three decades of Ann Arbor Railroad operations; Kathleen Osterhaus, curator/director of the Benzie Area Historical Society in Benzonia, Michigan, for contributing items from the organization's grand collection of historical photos; Karen Jania and Malgorzata Myc of the Bentley Historical Museum of the University of Michigan in Ann Arbor, for providing the excellent material from the lens of Claude Thomas Stoner; and the Tuscola & Saginaw Bay Railway Company of Owosso, Michigan, for contributing the map of Michigan's contemporary railroad routes.

Thanks also to the many contributors of photographs and memorabilia and other support: Larry Yaek, St. Clair, Michigan; Marie Groshans, Ypsilanti, Michigan; Jim Rees, Ann Arbor, Michigan; Kelly Fairchild, Frankfort, Michigan; Ron Morse, Springfield, Missouri; Bill Bunch, Terre Bonne, Missouri; Jim King, Waseca, Minnesota; James Hannum, Olympia, Washington; Joseph Geronimo, Endwell, New York; Bob Dobyne, Bingen, Washington; Lee Hillier, Owosso, Michigan; Chelsea White, Ann Arbor, Michigan; and Michael Leon, Okemos, Michigan. Special appreciation to the Friends of the Betsie Valley Trail, in Beulah, Michigan, for helping to create a sweet trail on the former Ann Arbor Railroad corridor between Thompsonville and Frankfort. And many thanks to all those who provided information via the www.MichiganRailroads.com Web site—it is an outstanding resource.

INTRODUCTION

Despite the richly deserved focus on its carferry operations, the Ann Arbor Railroad was a strong freight carrier at its core. With a mainline that originated in the industrial Lake Erie port city of Toledo, Ohio, the Ann Arbor stretched northwest in a diagonal line across almost the full length of the Lower Peninsula of Michigan to reach Frankfort and neighboring Elberta, Michigan.

At Elberta, the AA's tracks terminated literally on the shore of Lake Michigan, at the romantically named Boat Landing Yard. From that facility, the Ann Arbor Railroad blended trains and carferries to operate a unique, seamless transportation system that thrived for nearly a century.

The Ann Arbor's origins can be traced back to the 1880s, when the Toledo, Ann Arbor & North Michigan Railway was incorporated, with entrepreneur and former Montana governor James Mitchell Ashley serving as its first president. Tracks finally connected Toledo with Frankfort in 1892, and in November of that year, the first Lake Michigan carferry—the 260-foot, wood-hulled *Ann Arbor #1*—made its inaugural 62-mile run between Elberta and Kewaunee, Wisconsin. Less than three years after that milestone—on September 21, 1895—the Toledo, Ann Arbor & North Michigan was reorganized as the Ann Arbor Railroad Company.

At its peak, the "Double A" operated out of its Elberta terminal with boats that carried freight cars and passengers to four different ports: Kewaunee and Manitowoc in Wisconsin, and Manistique and Menominee in Michigan's Upper Peninsula. (For a brief period beginning in 1895, the AA also hauled freight cars to Gladstone, Michigan, on a seasonal basis. Boats alternated between landing at Gladstone in the warm months and at Manistique in the winter, but in 1902 the Gladstone route was dropped and service was shifted permanently to Manistique.) The combined mileage of the 4 carferry routes—approximately 320 miles over the water—actually exceeded the distance covered by the railroad's land route from Toledo to Elberta, which was 292 miles.

The railroad was conceived as a Chicago bypass that could shave as much as a week off east-west transit times for freight cars that would otherwise have to move through Chicago's maze of tracks and yards, and its carferry fleet included a total of nine different boats. Depending on the carferry's design and the size of the freight cars, each boat carried between 20 and 32 cars on tracks attached to the floor of the hold. Loading and unloading operations at the docks required a delicate and experienced hand; crews switching the ferries had to follow strict procedures or risk having the weight of the freight cars become unbalanced and possibly capsize the boat.

For decades, the identity of the communities of Elberta and Frankfort revolved around the ferry system. Its economic impact on the city was tremendous, as the railroad and ferry operations were the biggest employer in the area.

The Ann Arbor Railroad moved commodities such as lumber, grain, farming machinery, automobile parts, coal, sand, and cement along its scenic route. The "Annie" also served connections with many other railroads. In the 1950s, it linked with no fewer than nine other carriers at its southern terminus of Toledo. Heading north from Toledo, the steel rails of the Ann Arbor crossed and interchanged traffic with a long list of connecting railroads, with names that read like an index of American transportation history. Included in the venerable register were the following: the Wabash Railroad at Milan, the New York Central at Ann Arbor, the Grand Trunk Western at Durand, the Chesapeake & Ohio at Clare, and the Pennsylvania Railroad at Cadillac.

The extensive carferry fleet then lined up the Ann Arbor's rails with those of the Green Bay & Western (in Kewaunee), the Chicago & North Western (Menominee and Manitowoc), the Manistique & Lake Superior (Manistique), the Chicago, Milwaukee, St. Paul & Pacific (Menominee), and the Soo Line (Manitowoc and Manistique). With its many connecting lines, the Ann Arbor Railroad was a virtual transcontinental player on America's railroad map.

The Ann Arbor also made a series of business moves over the years in efforts to expand its reach. It acquired control of the Manistique & Lake Superior Railroad in 1911, which gave the railroad an additional 40 miles of trackage in Michigan's Upper Peninsula. The M&LS operated from the AA ferry slip in Manistique north to Doty, where it connected with the Duluth, South Shore & Atlantic (later to become part of the Soo Line Railroad). As traffic declined in the 1960s, however, the M&LS became an economic drain to the Ann Arbor, and the entire line was abandoned in 1968.

In 1925, the Ann Arbor came under the control of the Wabash Railroad through a stock purchase, thus making the AA part of a larger rail system. The arrangement with the Wabash lasted until 1963, when the Detroit, Toledo & Ironton Railroad purchased the Ann Arbor, and the Double A traded Wabash blue for the orange and black paint of new parent DT&I.

The beginning of the end for the Ann Arbor Railroad came when the carrier declared bankruptcy on October 15, 1973. Ironically, the bankruptcy came, in part, because the Ann Arbor could not repay a loan to the DT&I, which had provided $2.5 million in 1965 for the rebuilding of one of its carferries, *Ann Arbor #7*.

By the early 1970s, only two of the Ann Arbor's carferry routes were still operating—those to Kewaunee and to Manitowoc. Service to Manistique had ended with the demise of the M&LS in 1968, and the Menominee run was dropped in 1970.

As the Penn Central bankruptcy and reorganization was taking place in the mid-1970s, operation of the Ann Arbor was briefly conveyed to the freshly minted Conrail system. Conrail ran the Ann Arbor's trains and carferry system from April 1, 1976, until September 30, 1977, as its "Ann Arbor Division."

In order to preserve service in the corridor, the state of Michigan purchased the entire Ann Arbor route, and on October 1, 1977, freight and ferry operations were turned over to the Michigan Interstate Railway. That deal worked for five years, but in April 1982, Michigan Interstate stopped running trains north of the city of Ann Arbor, and the ferry system soon succumbed. *Viking*, the last carferry operating out of Elberta, steamed to Kewaunee for the final time on April 27, 1982.

In the contemporary era, the Ann Arbor has been sharply abbreviated from its once-long reach. In October 1988, the Ann Arbor Acquisition Corporation purchased the 50-mile stretch of track linking Toledo and Ann Arbor, and formed a privately-owned shortline that retained the name Ann Arbor Railroad.

Another carrier, however, has kept almost all of the rest of the original Ann Arbor's route active. The Tuscola & Saginaw Bay Railway stepped in after Michigan Interstate dropped out in 1982, and operates from where it connects with the "new" Ann Arbor Railroad at Osmer—5 miles north of the city of Ann Arbor—all the way to a sand pit at Yuma, a total of nearly 200 miles. The state of Michigan maintains ownership of the Osmer-Yuma trackage. As of 2005, the only section of the original AA trackage no longer in service is the stretch northwest from Yuma to Elberta. That 44-mile portion was abandoned in the late 1980s. The last freight train out of Elberta—a "clean-up" run to haul the remaining rolling stock left in Boat Landing Yard—pulled outbound for Cadillac on July 21, 1988.

Beyond the nuts and bolts of the history and economics of the Ann Arbor Railroad, there remains something grand and wonderful in the immeasurable sensation—now lost forever—of crossing Lake Michigan on the *Arthur K. Atkinson* under the full Midwestern moonlight; or feeling the *Viking's* four 16-cylinder Electro-Motive Division diesels throbbing with restrained roar as the boat cut through the water at a top speed of 21 miles per hour.

There was always something mysterious and ritualistic about the carferries, crossing the lake with their bellies full of freight cars bound for unseen ports. That heritage is dearly missed, not only by the mariners who operated the legendary boats, but also by so many who witnessed the Ann Arbor Railroad's operations. Those of us who watched freight cars being swallowed up by the Ann Arbor's distinctive fleet will never forget.

D. C. Jesse Burkhardt
White Salmon, Washington
April 12, 2005

One

Rolling Tonnage: Moving the Double A's Freight

A distant air horn reached me, and soon an Ann Arbor northbound came through Cadillac in a rush; the train was short and fast, apparently in a big hurry to get to Frankfort with its consist of boxcars and covered hoppers. The freight was probably the only northbound of the day.

—D. C. Jesse Burkhardt, journal entry, July 15, 1977

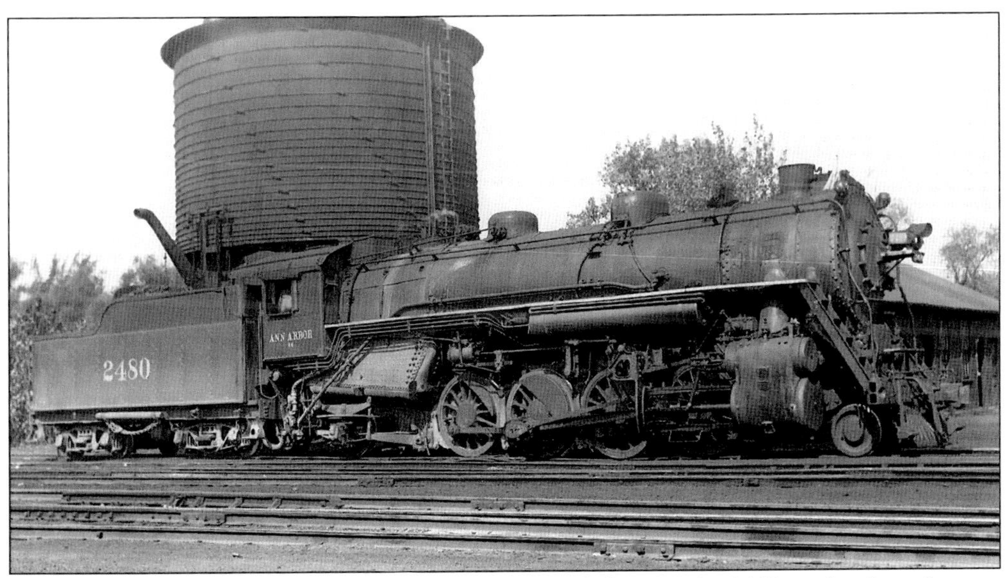

Resting by the Water Tank. The massive Ann Arbor 2-8-2 #2480, with white flags up front, idles next to the water tank at the railroad's yard in Owosso, Michigan, in an undated scene. (Collection of D. C. Jesse Burkhardt.)

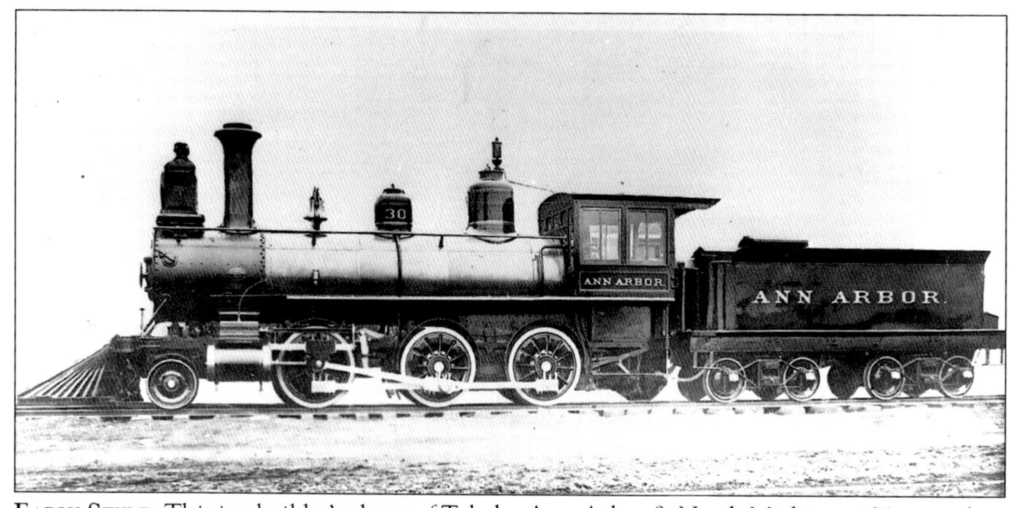

EARLY STYLE. This is a builder's photo of Toledo, Ann Arbor & North Michigan #30, a product of the Pittsburgh Locomotive & Car Works in Pittsburgh, Pennsylvania. TAA&NM #30, a 2-6-0 type, was built in 1887. The Pittsburgh Locomotive Works was one of seven locomotive manufacturers that merged with the Schenectady Locomotive Works in 1901, thus forming the famed American Locomotive Company. (Collection of Harold K. Vollrath.)

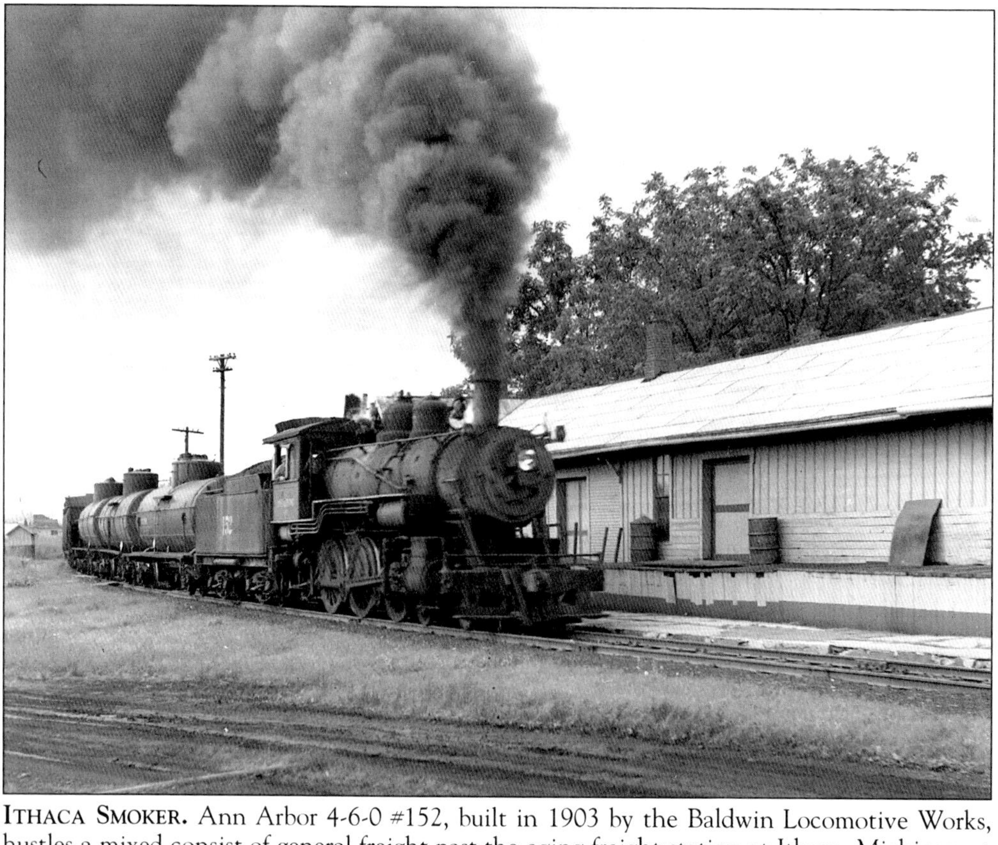

ITHACA SMOKER. Ann Arbor 4-6-0 #152, built in 1903 by the Baldwin Locomotive Works, hustles a mixed consist of general freight past the aging freight station at Ithaca, Michigan, at Milepost 138.3. This locomotive was scrapped in 1933. (Collection of D. C. Jesse Burkhardt.)

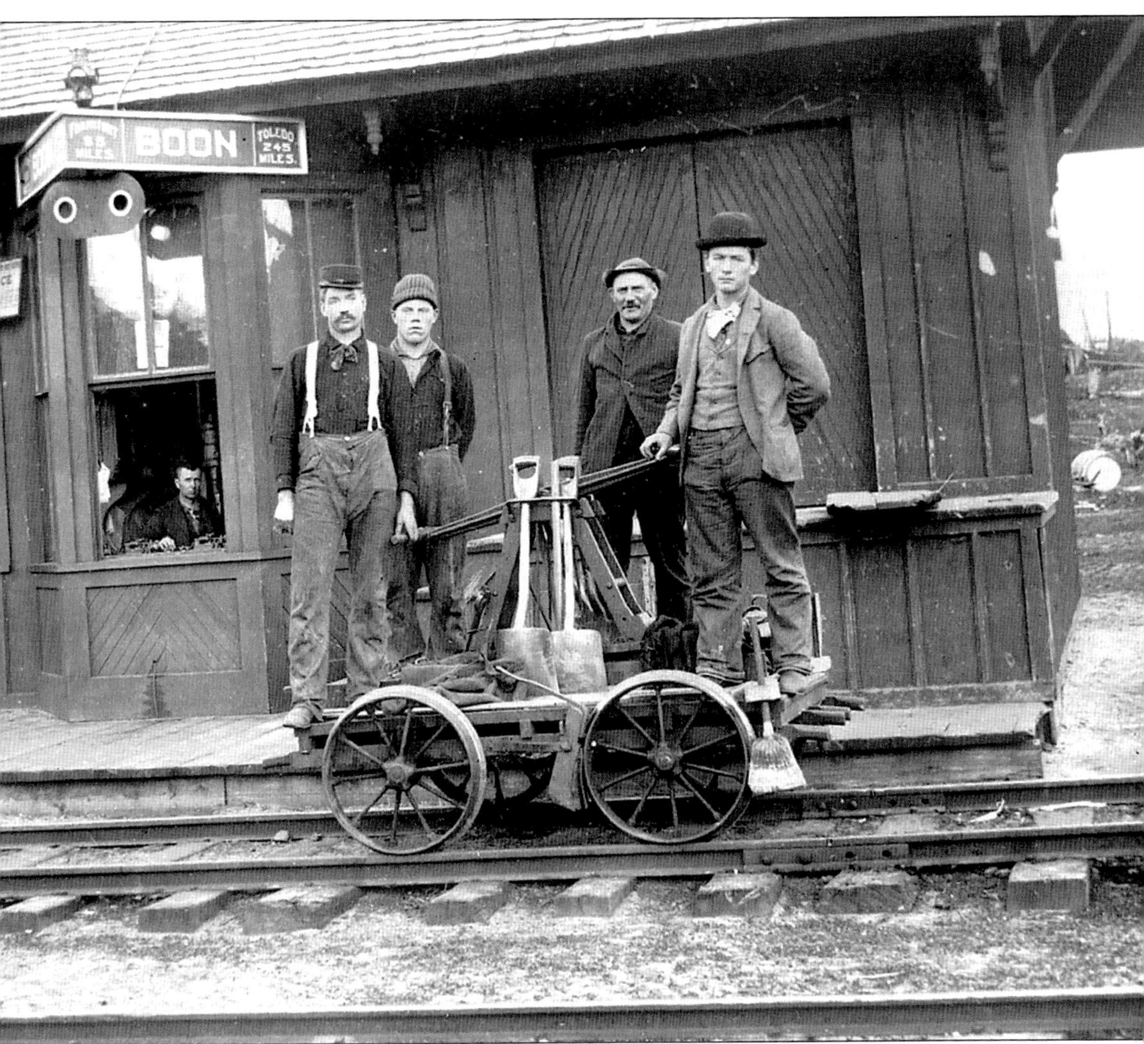

On the Job at Boon. An Ann Arbor Railroad section crew on a handcar loaded with shovels pauses for a photograph at Boon, Michigan, in the early 1890s. The telegrapher in the station has the bay window in front of his desk wide open. Note the station sign, which reveals that Boon is 55 miles from the railroad's northern terminus at Frankfort, and 245 miles from its southern terminus at Toledo. A track realignment project in 1895 reduced the distance of the railroad's trackage between Toledo and Frankfort by roughly eight miles. Originally, the tracks went northeast from Ann Arbor to the Washtenaw County town of Emery before cutting back to the northwest. The new alignment took the line almost due north after leaving Ann Arbor. (Courtesy of the Claude T. Stoner Collection, Bentley Historical Library, University of Michigan.)

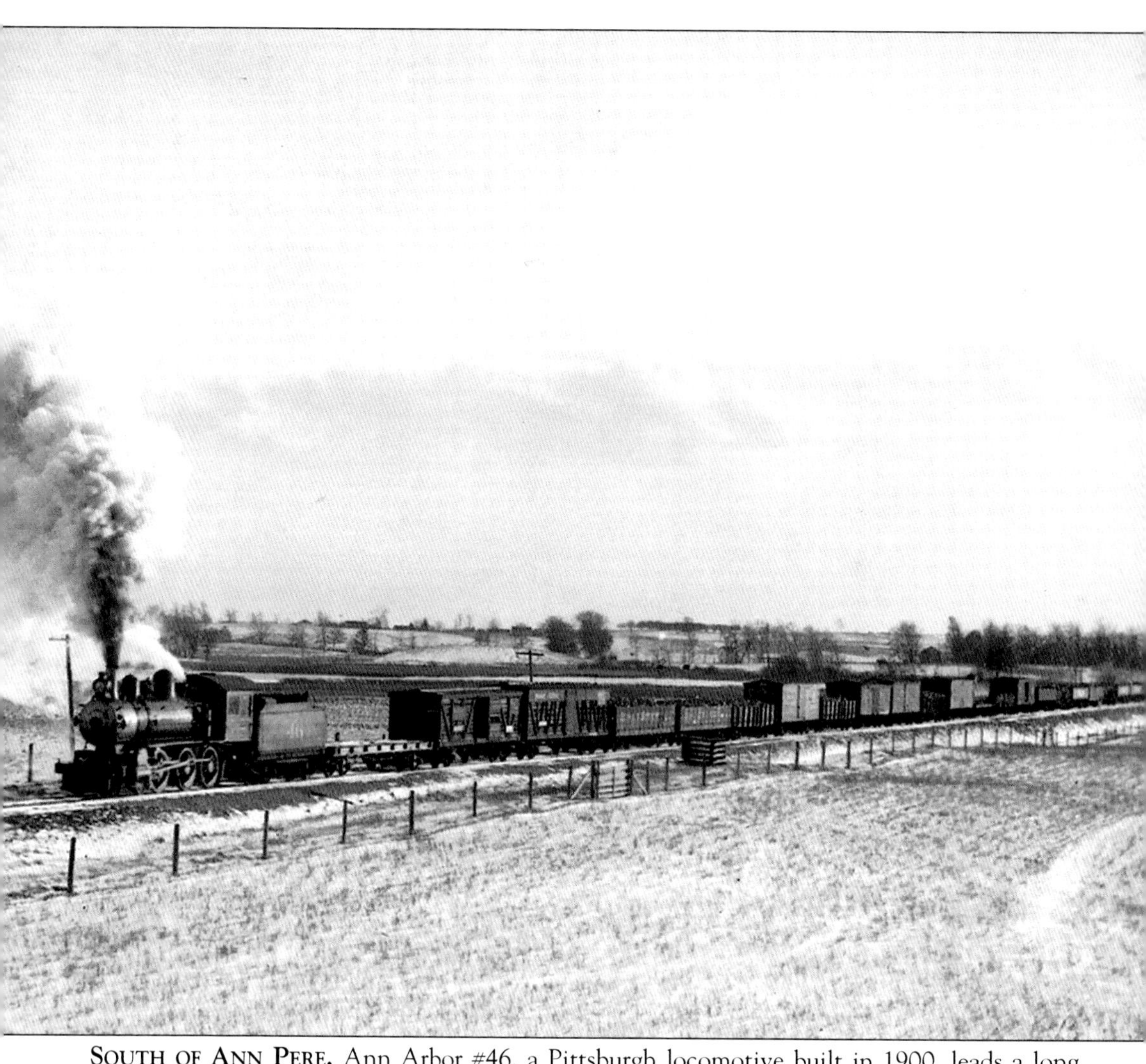

SOUTH OF ANN PERE. Ann Arbor #46, a Pittsburgh locomotive built in 1900, leads a long freight train past farmer's fields near Chilson, Michigan, in 1905. Chilson, at Ann Arbor Railroad Milepost 66.9, was about 5 miles south of Ann Pere, the AA's crossing with the Grand Rapids-Detroit mainline of the Pere Marquette Railroad. (Courtesy of the Claude T. Stoner Collection, Bentley Historical Library, University of Michigan.)

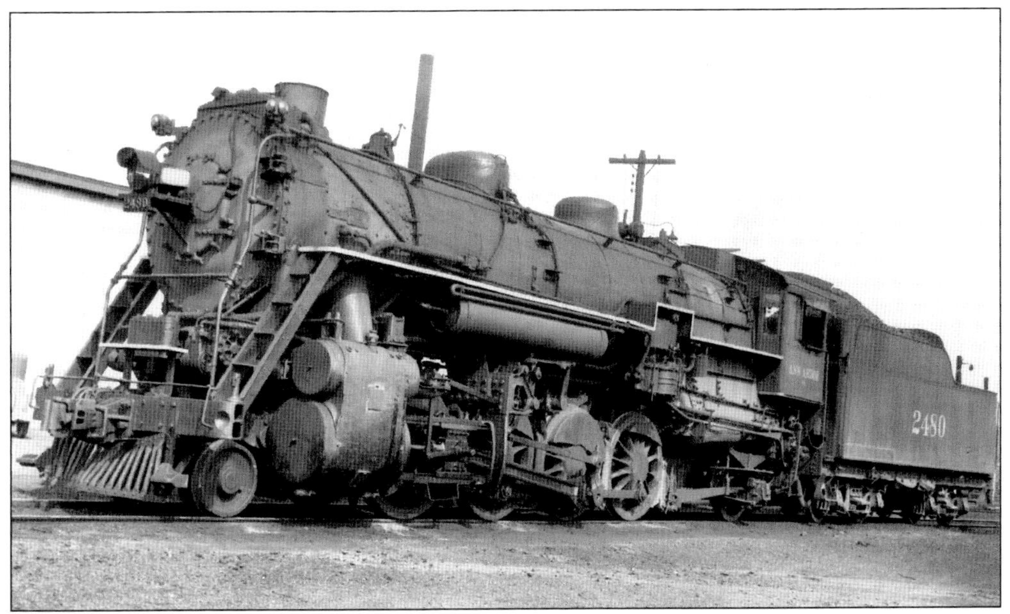

THE NEXT TRAIN. Built in 1916 by the Brooks Locomotive Works, Ann Arbor #2480—pictured in July 1939 with its coal tender full to the brim—waits at Elberta's Boat Landing Yard for the next train to pull. (Collection of Harold K. Vollrath.)

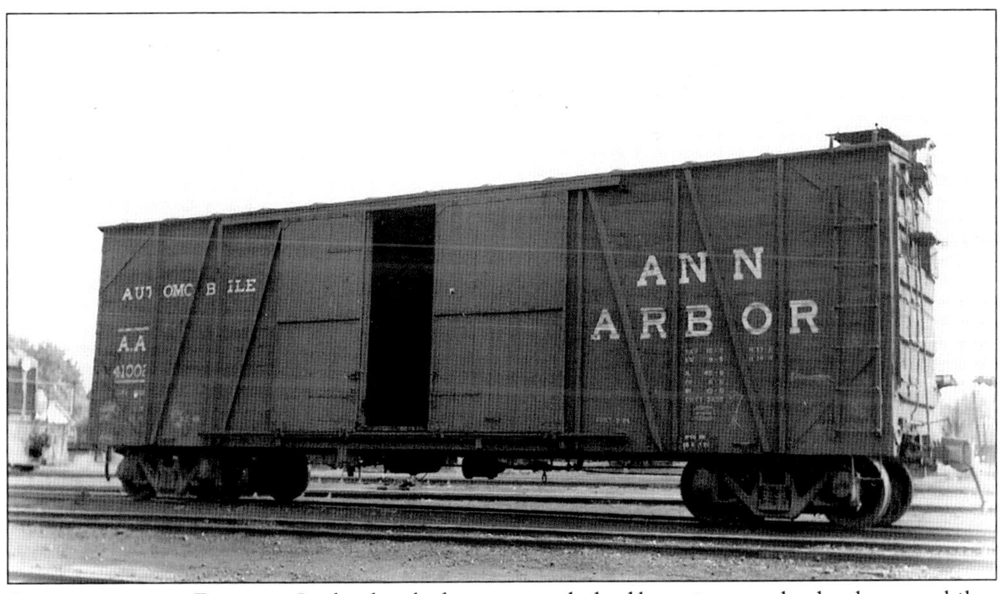

AUTOMOBILES BY BOXCAR. In the days before auto-racks had been invented to haul automobiles, boxcars like Ann Arbor #41002 were used to transport finished cars. These boxcars could carry several automobiles, which would be loaded on an angled ramp to take advantage of the freight car's "vertical space." This outside-braced wooden boxcar, photographed in September 1946 at Pontiac, Michigan, was built in 1924. (Collection of D. C. Jesse Burkhardt.)

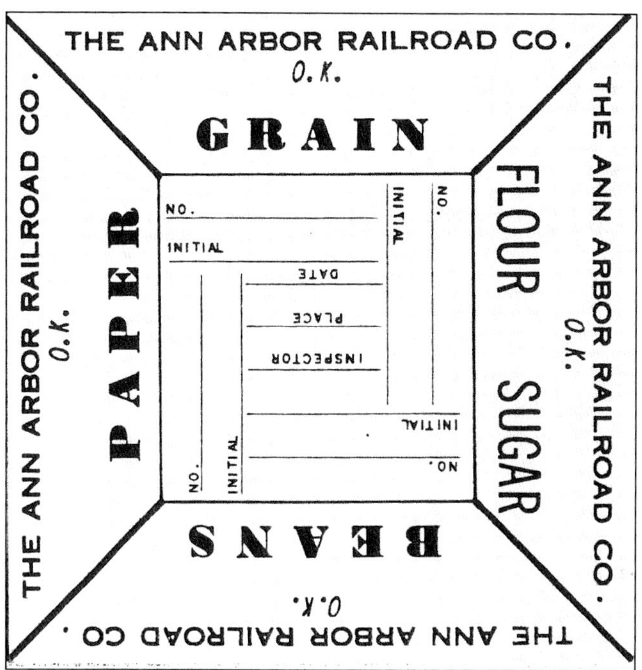
THE ANN ARBOR RAILROAD CO.
O.K.
GRAIN
THE ANN ARBOR RAILROAD CO.
O.K.
FLOUR SUGAR
THE ANN ARBOR RAILROAD CO.
O.K.
BEANS
THE ANN ARBOR RAILROAD CO.
O.K.
PAPER
NO.
INITIAL
DATE
PLACE
INSPECTOR
INITIAL
NO.

MANY COMMODITIES. Long before computerization, cards like this one from 1949 were tacked to the wooden route boards of freight cars to make sure railroad inspectors knew what the car was carrying. The side that was facing up represented the commodity inside the car, and the car number would be added before the shipment went in transit. The forms were printed back to back to maximize the types of goods represented. (Collection of D. C. Jesse Burkhardt.)

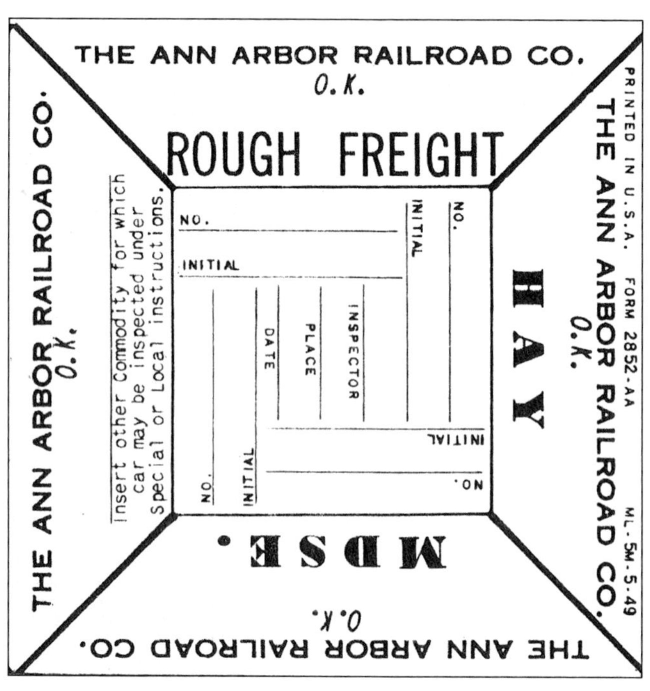
THE ANN ARBOR RAILROAD CO.
O.K.
ROUGH FREIGHT
PRINTED IN U.S.A. FORM 2852-AA ML-5M-5-49
THE ANN ARBOR RAILROAD CO.
O.K.
HAY
THE ANN ARBOR RAILROAD CO.
O.K.
MDSE.
THE ANN ARBOR RAILROAD CO.
O.K.
Insert other Commodity for which car may be inspected under Special or Local instructions.
NO.
INITIAL
DATE
PLACE
INSPECTOR
INITIAL
NO.

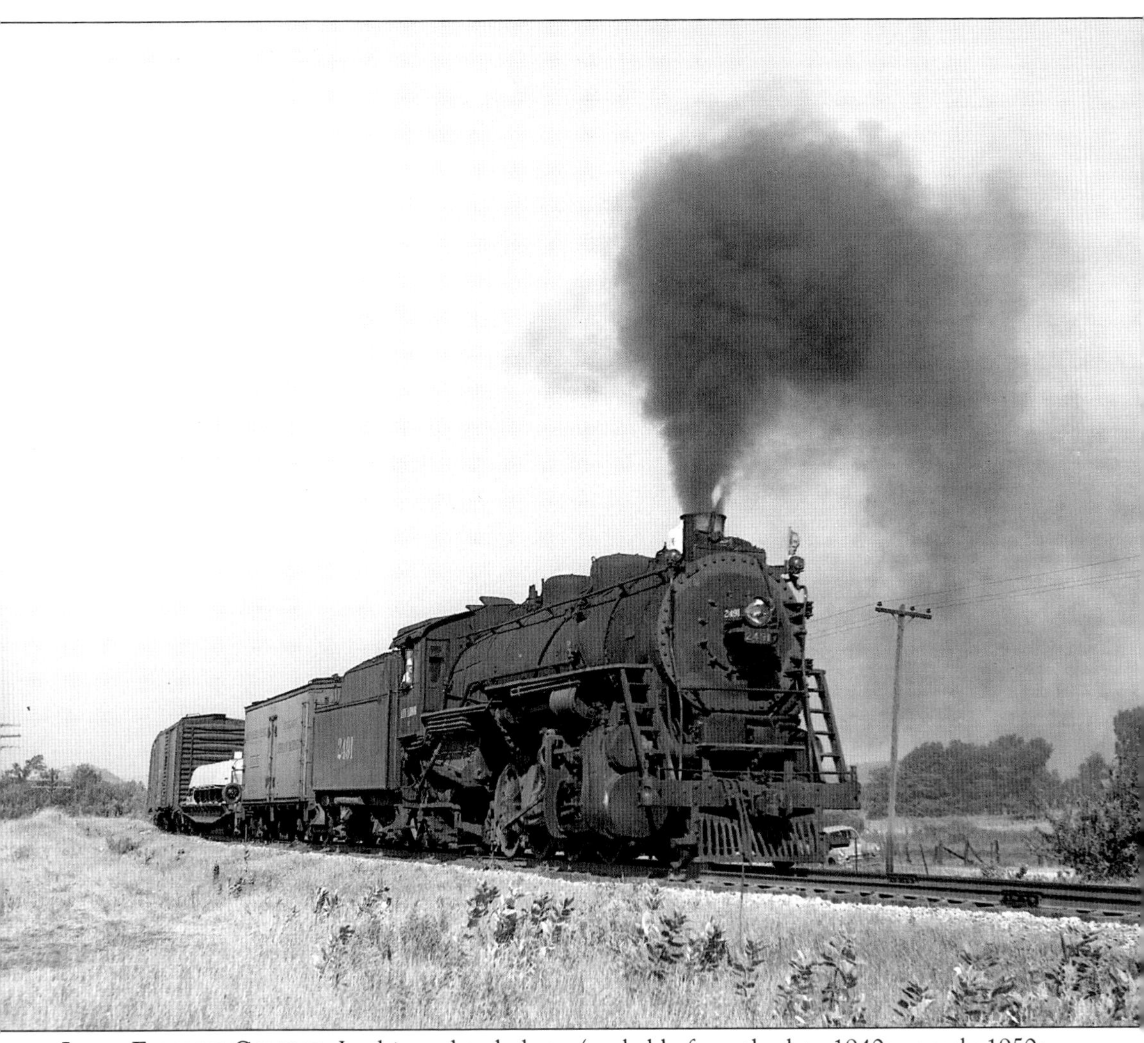

LONG FREIGHT COMING. In this undated photo (probably from the late 1940s or early 1950s, judging by the car visible behind the locomotive), Ann Arbor #2491 puffs grandly as it moves tonnage north. The white flags flying on the locomotive, used in the era before radios allowed communication between trains, signified that the train was an extra, not scheduled in the timetable. AA #2491, a 2-8-2 type, was built in 1923 and scrapped in late 1951. (Collection of D. C. Jesse Burkhardt.)

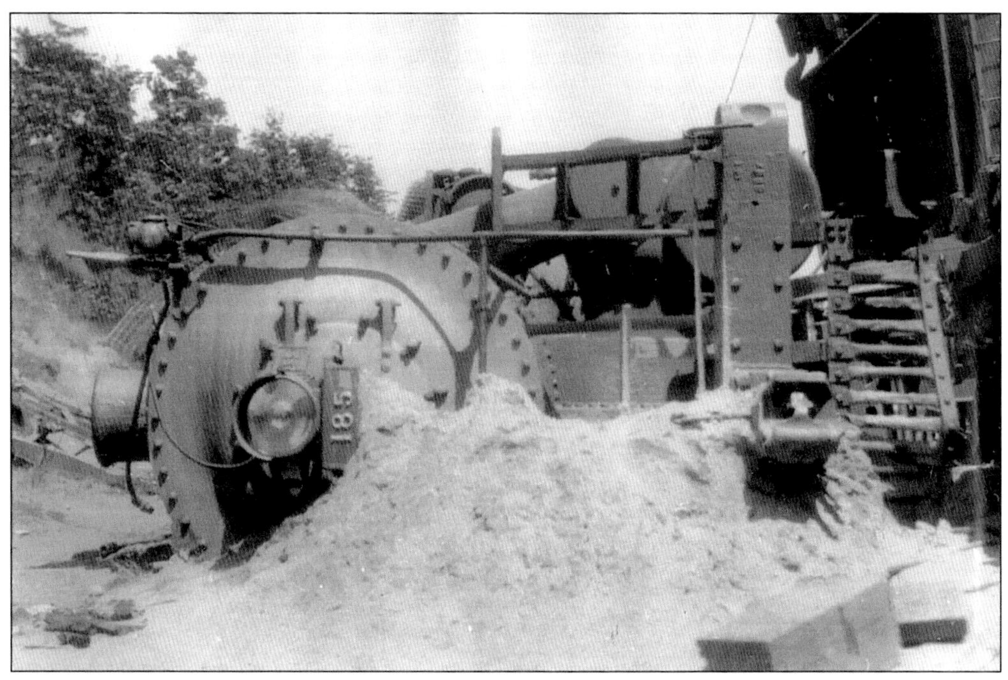

Derailment at Pomona. Ann Arbor locomotive #185 rests on its side, half buried in sand after coming off the tracks at Pomona, a village between Mesick and Copemish. This accident, which happened at about 1:35 a.m. on July 4, 1929, left cars twisted and torn alongside the tracks and made the clean-up workers armed only with shovels look silly. (Both photos courtesy of the Benzie Area Historical Society.)

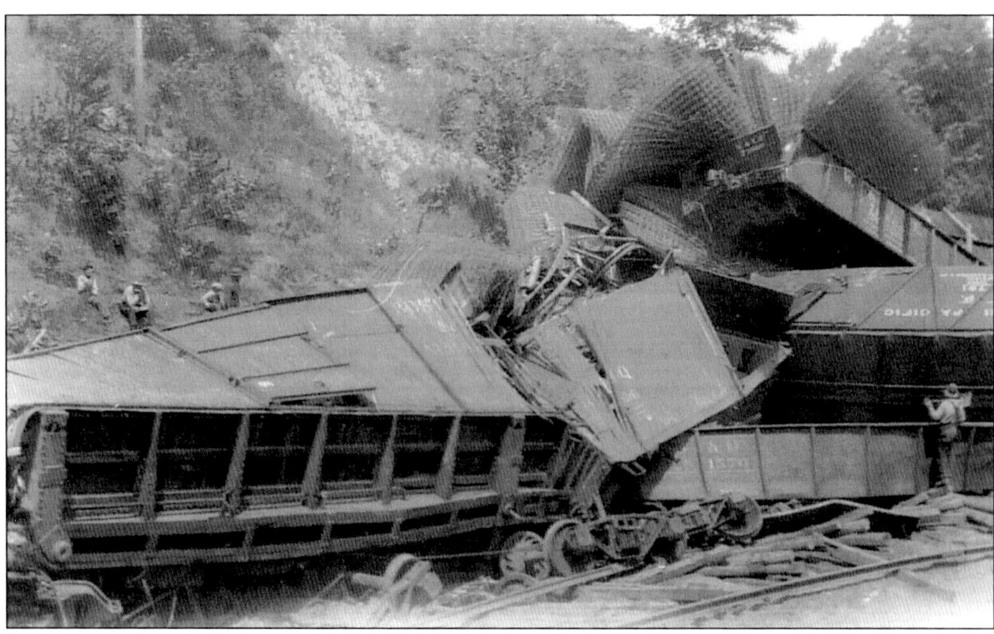

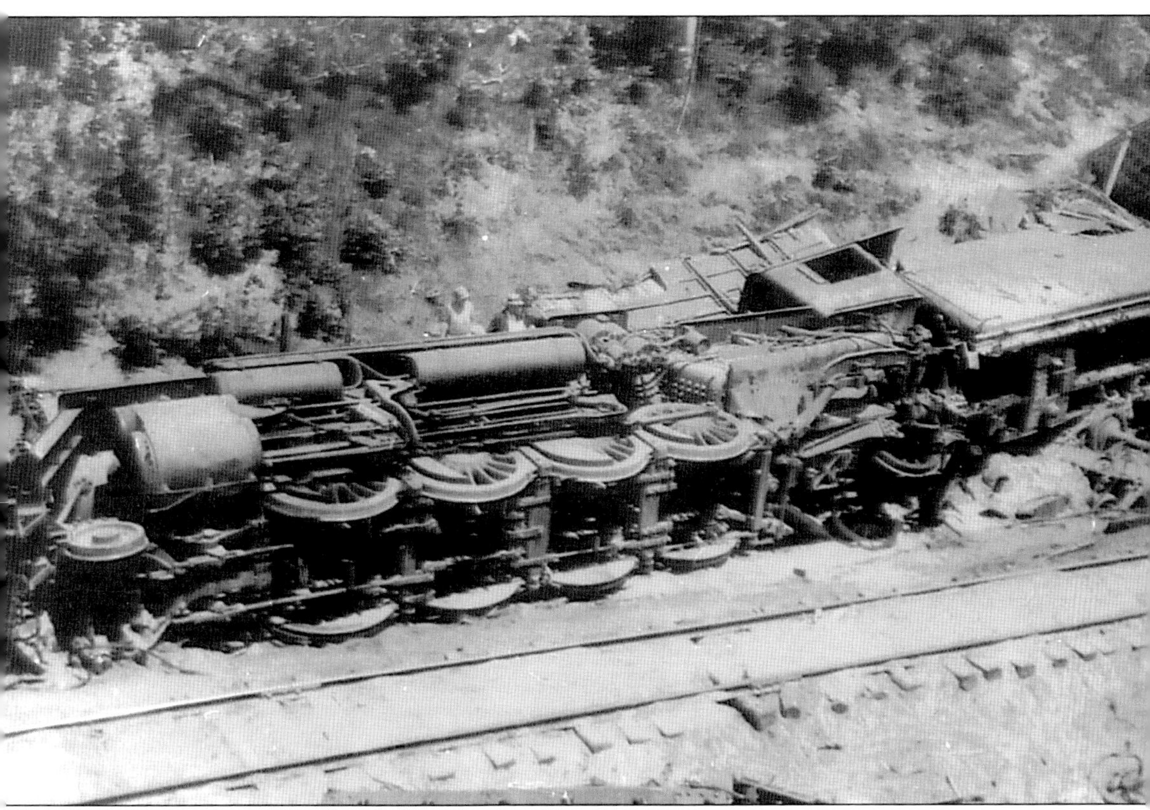

Now What? Ann Arbor locomotive #185 lies where it fell after the derailment at Pomona, in northwestern Michigan's Manistee County. The wreck was caused by heavy rains, which washed out a section of track. According to the railroad's accident report, the westbound freight was traveling at about 30 miles per hour when it hit the washout, and the engineer and fireman were killed. Despite the seriousness of this wreck and the apparent helplessness of the derailed engine, a steam crane was brought in, and eventually #185 was back in service. The 2-8-2 locomotive, built by the Brooks Locomotive Works in 1923, was later renumbered as #2492 and served on the Ann Arbor line until it was scrapped in 1951. (Courtesy of the Benzie Area Historical Society.)

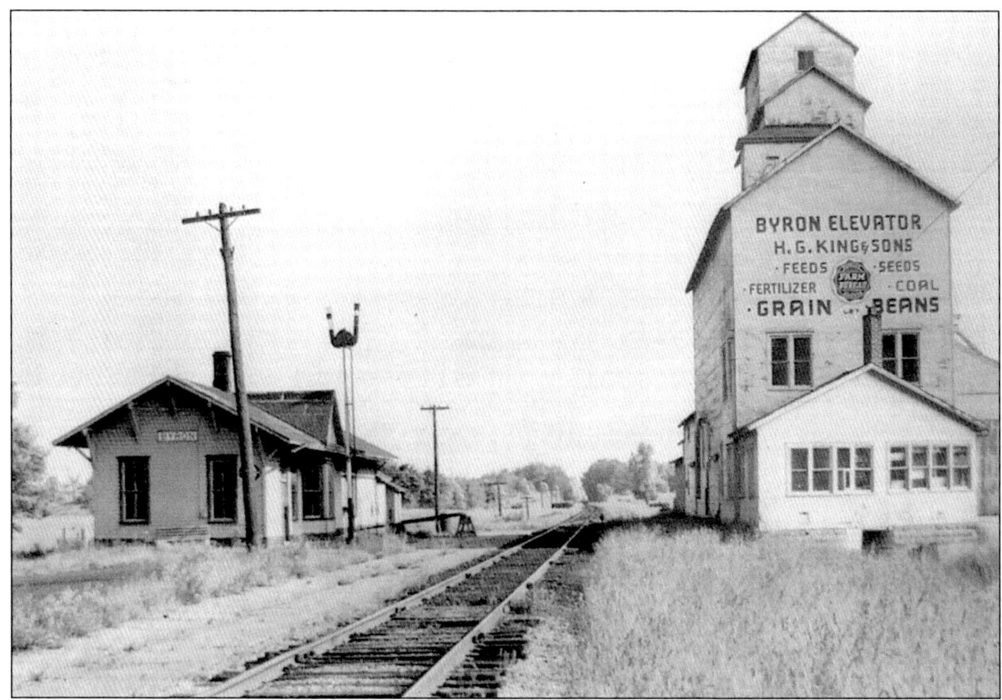

ALL QUIET AT BYRON. This lonely scene from Byron, Michigan, Milepost 88.93 on the Ann Arbor Railroad, was captured in the early 1950s. The setting reflects the end of an era, as the station on the left has already seen its last passenger train and the grain elevator on the right no longer ships its goods by rail. Even the semaphore signal towers will soon fade from Michigan's railroad landscape. (Courtesy of the Benzie Area Historical Society.)

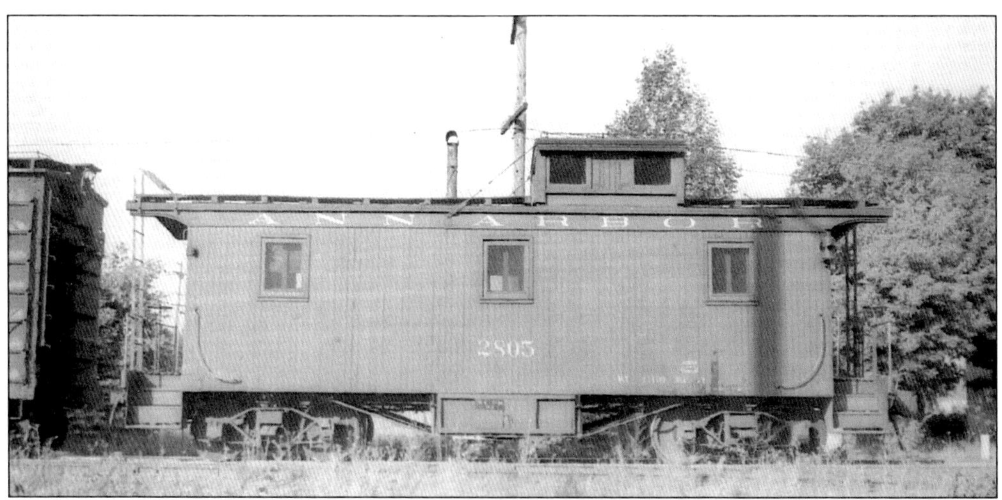

STEEL TRUMPS WOOD. Ann Arbor caboose #2805 rolls through Ann Arbor in 1950. New steel cabooses, delivered beginning in 1952, soon replaced the railroad's wood cabooses, including this one. After being taken out of regular freight service, the wood cabooses were often used in maintenance of way operations. In 1957, this particular caboose was converted into a maintenance of way car and renumbered #4614. (Courtesy of the Benzie Area Historical Society.)

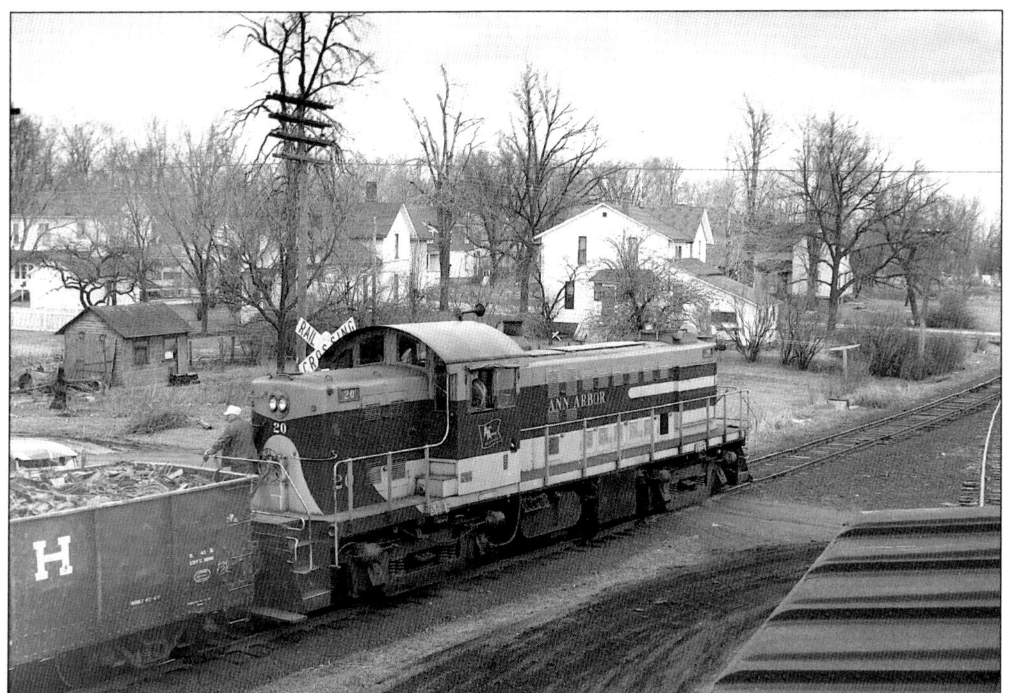

SCRAP HAULER. Ann Arbor #20 picks up a gondola load of scrap metal as it works a spur track behind a residential neighborhood at Ithaca. The Alco locomotive, built in 1950, is still sharp and its paint appears relatively fresh in this scene. (Collection of D. C. Jesse Burkhardt.)

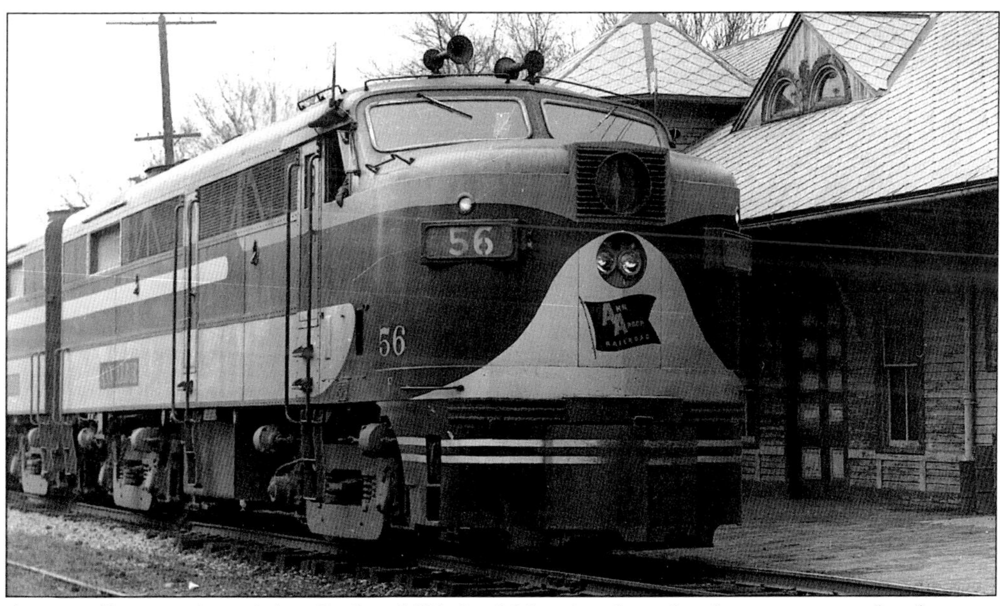

AT THE DEPOT. Ann Arbor Railroad FA-2 #56 heads a long freight as it passes the depot at Ann Arbor in 1954. The 1,600-horsepower FAs were Alco-GE products; AA #56 was built new for the railroad in 1950. The FAs hauled freight between Toledo and Elberta until they were retired in 1964 and replaced by 10 new GP35s. (Photo by Ron Morse.)

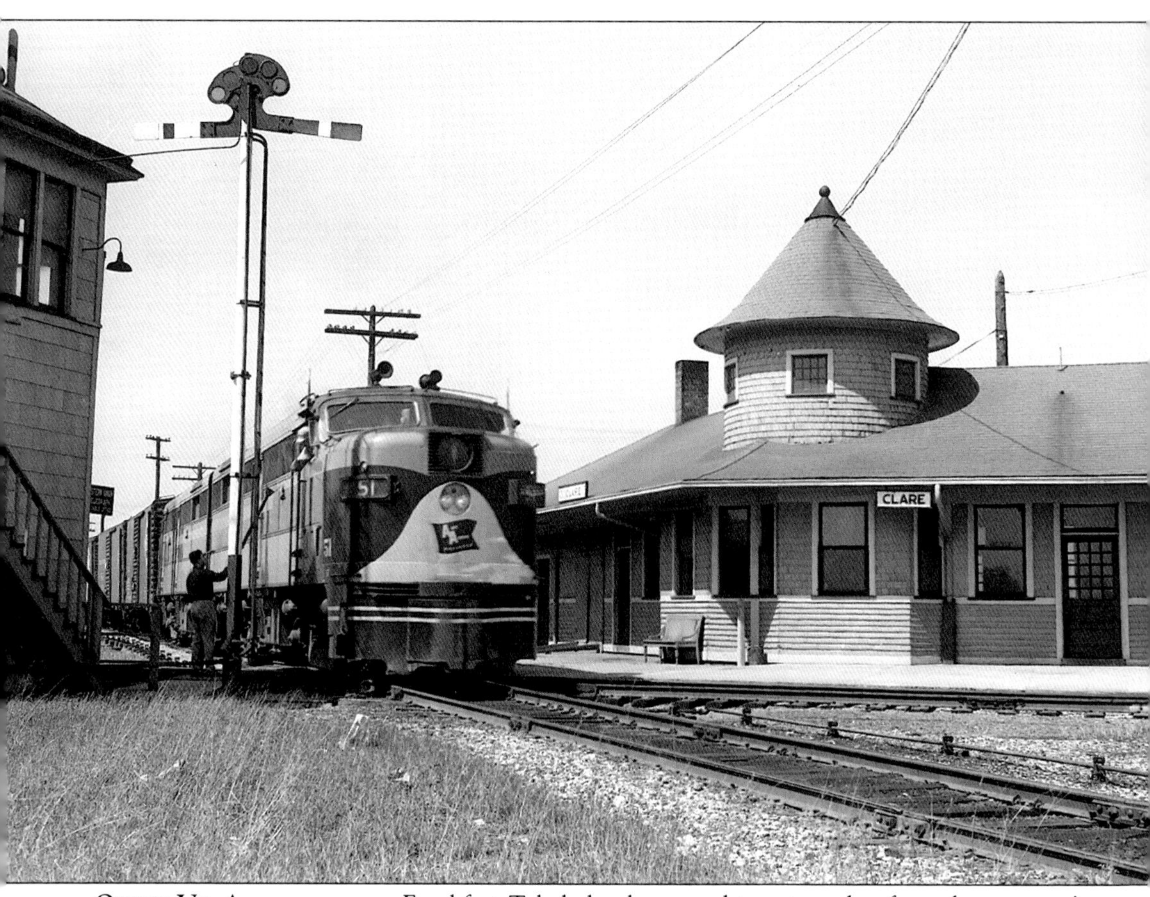

ORDER UP. A crewman on a Frankfort-Toledo hauler snags his train orders from the operator's hoop as a long freight rolls southbound (eastward by timetable) past the semaphore signal tower and across the Chesapeake & Ohio's Ludington-Saginaw line at Clare, Michigan, in 1953. When this scene was captured, the unique, 1895-era Ann Arbor depot on the right was no longer being used by passengers; the railroad had ended its passenger train service three years earlier. Note the sign on the interlocking tower: "Western Union Telegraph Cable Office." (Collection of D. C. Jesse Burkhardt.)

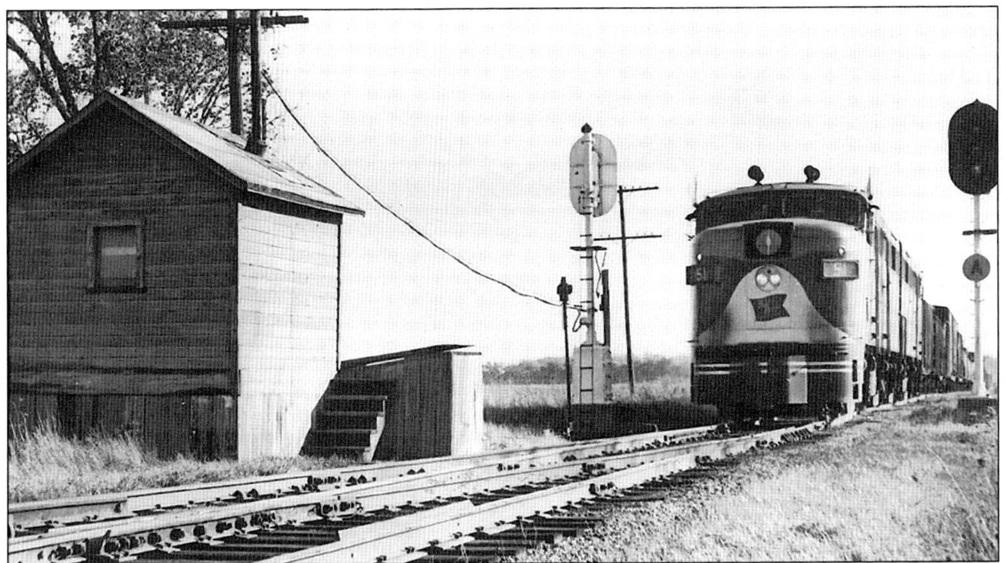

Blasting Through Urania. A Toledo-Frankfort freight rocks north past the block signals at Urania, Michigan, in October 1951, with FAs #51 and #51A in the lead. Block signals were a rarity on the Ann Arbor Railroad. They were employed in only 2 territories: between Toledo and Alexis, a 5-mile segment; and between Milan and Ann Arbor, about 14 miles. The blocks pictured here were in place to protect the New York Central crossing at Pittsfield, Michigan, about four miles north from this location. (Courtesy of the Claude T. Stoner Collection, Bentley Historical Library, University of Michigan.)

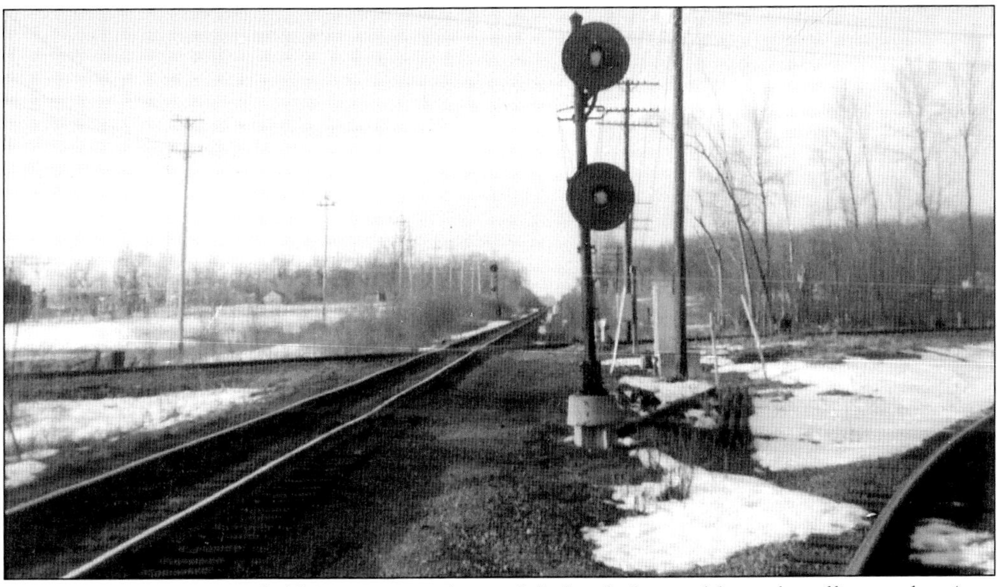

Red Signals. At Pittsfield Junction, red signal lights halt northbound traffic on the Ann Arbor at the crossing of a New York Central line between Ypsilanti and Hillsdale. From the AA's timetable: "Normal position of signals is proceed on Ann Arbor and stop on New York Central. If proceed indication is not displayed for Ann Arbor train, a member of crew will go to crossing, and after ascertaining that no trains are approaching on New York Central, may proceed at restricted speed." (Photo by D. C. Jesse Burkhardt.)

TOLEDO—OWOSSO
1st SUB-DIVISION

Distance from Toledo (Cherry Street)	Time Table No. 113 In Effect Sunday, October 11, 1964 STATIONS	Capacity Sidings In 50 ft. Cars Exclusive of Engine & Caboose
.0	.... TOLEDO	Yard
	BLK SIGS / TT Crossing 2.24 / DBL TRK	
2.24	I........ BOULEVARD	....
	C&O-TT 1.49 Crossing	
3.73	I........ HALLETT.... R DN	....
	NYC-C&O 1.20 Crossing	
4.93	I........ ALEXIS .... DN	....
	4.40	
9.33	.... TEMPERANCE	....
	2.08	
11.41	.... SAMARIA	98
	7.23	
	NYC Crossing	
18.64	I........ FEDERMAN	....
	DT&I Crossing 1.90	
20.54	I........ DIANN ....DN	84
	2.29	
22.83	.... DUNDEE ....D	34
	BLK SIGS / Wabash 8.03 Crossing	
30.86	I........ MILAN ....DN	76
	5.67	
36.53	.... URANIA	77
	NYC 3.92 Crossing	
40.45	I........ PITTSFIELD	....
	4.01	
44.46	.... FERRY (ANN ARBOR) ..D	Yard
	5.99	
50.45	.... OSMER	80
	6.22	
56.67	.... WHITMORE LAKE	34
	5.15	
	GTW Crossing	
61.82	I........ LAKELAND	....
	5.12	
66.94	.... CHILSON	121
	C&O Crossing 5.07	
72.01	I........ ANNPERE	....
	1.89	
73.90	.... HOWELL .... D	74
	6.04	
79.94	.... OAK GROVE	40
	4.79	
84.73	.... COHOCTAH	72
	4.20	
88.93	.... BYRON	27
	GTW Cross. 6.58 Not Intl'kd-Stop	
95.51	.... DURAND	....
	0.69	
96.20	.... YORK ....D	61
	2.53	
98.73	.... VERNON	....
	5.29	
104.02	.... CORUNNA	....
	2.05	
106.07	.... OWOSSO .... RDN	Yard

STATIONS & SIDINGS NOT SHOWN

Dundee Cement Co. at MP-25—7155 Ft. long connected both ends.

Wickes—2½ Mi. east of Milan, 1465 Ft. connected west end.

Reynolds Chemical Co. spur track, 2000 Ft. west of MP-57, connected at west end — 570 Ft. in length.

TIMETABLE, SUBDIVISION #1. This image was taken from the Ann Arbor Railroad's Timetable #113, which was in effect in 1964—almost immediately after the Detroit, Toledo & Ironton took over the railroad. The timetable divided the AA's 292-mile land route into 2 separate subdivisions. Here is the 1st Subdivision, from Toledo to the freight yard in Owosso; it covered about 106 miles.

OWOSSO—BOAT LANDING
2nd SUB-DIVISION

Distance from Toledo (Cherry Street)	Time Table No. 113 In Effect Sunday, October 11, 1964 STATIONS	Capacity Sidings In 50 ft. Cars Exclusive of Engine & Caboose
106.07	OWOSSO ...... R DN	Yard
	NYC Crossing 1.70 Not Intl'kd-Stop	
107.77	OWOSSO JCT.	
	1.02	
108.79	KING	57
	6.63	
115.42	CARLAND	60
	4.89	
120.31	ELSIE	35
	3.85	
124.16	BANNISTER	
	4.19	
128.35	ASHLEY ...D	41
	5.34	
133.69	NORTH STAR	27
	4.65	
138.34	ITHACA ...D	
	6.33	
144.67	WRIGHT	77
	C&O Crossing 1.13 Not Intl'kd-Stop	
145.80	ALMA ...D	
	4.36	
150.16	FOREST HILL	59
	6.00	
156.16	SHEPHERD ...D	40
	7.60	
163.76	MT. PLEASANT ...D	39
	6.70	
170.46	ROSEBUSH	33
	C&O Crossing 8.36	
178.82	I ... CLARE ...D	101
	15.00	
193.82	LAKE GEORGE	83
	6.89	
200.71	TEMPLE	24
	7.90	
208.61	MARION ...D	82
	7.82	
216.43	McBAIN	36
	4.39	
220.82	LUCAS	45
	PRR Crossing 6.09	
226.91	I CADILLAC D	
	PRR Cross. (Spur) 1.16 Not Intl'kd-Gate	
228.19	SELMA	Yard
	9.45	
237.64	BOON	28
	10.39	
248.03	YUMA	99
	6.08	
254.11	MESICK	28
	7.38	
261.49	HARLAN	93
	6.09	
267.58	COPEMISH	
	C&O Crossing 2.81	
270.39	I ... THOMPSONVILLE ...D	
	6.25	
276.64	WELDEN	63
	6.19	
282.83	BEULAH	
	7.46	
290.29	JUNCTION SWITCH	
	1.51	
291.80	BOAT LANDING ... R DN	Yard
290.29	JUNCTION SWITCH	
	1.87	
292.	FRANKFORT	

STATIONS AND SIDINGS NOT SHOWN

Pomona—2½ miles east of Copemish, lgth. 740 ft., connected west end.

Case's—1 mile east of Beulah, lgth. 400 ft., connected east end.

TIMETABLE, SUBDIVISION #2. Taken from the same timetable, this image displays the Ann Arbor's 2nd Subdivision, which went from Owosso Yard to Frankfort and Boat Landing Yard in Elberta. The 2nd Sub covered about 186 miles. (Collection of D. C. Jesse Burkhardt.)

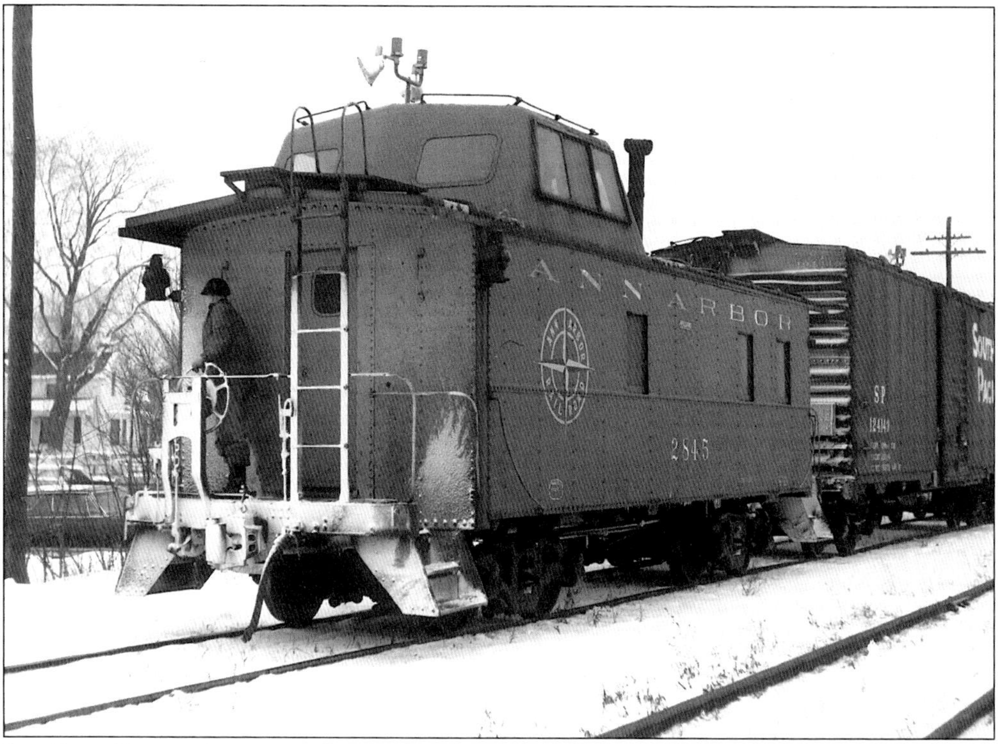

ICE COLD DUTY. A crewman leaves the warm confines of frost-encrusted Ann Arbor caboose #2845 as his train pulls into Alma, Michigan, on a bitterly cold January 28, 1968. The Wabash Railroad built this caboose in 1952, but #2845 has been repainted with a compass logo to reflect the AA's new owner, the Detroit, Toledo & Ironton, which took over in 1963. The old lanterns hanging at the rear of the caboose were rare for the late 1960s. (Photo by Dennis Schmidt.)

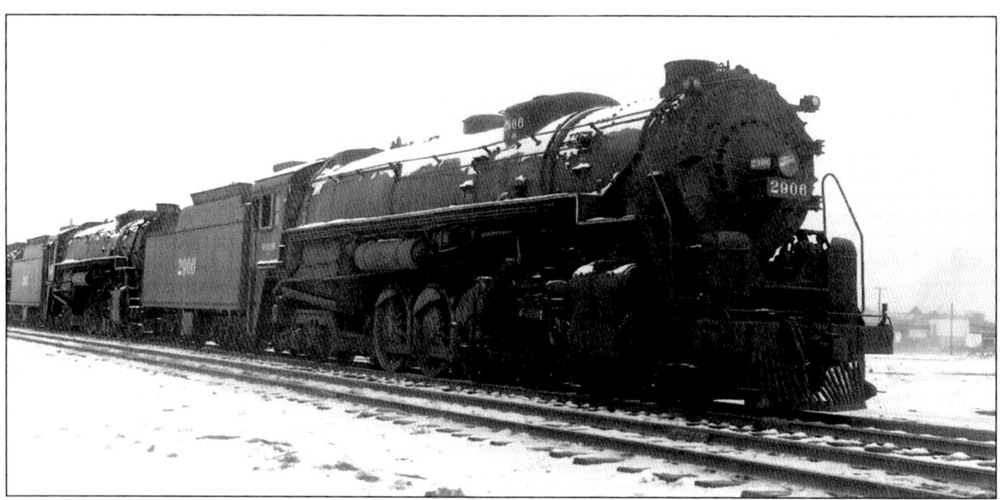

WABASH DEADLINE. Covered with snow, a line of retired Wabash Railroad 4-8-4 steam locomotives endure the cold on a deadline track in Decatur, Illinois, in 1969, six years after the historic carrier was absorbed into the Norfolk & Western Railway. With its merger into the N&W, the Wabash gave up its controlling interest in the Ann Arbor Railroad, clearing the way for the DT&I to step in. (Collection of D. C. Jesse Burkhardt.)

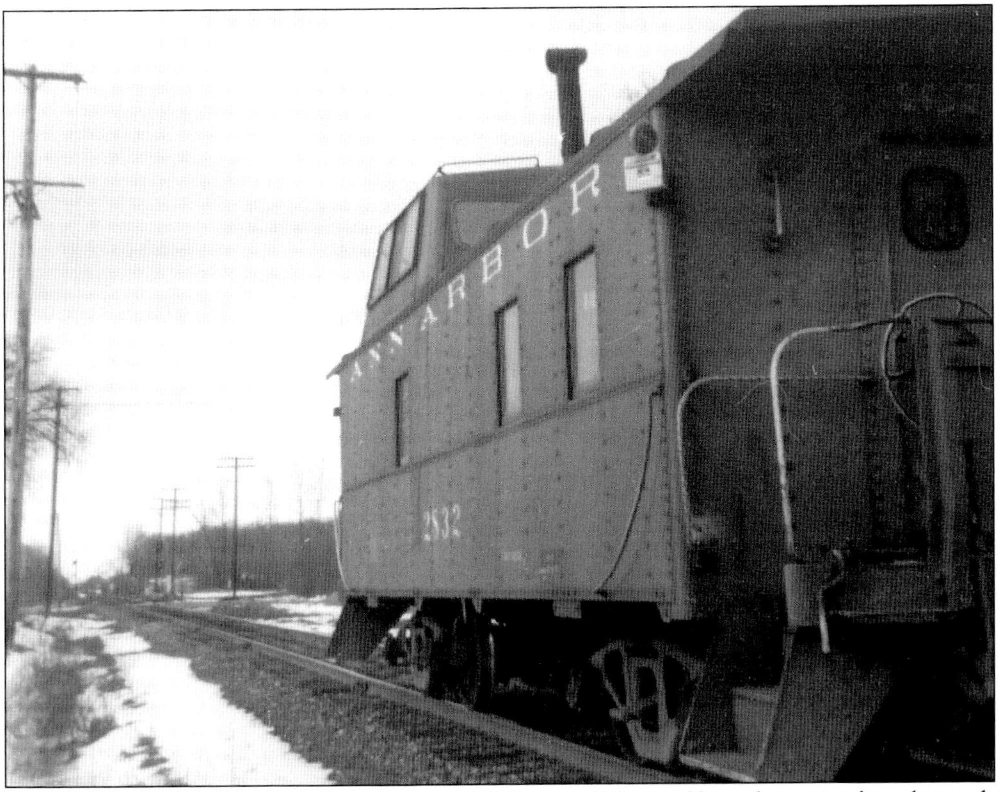

CABOOSE WAITING. Ann Arbor caboose #2832 rests all by itself on the main directly south of Pittsfield Junction while the locomotive and crew switch industries in Saline, at the end of the Saline Branch. Saline is about five miles west of Pittsfield on a branchline the Ann Arbor inherited from the remnant of the former New York Central route that crossed the AA here. (Photo by D. C. Jesse Burkhardt.)

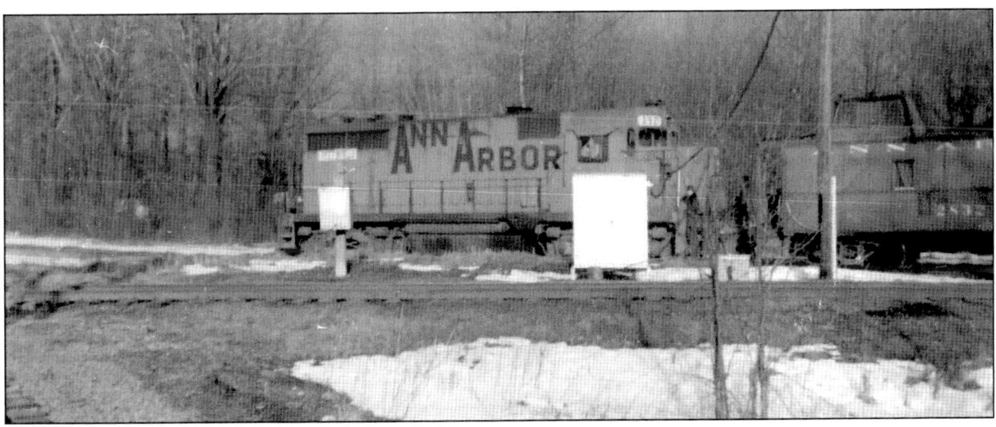

BOUND FOR SALINE. In this image taken during the winter of 1973, Ann Arbor GP35 #392 hauls caboose #2832 around the wye at Pittsfield Junction, about five miles south of the city of Ann Arbor, to gain access to the railroad's Saline Branch. In this era, the branchline served a Ford Motor Company plant in Saline. The Ann Arbor began operating the branch in 1968, after the New York Central trackage from Pittsfield Junction east to Ypsilanti was abandoned. (Photo by D. C. Jesse Burkhardt.)

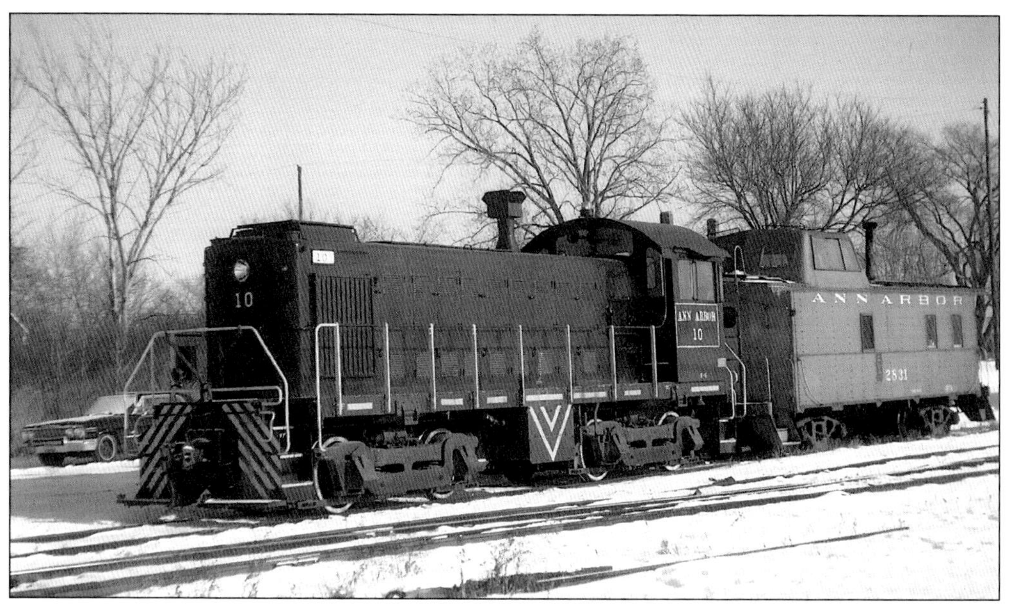

Forever Changes. Ann Arbor #10, an Alco S3 built in 1952, displays two different chapters of the railroad's history in these virtually identical scenes. In the top view, #10 rests in the AA yard in Owosso in January 1970 with caboose #2831. The locomotive is still in the black dress with yellow trim of its ex-owner, the Manistique & Lake Superior Railroad, under which its identity was M&LS #1. This engine was sold to the AA in 1968, the year the M&LS—an Ann Arbor subsidiary—was abandoned. In the lower photo, taken in the same location in November 1979, the unit is in weathered orange and bears a compass logo, a holdover from the years (1963–1973) when the Detroit, Toledo & Ironton Railroad controlled the Ann Arbor. Note freshly painted caboose #2835 with its new logo. (Both photos by Dennis Schmidt.)

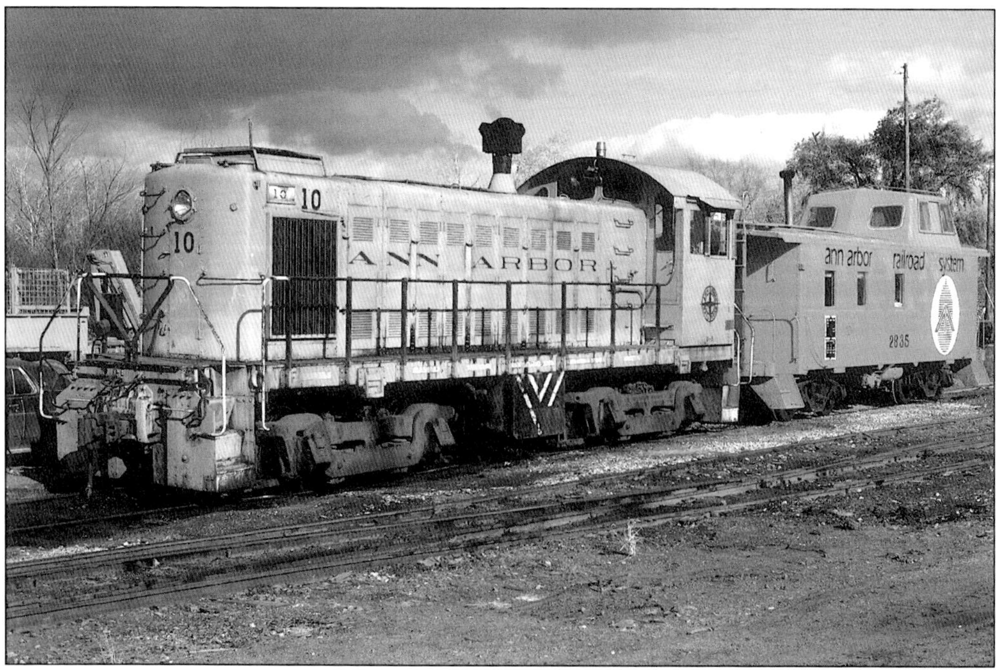

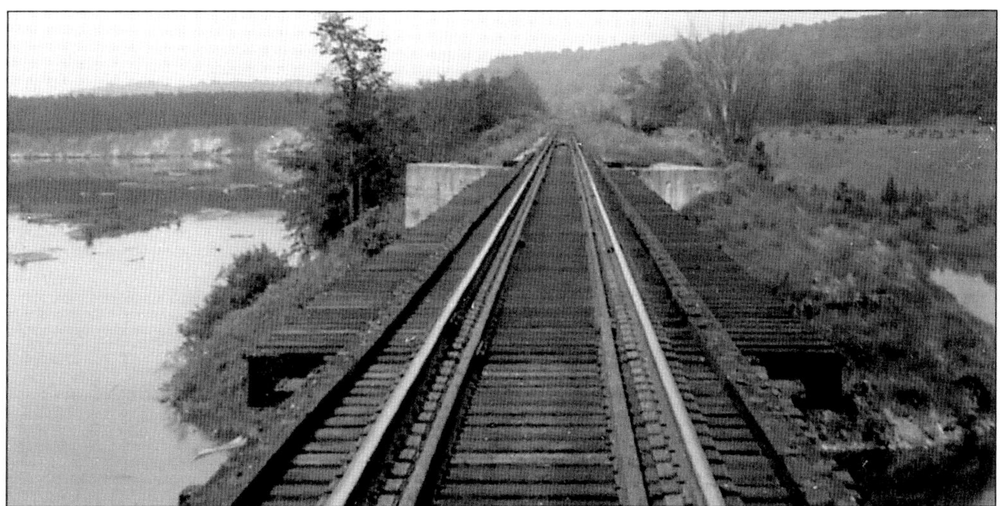

CROSSING THE MANISTEE. Shiny rails cut to the northwest across an open-deck bridge over the Manistee River in this scene from 1971. The Ann Arbor Railroad's river crossing here is located at Milepost 254.3, in Wexford County just west of Mesick. (Photo by D. C. Jesse Burkhardt.)

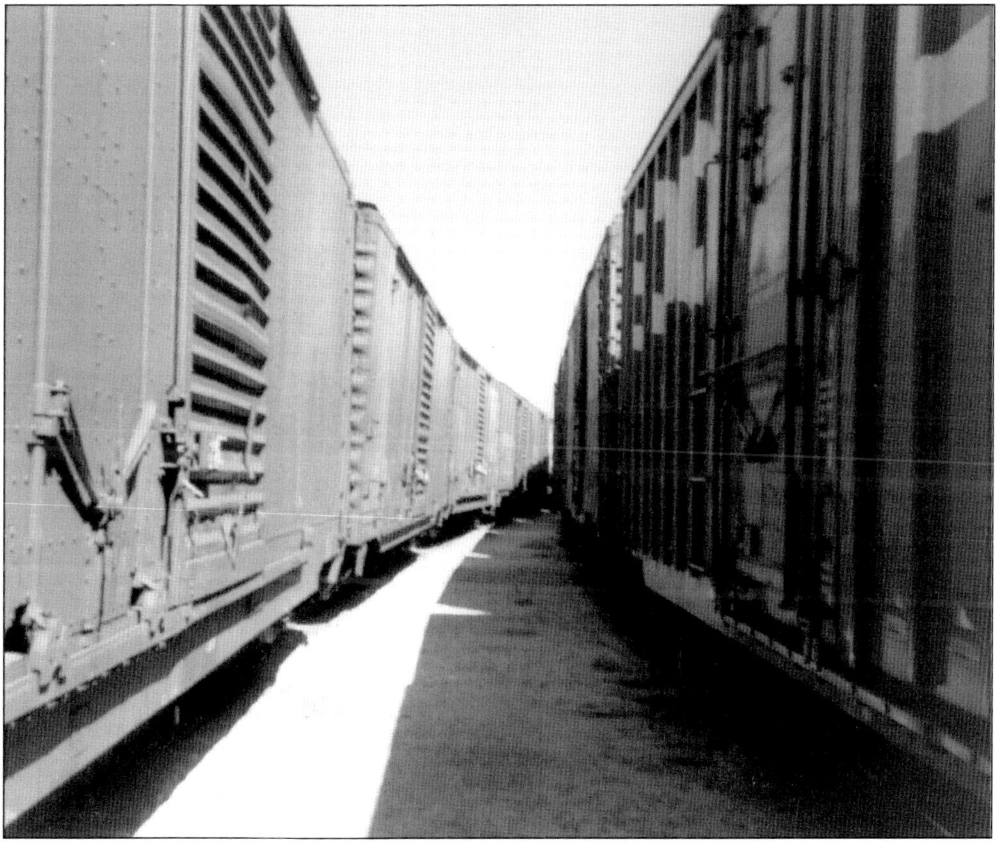

BOXCARS AND SAND. In the summer of 1971, Boat Landing Yard in Elberta is packed with boxcars waiting to be loaded onto westbound carferries at the northern terminus of the Ann Arbor Railroad's mainline. (Photo by D. C. Jesse Burkhardt.)

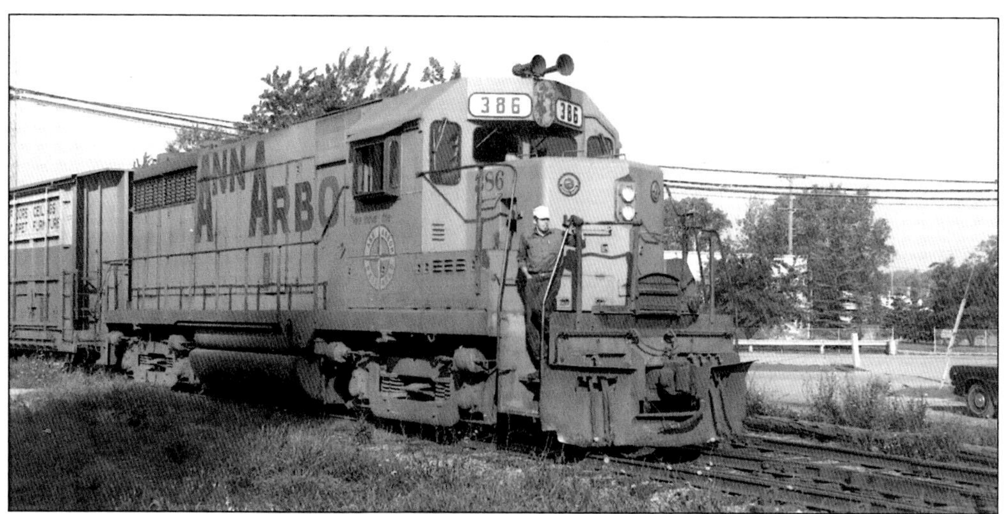

Switching Duties. Ann Arbor GP35 #386 switches at Alma, Michigan, in June 1974. Note the bold, dramatic "Ann Arbor" lettering on the side of the GP35, and the attractive compass logo. (Collection of Harold K. Vollrath.)

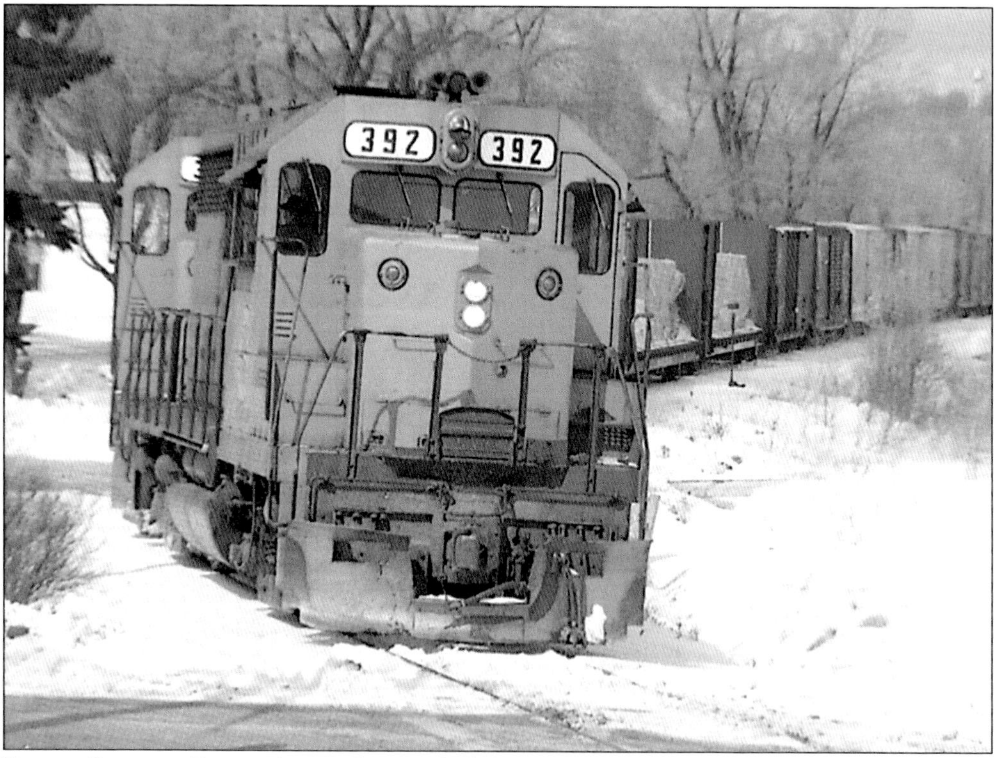

Right Off the Boat. Ann Arbor symbol freight FT2 pulls out of Boat Landing Yard in this Christmas card scene captured by photographer Bob Lenardson on March 6, 1976. The "Gyralite" safety light package between the lead locomotive's numbers featured a rotating headlamp designed to alert motorists at railroad crossings. If a train had to make an emergency stop, the gyrating lamp could be switched to a red beam—reportedly visible as far as five miles away—to warn oncoming trains. (Collection of D. C. Jesse Burkhardt.)

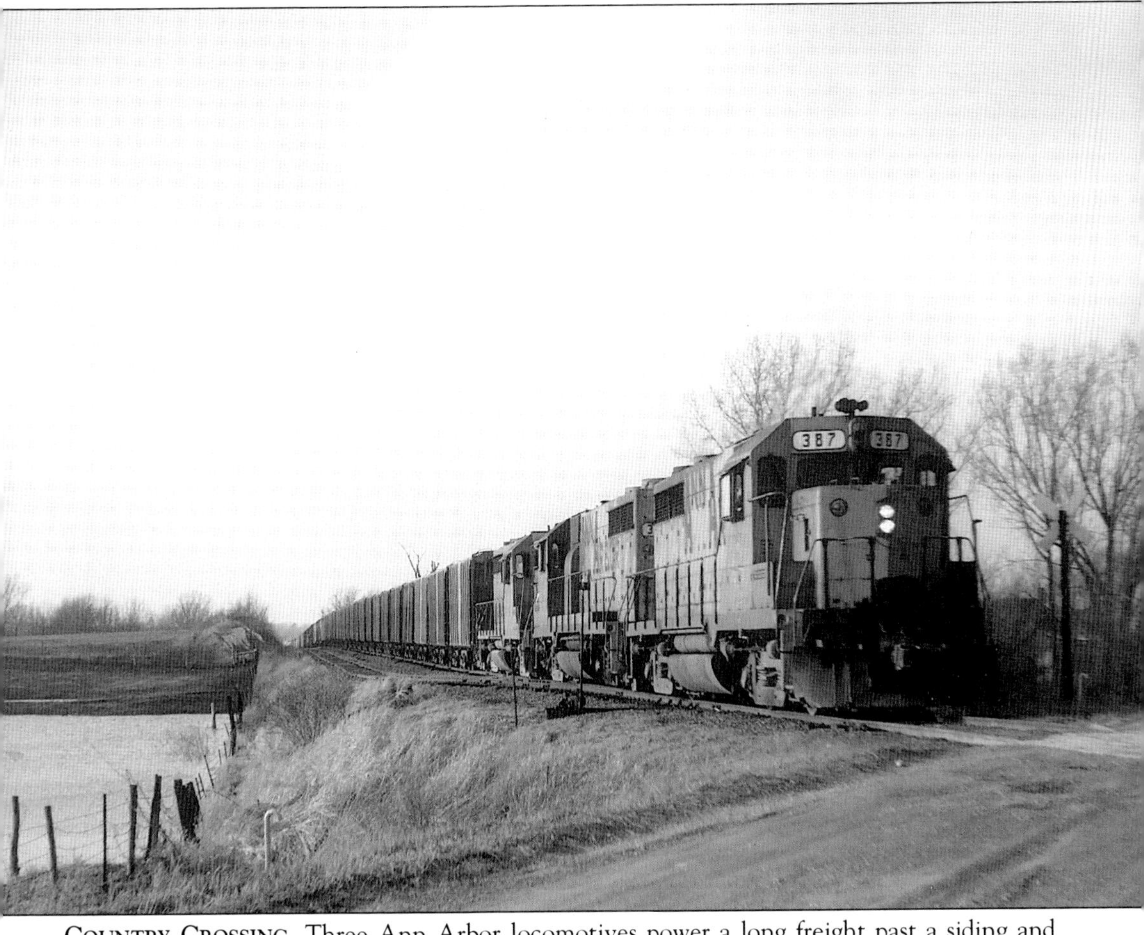

Country Crossing. Three Ann Arbor locomotives power a long freight past a siding and over the undulating landscape outside of Alma in this image captured on March 7, 1974. Note the many covered hoppers up front; these cars haul foundry sand from the Fairmount Minerals sand pits at Yuma, Milepost 248. Most of the sand goes to a Ford Motor Company plant in Cleveland, where it is used to make casting molds for automobile engines. Approximately 250,000 tons of sand a year move by rail out of the Yuma pits. (Photo by Dennis Schmidt.)

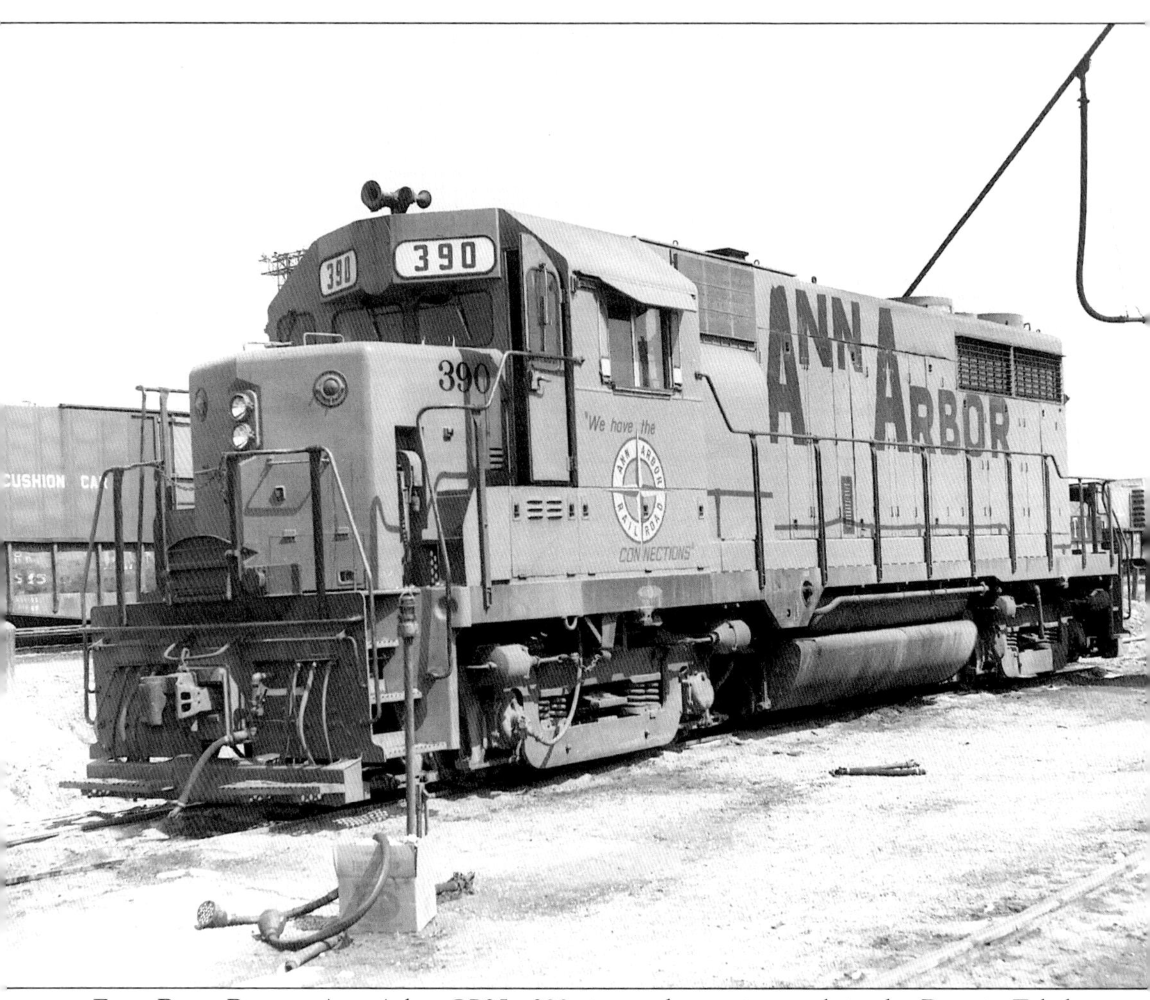

FLAT ROCK POWER. Ann Arbor GP35 #390 sits on the service track in the Detroit, Toledo & Ironton yard at Flat Rock, Michigan, in April 1972. Ann Arbor parent DT&I occasionally borrowed the AA's motive power, much to the displeasure of the Ann Arbor train crews, who appreciated the reliable and powerful GP35s on the AA's roster—each of which delivered 2,500 horsepower of pulling effort. After the Ann Arbor went bankrupt in 1973 (by the end of 1973, it was no longer under the ownership of the DT&I), a disillusioned employee altered the *We Have the Connections* slogan on one of the GP35s to read: *We Had Connections*. (Photo by Dennis Schmidt.)

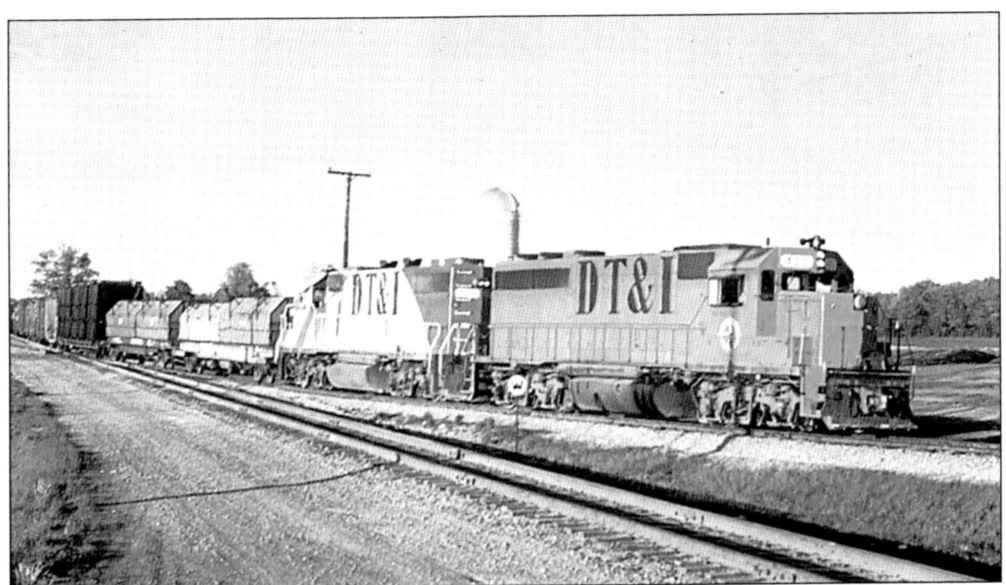

Visiting Freight. On May 13, 1977, a westbound Detroit Toledo & Ironton freight—on its way from Flat Rock to Toledo—switches off DT&I rails at Diann, Michigan, and heads south onto the Ann Arbor Railroad's main to finish its journey. Although the DT&I had relinquished control of the Ann Arbor several years prior to this date, the carrier maintained running rights on the Ann Arbor between Diann and Toledo. The second unit, DT&I #1776, is dressed in red, white, and blue in honor of the nation's bicentennial. (Collection of D. C. Jesse Burkhardt.)

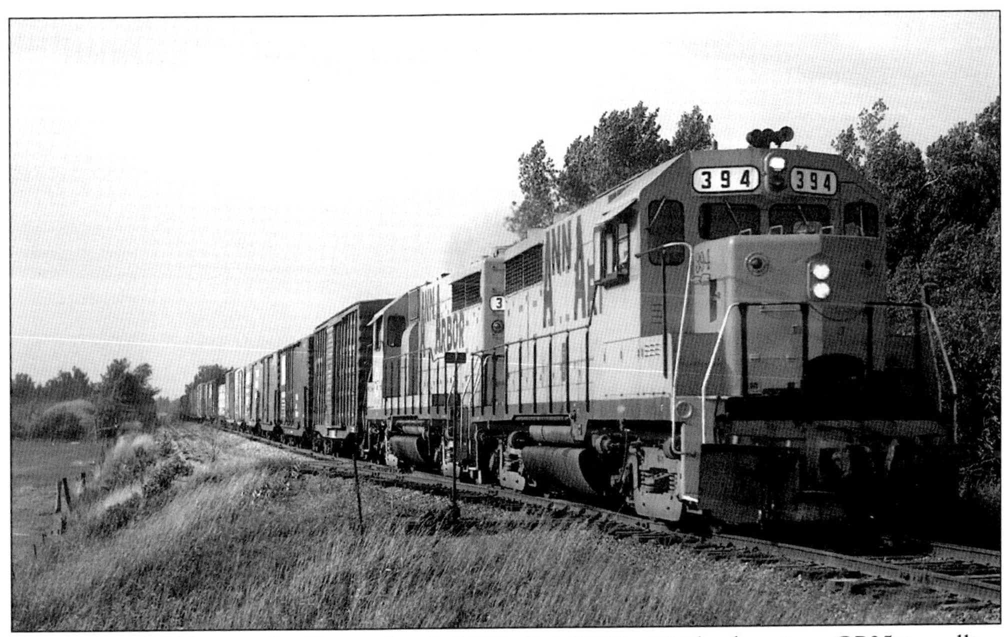

Cars For the Boats. On September 1, 1978, AA GP35 #394 leads a sister GP35 in pulling a long, mixed manifest freight across the grassy, windswept central Michigan countryside near Alma. This photo represents a typical 1970s-era scene of a "boat train" moving back and forth between Toledo and Frankfort. These trains were almost entirely comprised of traffic coming off or heading to the carferries. (Photo by Dennis Schmidt.)

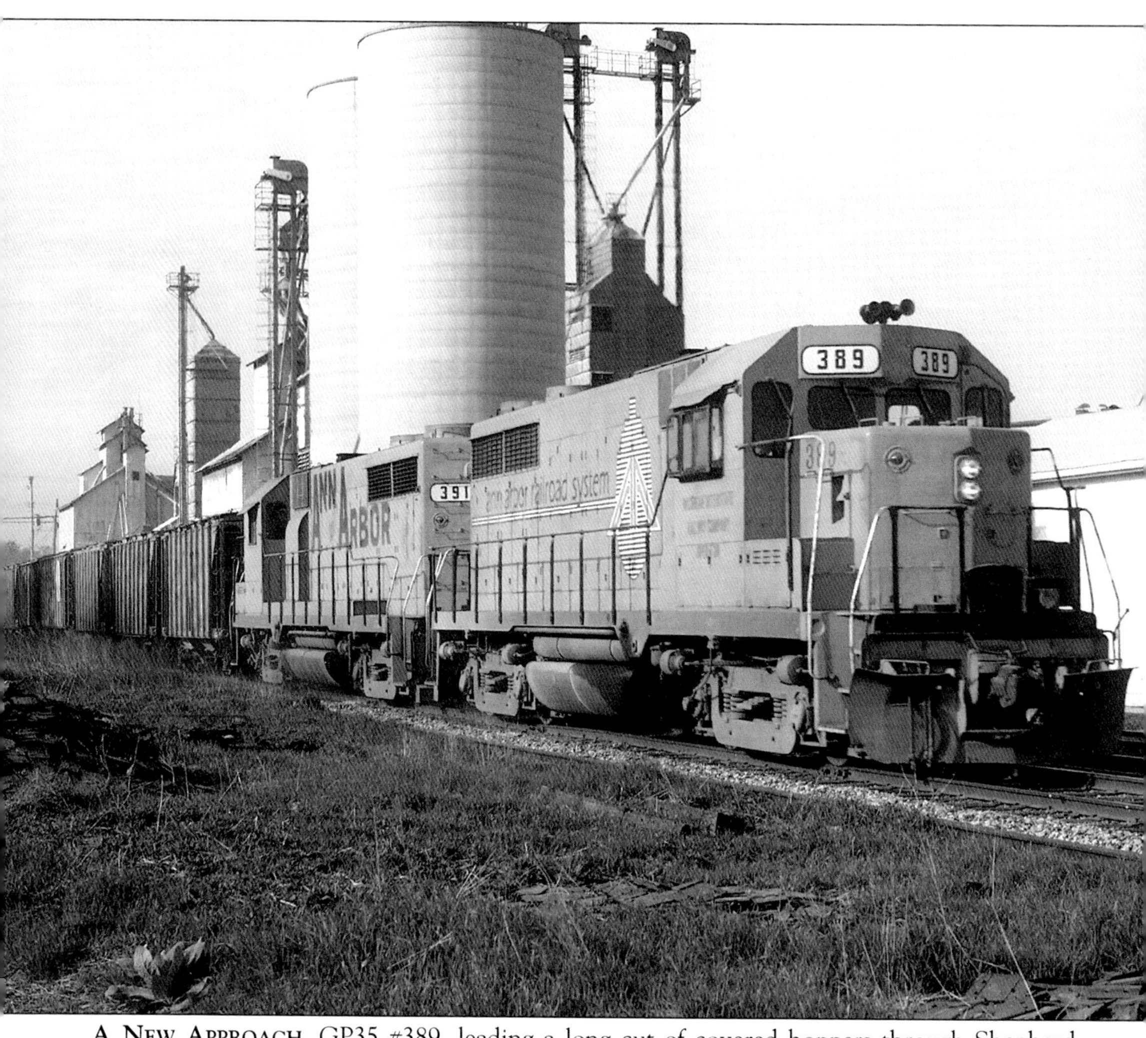

A New Approach. GP35 #389, leading a long cut of covered hoppers through Shepherd, Michigan, displays a revamped "Double A" logo superimposed over the outline of a carferry. The name of the railroad itself has also been subtly changed, from Ann Arbor Railroad to Ann Arbor Railroad System. And in a further twist of confusion, the lettering on the side of the cab reads: "Michigan Interstate Railway Company Operator." At this time, the state of Michigan owned the AA's trackage, and on October 1, 1977, contracted with the Michigan Interstate to operate the line and keep the ferries running through a lease agreement. Less than a year after this photo was taken in May 1981, however, the deal fell through; In April 1982, Michigan Interstate stopped moving freight north of the city of Ann Arbor, and the carferries were idled. (Photo by Dennis Schmidt.)

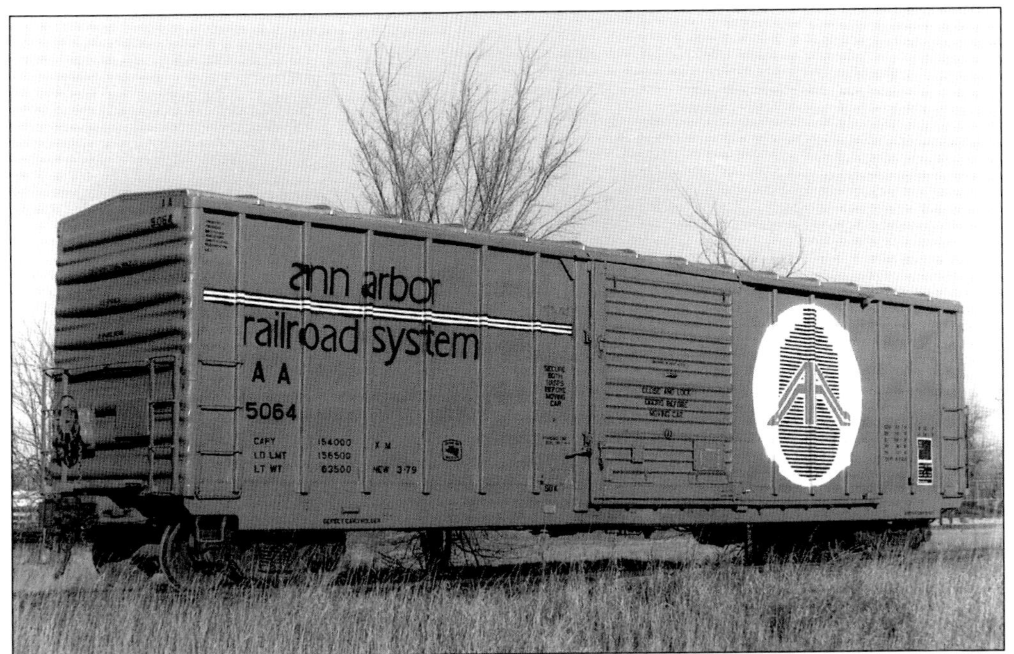

HECHO EN MEXICO. The Ann Arbor Railroad System placed a $4 million order for 100 new boxcars in the late 1970s. These 50-foot, single-door boxcars, road numbers 5000–5099, were built in Mexico in March 1979. Included in that order was AA #5064, pictured here in March 1980 in Alma, still looking fresh and new. (Photo by Dennis Schmidt.)

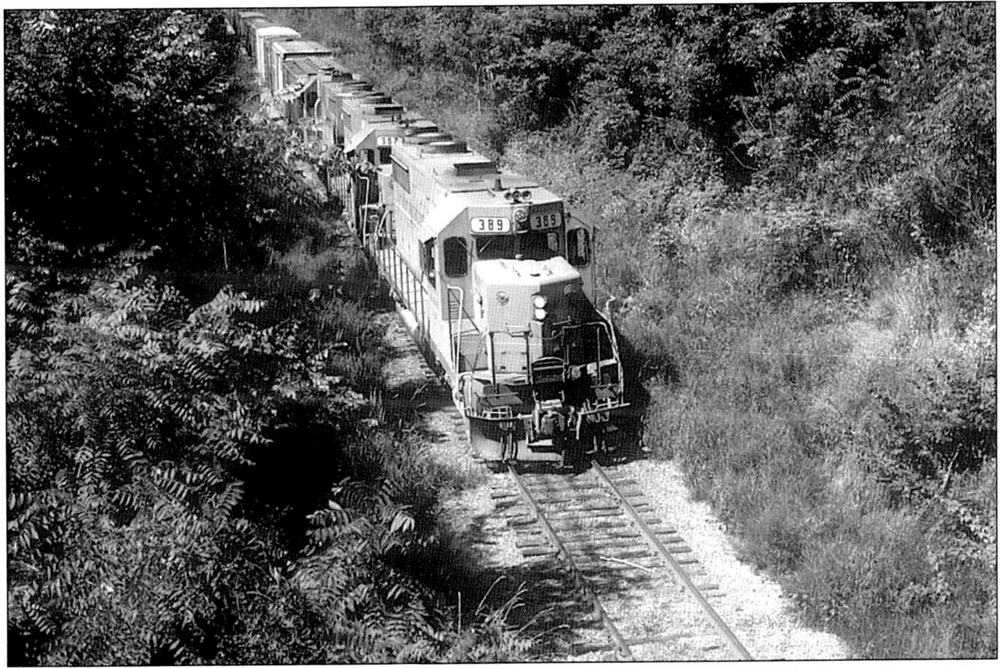

TUNNEL OF TREES. It is the height of summer—August 22, 1980—and three Ann Arbor Railroad GP35s, with AA #389 in the lead, pull a long mixed manifest freight train through overhanging trees near Ithaca. (Photo by Dennis Schmidt.)

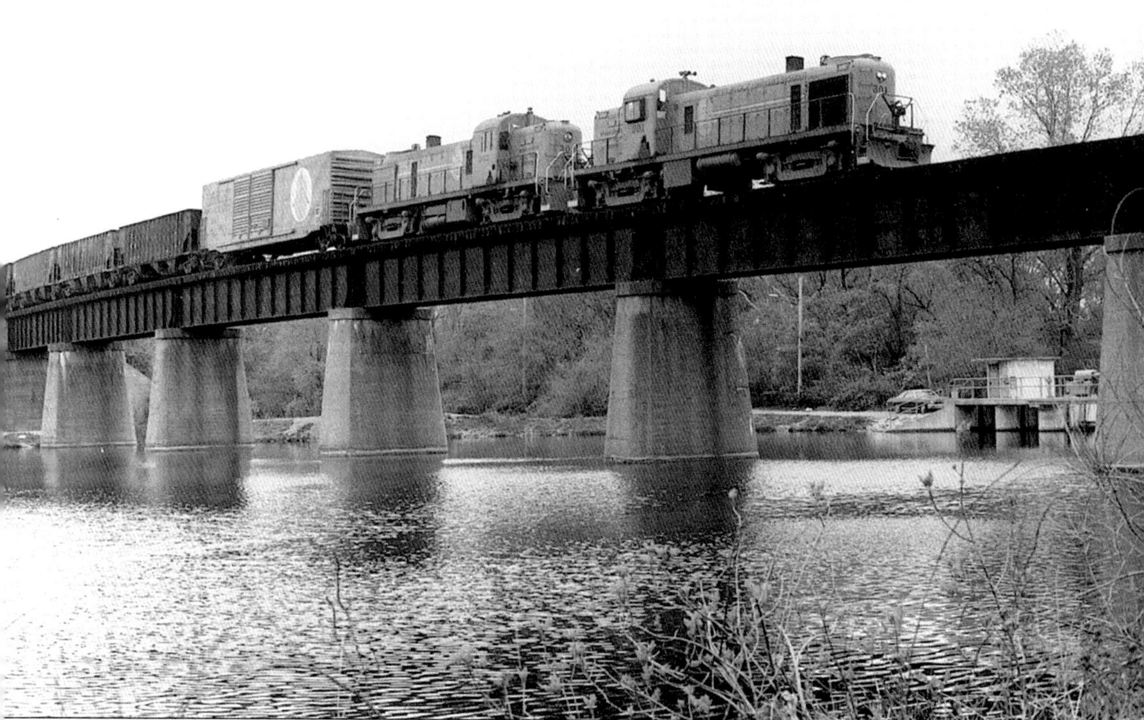

Over the River. Two Alco RS2s pull a cut of freight cars across the Huron River in Ann Arbor on May 15, 1980. The Alcos, #301 and #303, were built in February 1950 for the Green Bay & Western Railroad (with the same road numbers), and sold to the Ann Arbor in 1979. Although long out of freight service, both locomotives have so far staved off being sent to the scrapper; as of early 2005, #301 and #303 were owned by the Soo Line Historical & Technical Society, based in Duluth, Minnesota. (Collection of D. C. Jesse Burkhardt.)

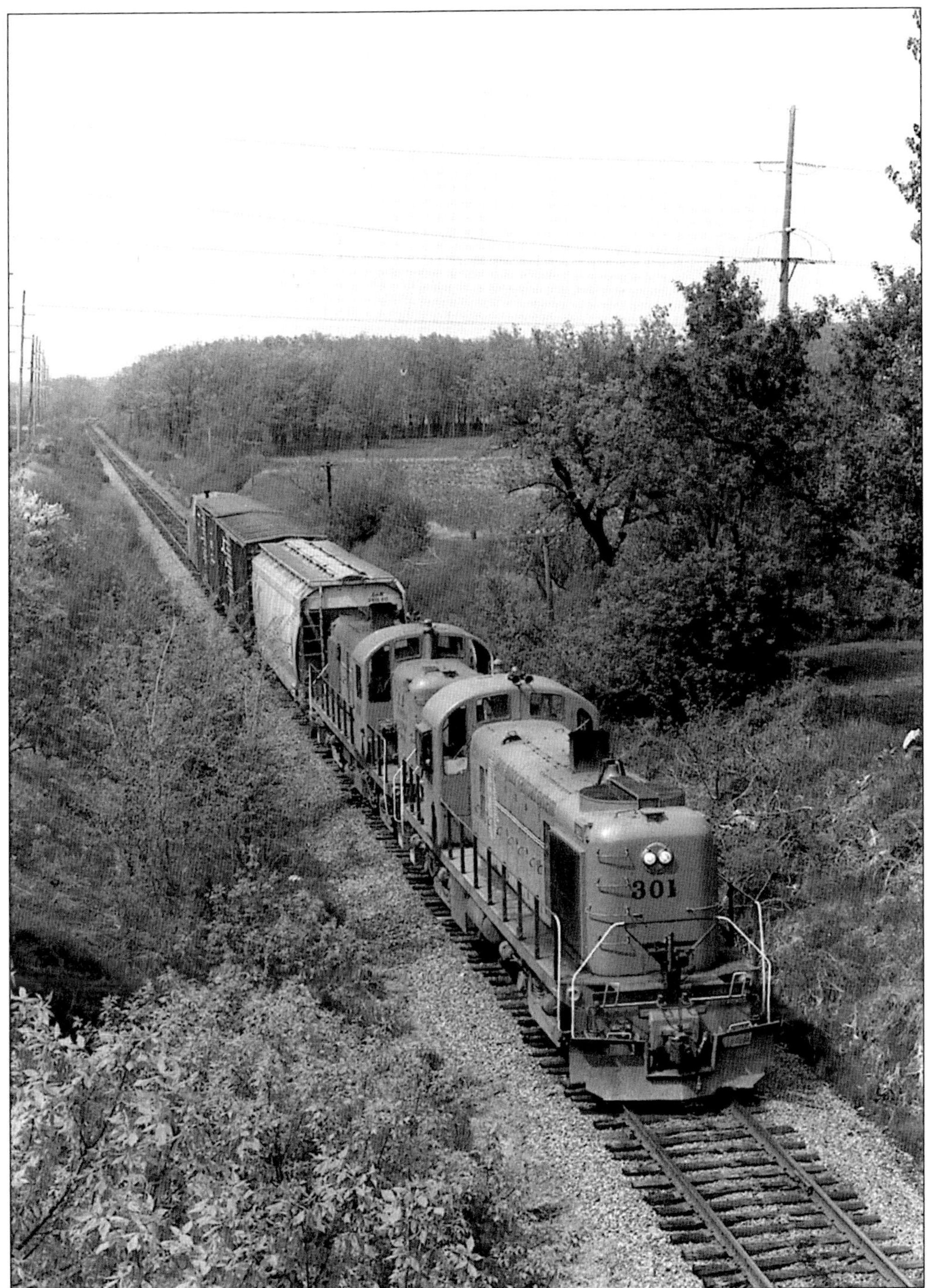

Three Cars Today. Later on the same day, the same pair of Alcos roll through the scenic landscape north of Howell, Michigan, with a short train that includes only a covered hopper, two boxcars, and a caboose. This local operated as an Ann Arbor-Owosso turn, switching industries along the route and hauling cars between the road's operating headquarters at Owosso and Ferry Yard in Ann Arbor. (Collection of D. C. Jesse Burkhardt.)

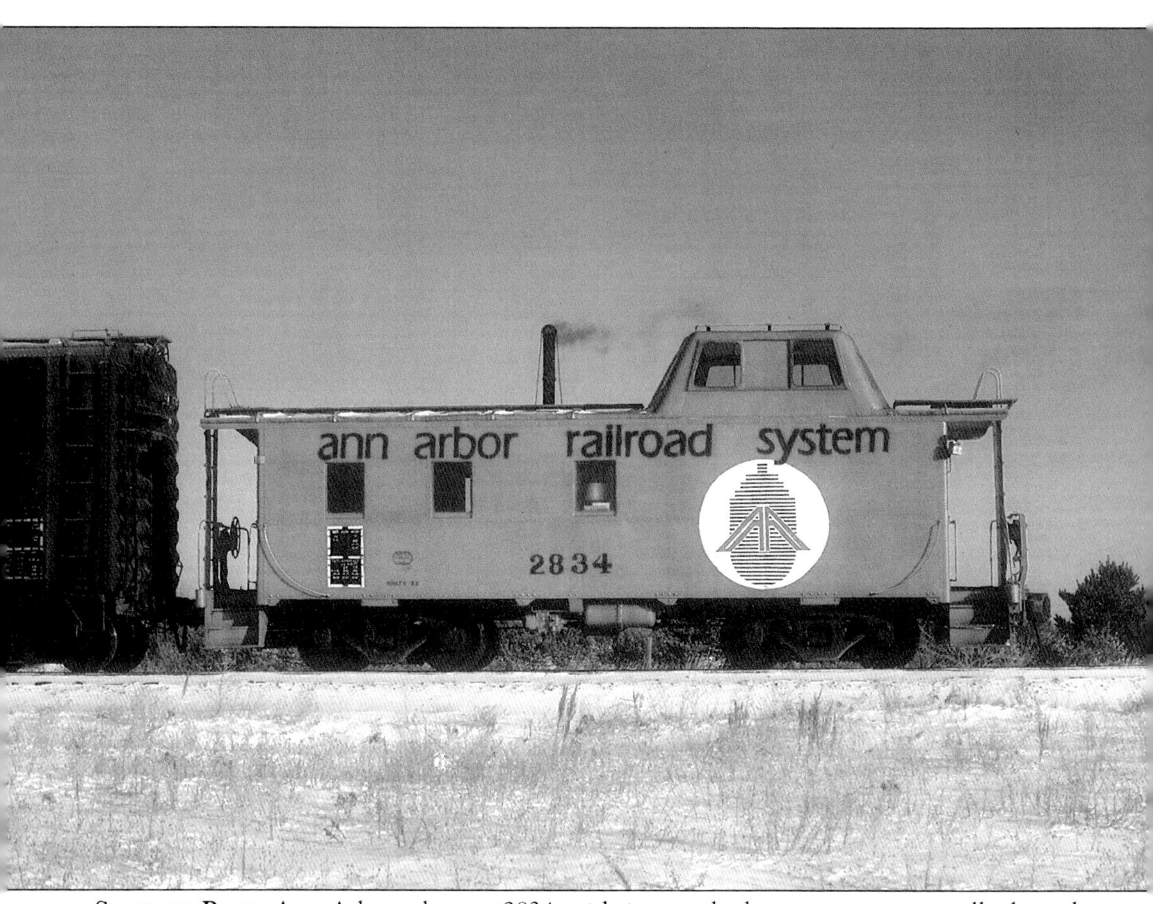

SMOKING PAST. Ann Arbor caboose #2834, with its new-look corporate image, rolls through snowy Cadillac, Michigan, on December 20, 1980. This caboose was built in the early 1950s when the Wabash Railroad controlled the AA. The new logo was created for the Michigan Interstate Railway, which operated the Annie's trains from 1977 to 1982. With the smoke trailing from the stovepipe, it's obvious the crew has a warm fire going in the coal stove on this cold winter's day in northern Michigan. (Photo by Dennis Schmidt.)

Two

PASSENGER TRAINS

The 20-mile stretch of track from Frankfort to Thompsonville, where the Ann Arbor once crossed the Chicago-Petoskey division of the old Pere Marquette railway, was immortalized in the pages of Bruce Catton's Waiting For the Morning Train. *The eminent Civil War historian spent his boyhood in nearby Benzonia and in his travels boarded the Ann Arbor trains at Beulah, which is just down a steep hill from Benzonia.*

—Harry Cook, "Forevermore, Waiting For the Morning Train," *Detroit Free Press*, October 4, 1985

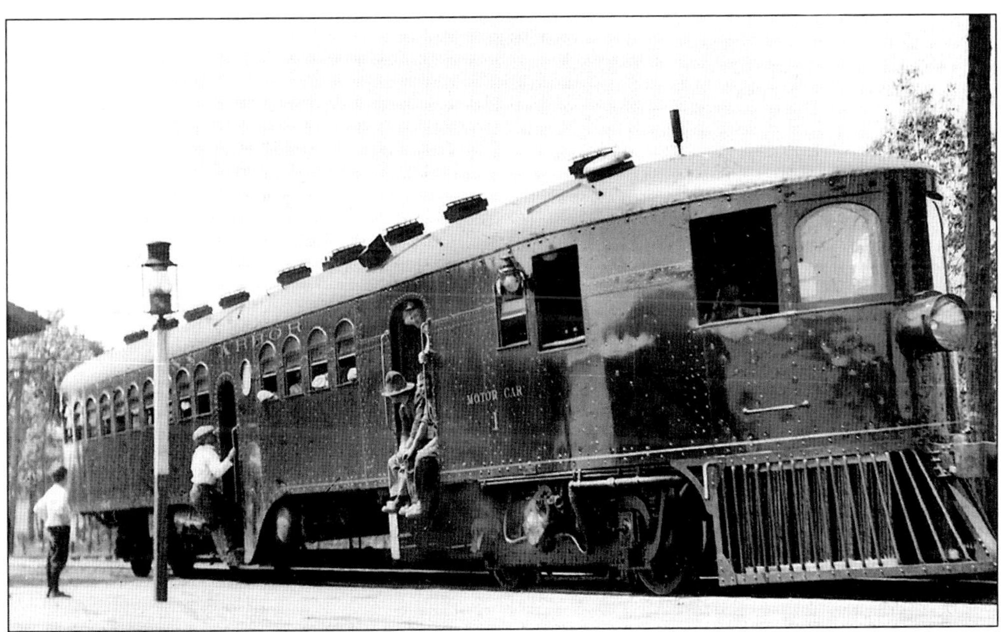

THIRTEEN-YEAR RUN. Ann Arbor Motor Car #1 pauses at the station at Lakeland, Michigan, on May 11, 1911. The Ann Arbor Railroad used these gasoline-powered, mechanical-drive railcars from 1911 to 1924. The Ann Arbor's McKeen cars were the first self-propelled passenger cars operating in Michigan. (Courtesy of the Claude T. Stoner Collection, Bentley Historical Library, University of Michigan.)

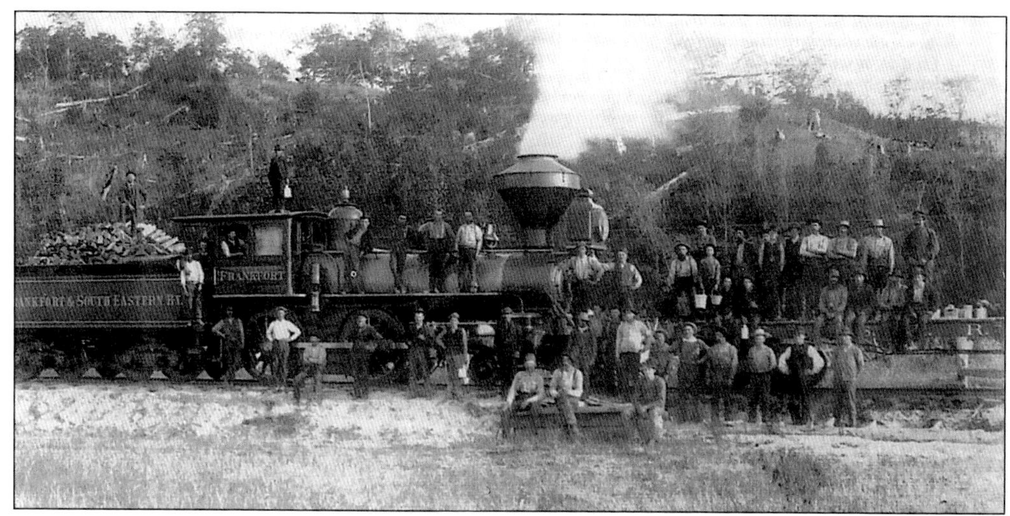

EMPLOYEE SPECIAL. On July 4, 1889, employees of the Frankfort & South Eastern Railway pose for a photo to commemorate the first passenger train on the newly opened rail line linking Frankfort and Copemish. Notice the name of the locomotive: *Frankfort*. (Courtesy of the Benzie Area Historical Society.)

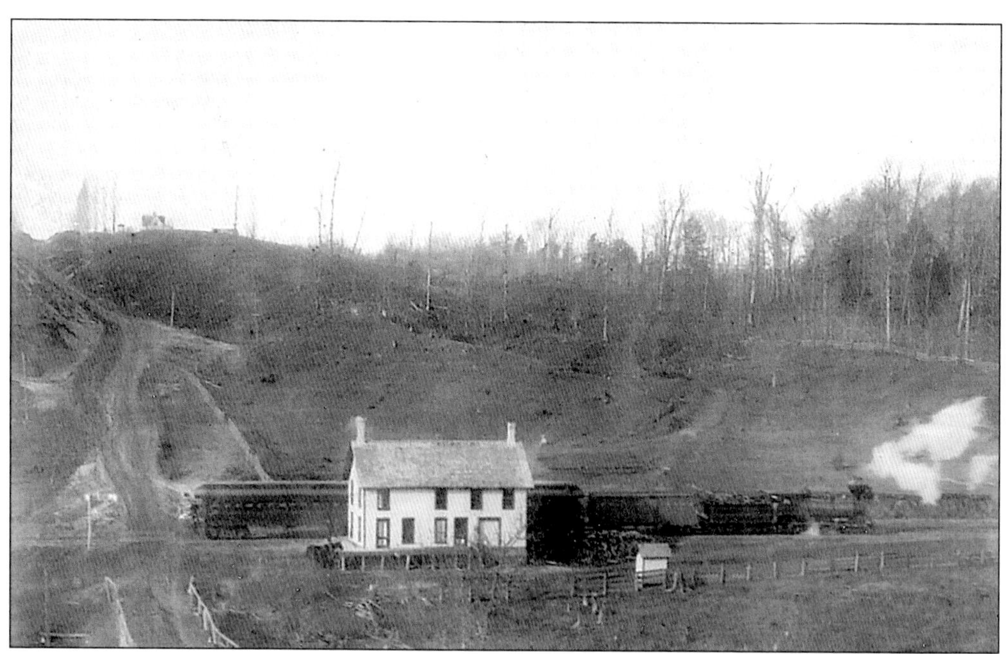

BENZONIA, 1890. A Frankfort & South Eastern Railway passenger train pulls away from the station at Benzonia, Michigan, in September 1890. This facility, about seven miles east of Frankfort, greeted passengers coming and going on the Frankfort & South Eastern. The F&SE became part of the Toledo, Ann Arbor & North Michigan Railroad about two years after this photo was taken. (Courtesy of the Benzie Area Historical Society.)

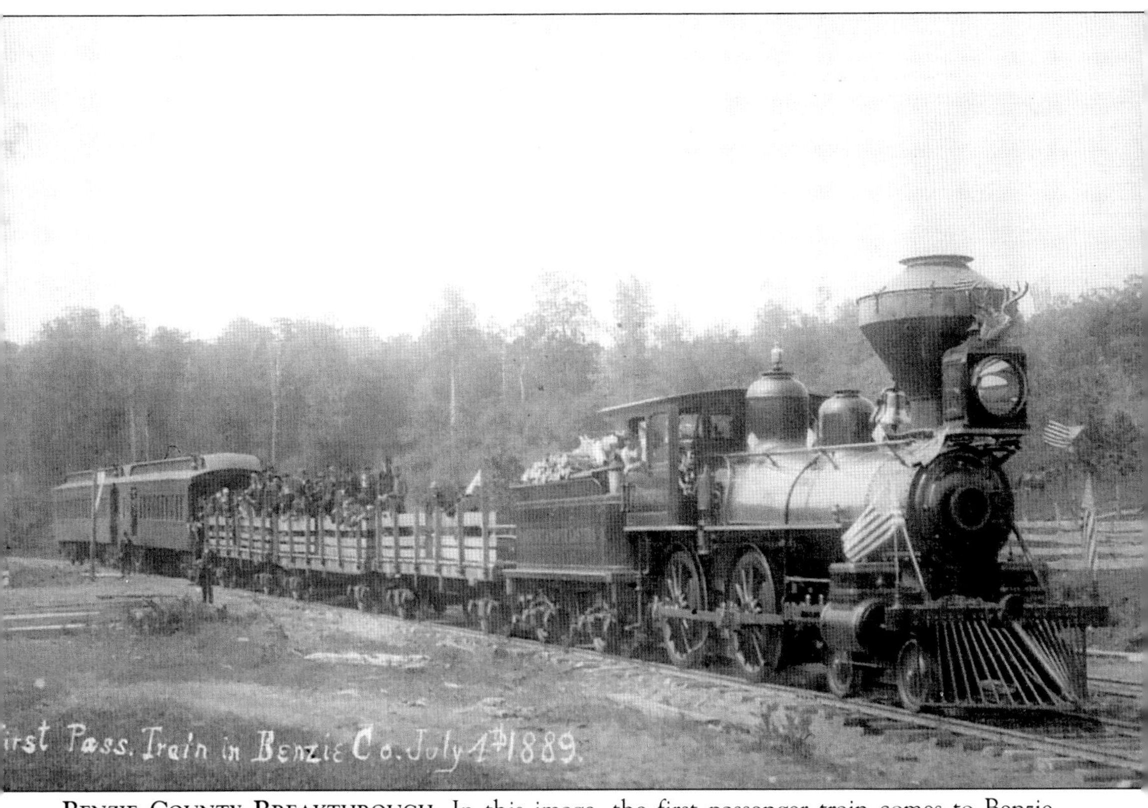

Benzie County Breakthrough. In this image, the first passenger train comes to Benzie County, in a northwest corner of Michigan's Lower Peninsula, on July 4, 1889. Traffic began to flow on the line that year after the Frankfort & South Eastern Railway completed its 25-mile line between Frankfort and Copemish. Festive flags adorn the locomotive, and there are many passengers aboard to celebrate the historic event. The Toledo, Ann Arbor & North Michigan purchased the F&SE in 1892, thereby providing access to the harbor at Frankfort and opening a direct link to Toledo, Ohio. Fittingly, the motto of the TAA&NM was: "The Key to Northern Michigan." (Courtesy of the Benzie Area Historical Society.)

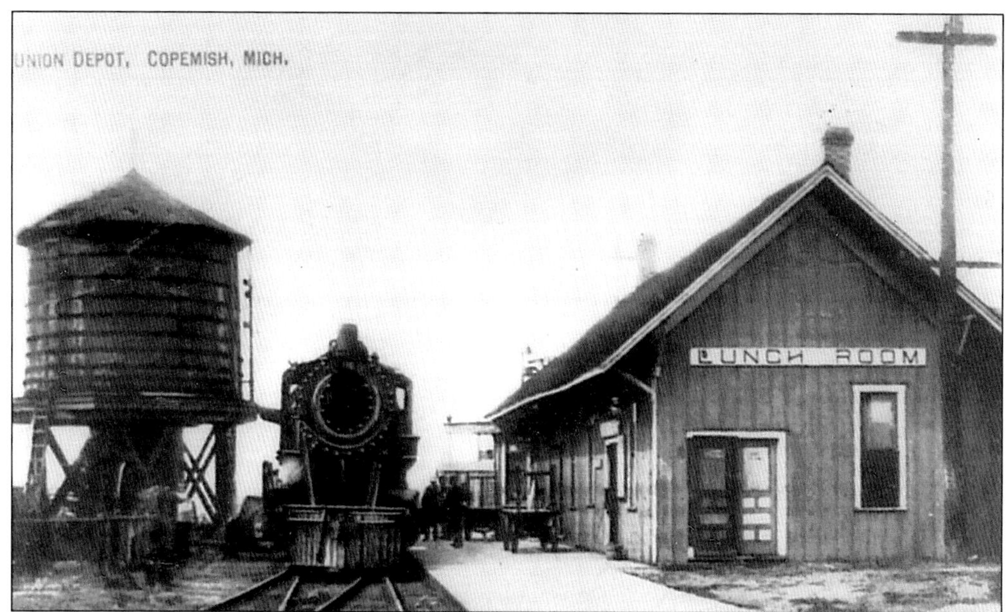

UNION DEPOT. A passenger train takes on water at the station at Copemish, Michigan, about 25 miles southeast of Frankfort, in this undated photo. The caption on the photo reads "Union Depot," as Copemish was also served by the Manistee & Northeastern for many years. The depot was built in 1892. (Courtesy of the Benzie Area Historical Society.)

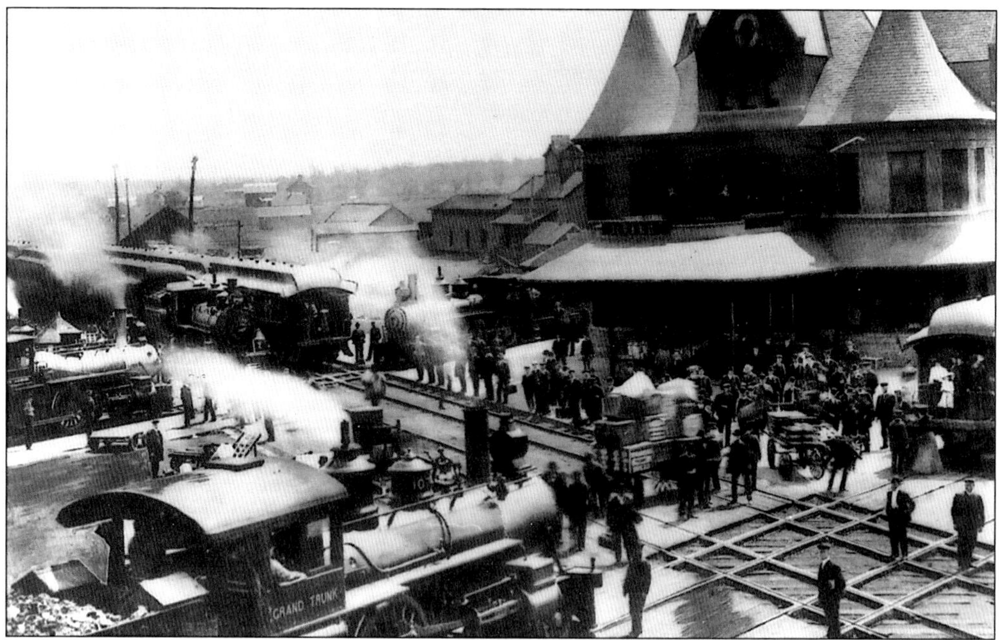

CONFLUENCE. Passenger trains of the Ann Arbor Railroad and the Grand Trunk Railway jam Durand Union Station in this 1905 scene. During this era, 42 passenger trains a day called on Durand's magnificent station, built where the tracks of the 2 railroads cross. Ann Arbor trains went north and south from here, while GT passengers could go in any of four directions. The station was built in 1903, then rebuilt in 1905 after a fire. (Collection of D. C. Jesse Burkhardt.)

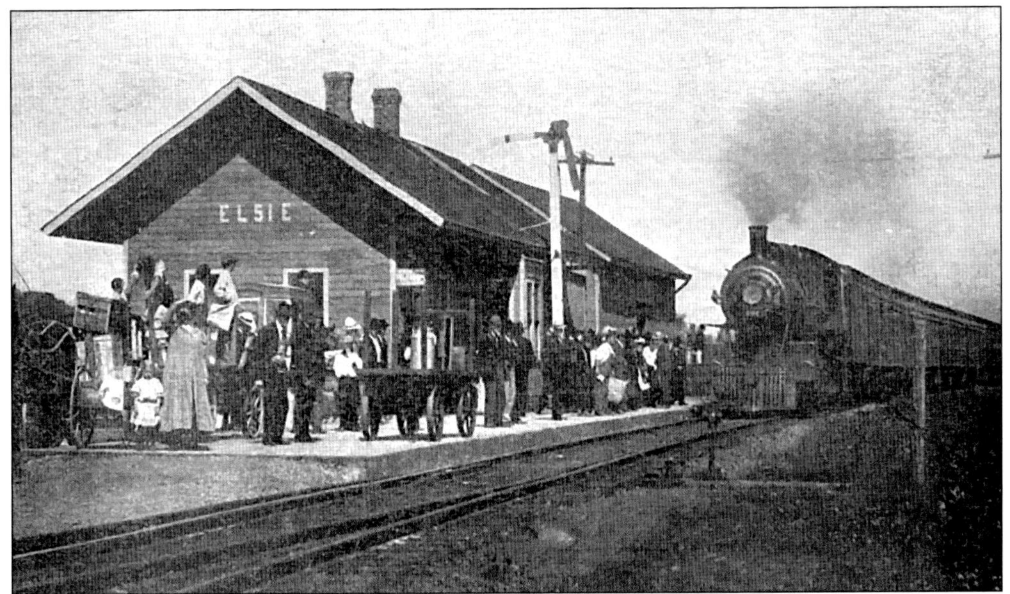

A CROWD AT ELSIE. Passengers wait for a train at the Ann Arbor Railroad depot at Elsie, Michigan, in this antique postcard scene. Elsie was located at Milepost 120, about 14 miles north of Owosso. (Collection of D. C. Jesse Burkhardt.)

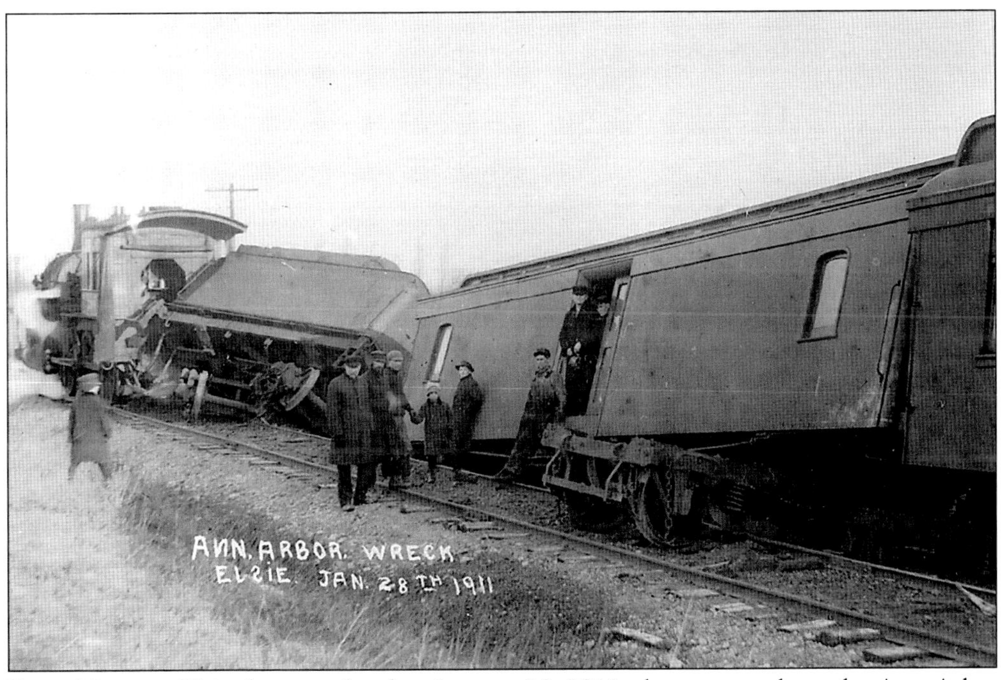

ELSIE MISHAP. This photograph taken January 28, 1911, shows a wreck on the Ann Arbor Railroad at Elsie. The tender of locomotive #108 has left the tracks, as well as several passenger cars. (Courtesy of the Claude T. Stoner Collection, Bentley Historical Library, University of Michigan.)

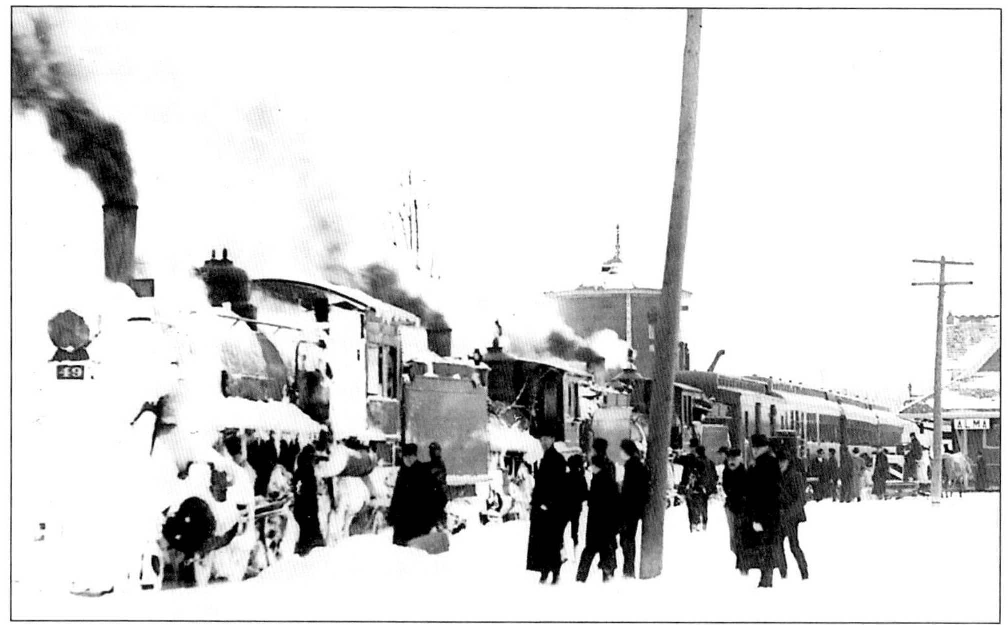

TRIPLE HEADER. Three locomotives, with Ann Arbor #49 in the lead, head a passenger train at the snowy depot at Alma on February 19, 1908. The extra power may have been needed to ensure the train would not get stuck in a snowdrift somewhere down the line. (Courtesy of the Claude T. Stoner Collection, Bentley Historical Library, University of Michigan.)

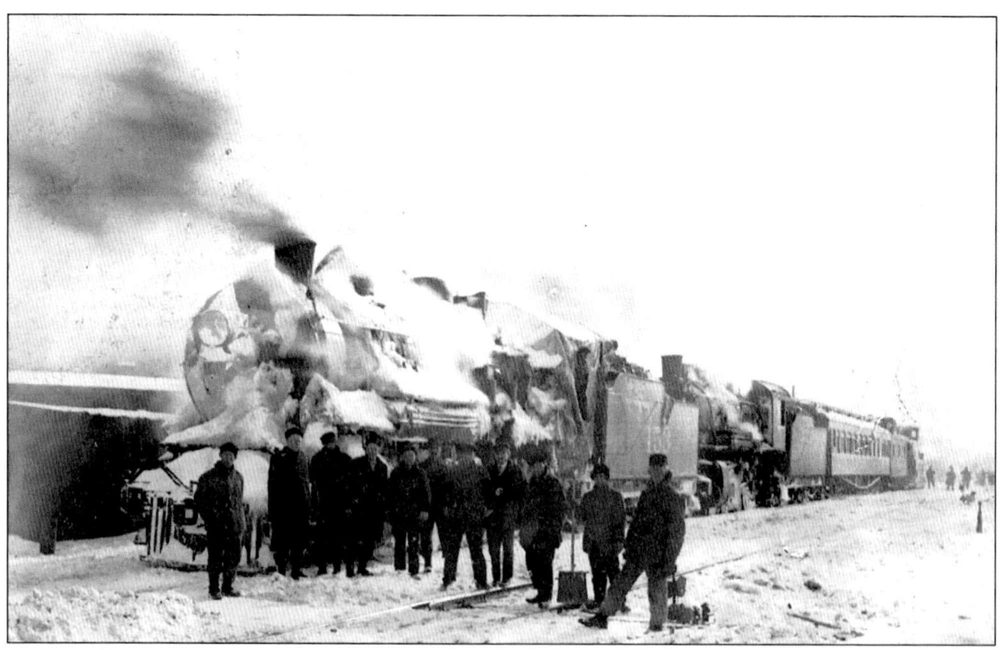

SHOVEL PATROL. Ann Arbor Railroad employees—some wielding snow shovels and others just waiting for the tracks to be cleared so they can get their passenger train moving again—pause for a photograph as crews work to get ice and snow out of the switch points at Ann Arbor. The date is January 14, 1918. (Courtesy of the Claude T. Stoner Collection, Bentley Historical Library, University of Michigan.)

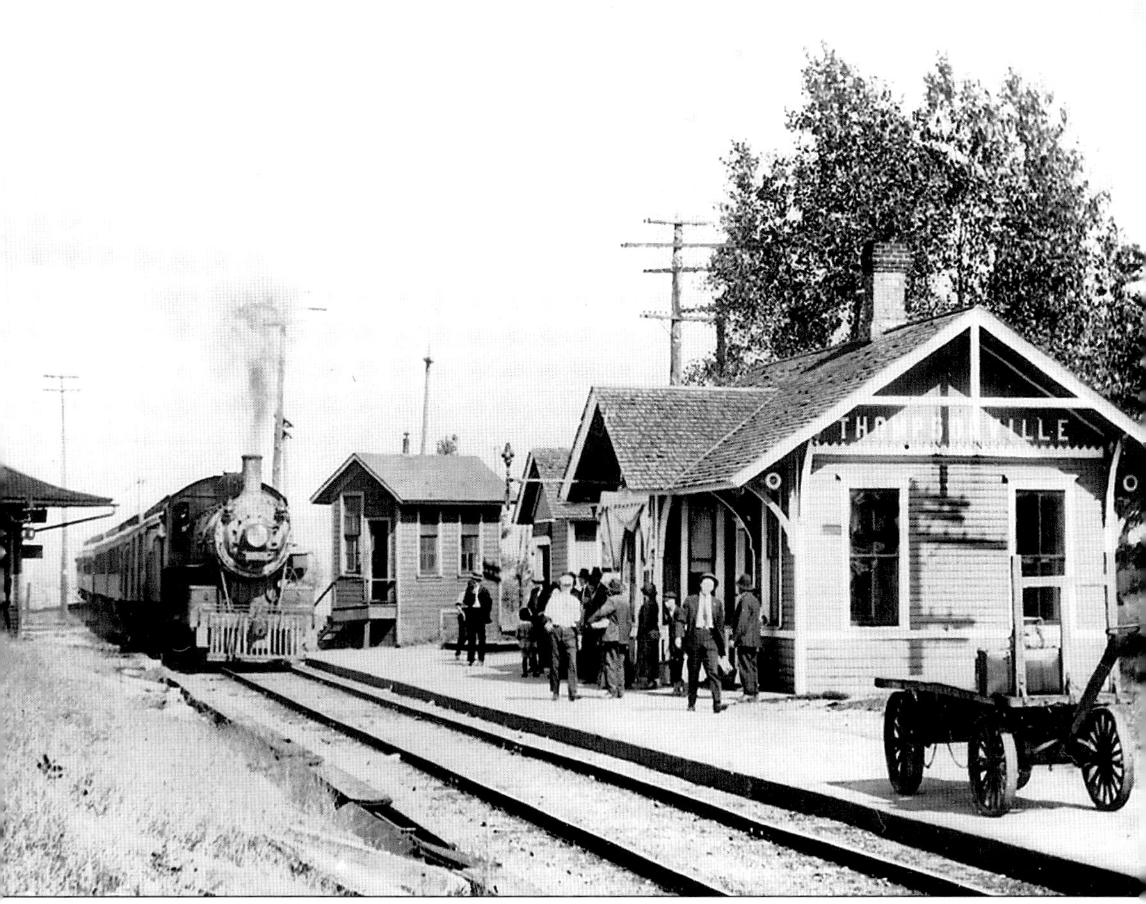

TRAIN TIME IN THOMPSONVILLE. A southbound passenger train headed by Ann Arbor locomotive #203, a 4-4-2 type built in 1907, pulls in to Thompsonville, Michigan, *c.* 1910. The train is crossing over the Petoskey-Grand Rapids line of the Pere Marquette Railroad, and the Pere Marquette depot is on the left in this view. Thompsonville is located about 22 miles southeast of Frankfort. (Courtesy of the Claude T. Stoner Collection, Bentley Historical Library, University of Michigan.)

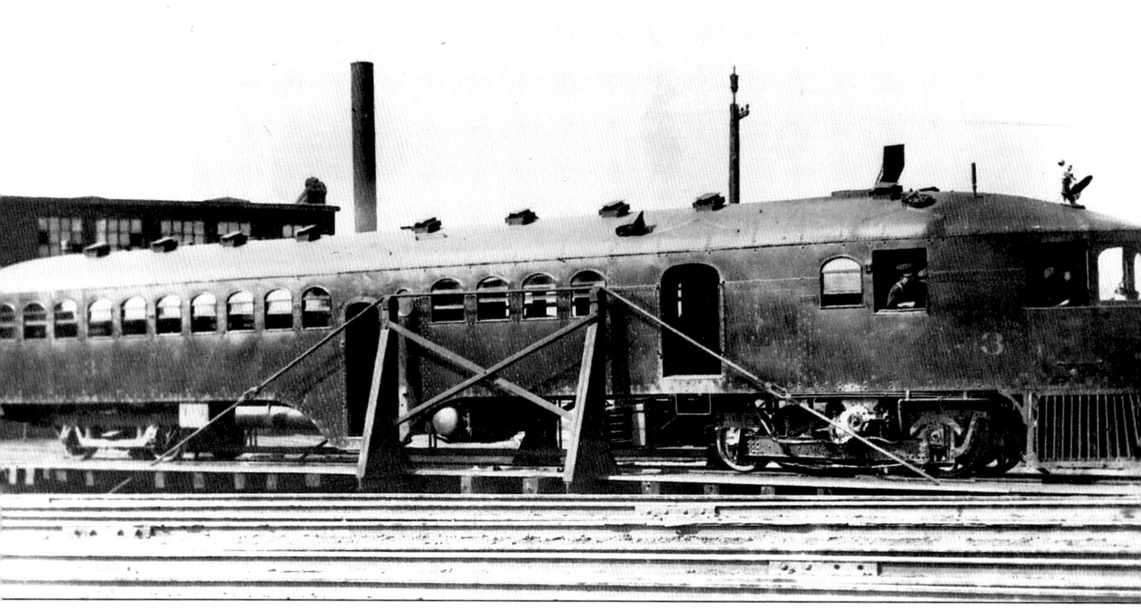

TURNTABLE RIDE. Ann Arbor #3, a McKeen "rail bus" built in 1911, takes a ride on the Owosso turntable in this scene from 1920. These ungainly machines, built by the McKeen Motor Car Company of Omaha, Nebraska, carried 56 passengers and light freight. The Ann Arbor had five of these gasoline-fired contraptions, which were intended to provide more economical passenger operations than a regular train could. The McKeen cars typically had round "porthole" windows, but the Ann Arbor requested a more traditional window design. On the Ann Arbor, the "windsplitters" ran only between Cadillac and Toledo. Steeper grades kept them from operating between Frankfort and Cadillac. (Collection of Harold K. Vollrath.)

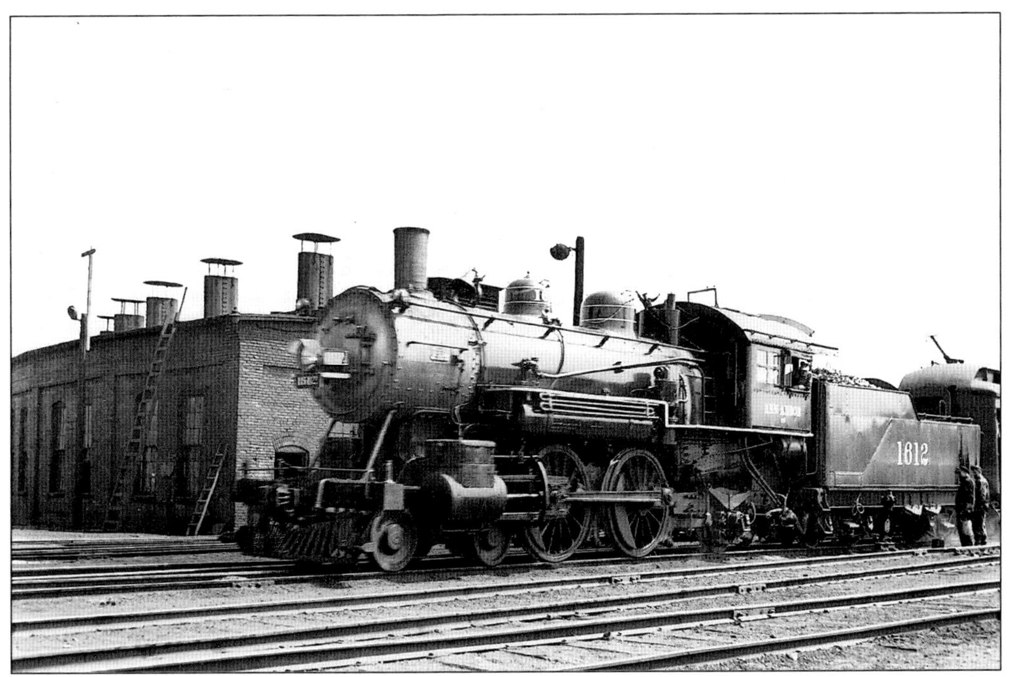

SLEEK POWER. A Schenectady-built 4-4-2 from 1907, Ann Arbor #1612—with a "heavyweight" passenger car attached—is seen in Owosso, c. 1940. (Collection of D. C. Jesse Burkhardt.)

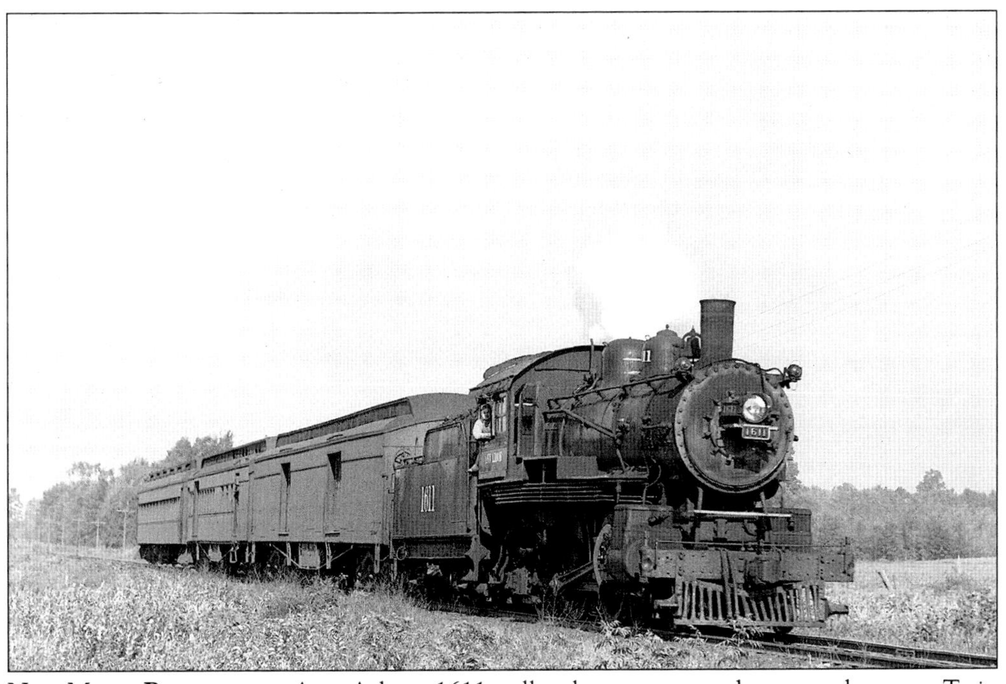

NOT MANY PASSENGERS. Ann Arbor #1611 pulls a baggage car and two coach cars as Train #12 rolls south in a scene from the early 1920s. The Ann Arbor's Train #12 operated between Ann Arbor and Toledo, Monday through Saturday. Train #11 ran Toledo to Ann Arbor on the same days. (Collection of D. C. Jesse Burkhardt.)

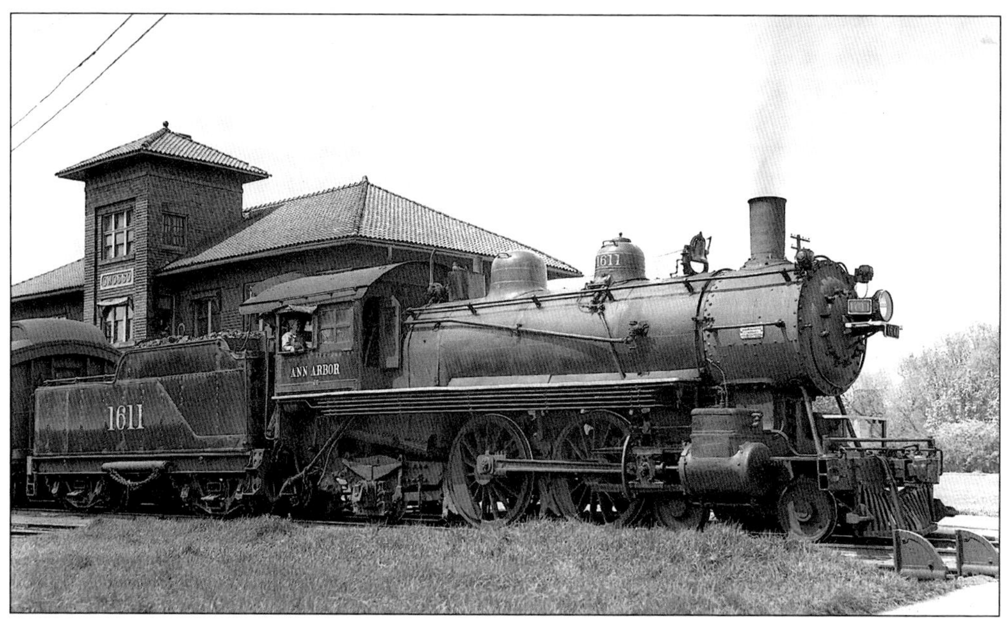

Waiting at the Station. In these two nearly identical scenes captured on two different days, Ann Arbor 4-4-2 Schenectady locomotives #1611 (top photo) and #1614 (bottom photo) pause alongside the classy brick passenger station in Owosso as they load and unload passengers in May 1938. The passenger trains are headed south toward Ann Arbor. Regrettably, both locomotives were sent to the scrapper in 1951. (Collection of D. C. Jesse Burkhardt.)

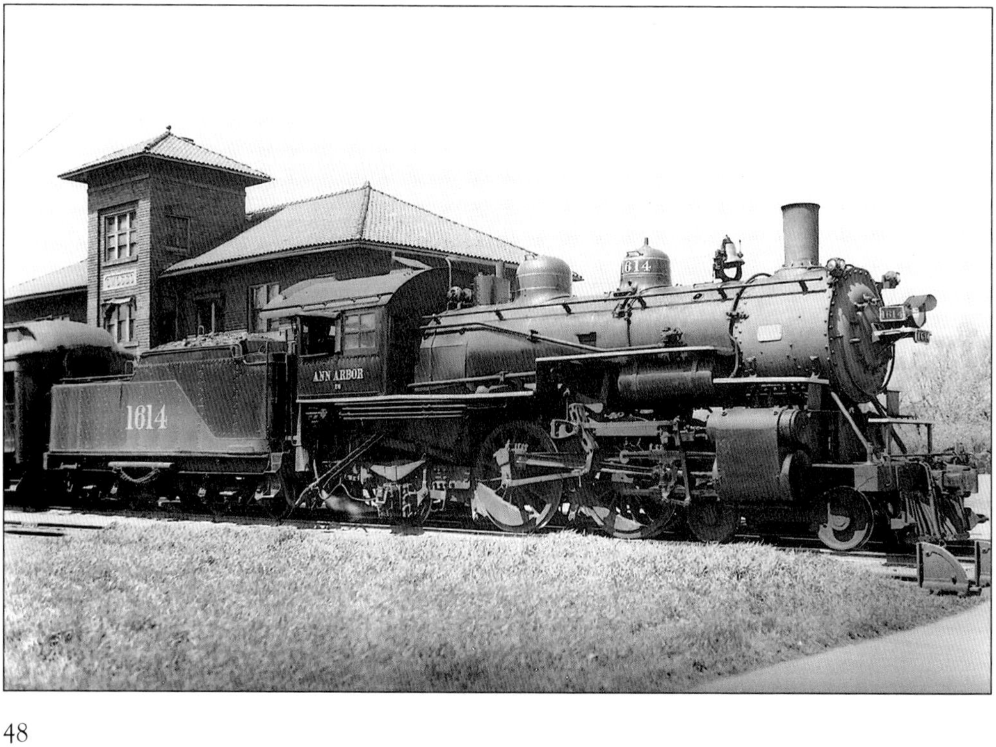

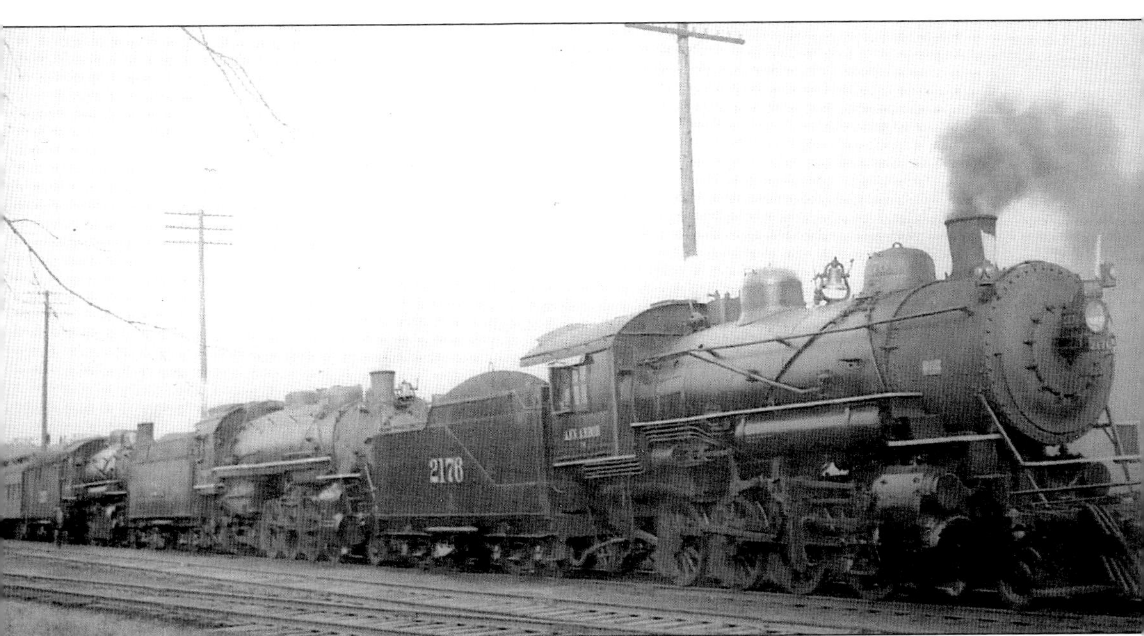

STADIUM SPECIALS. Trains carrying college football fans were once a common sight at the University of Michigan in Ann Arbor during the autumn football season. In this scene from the early 1940s, three locomotives, headed by Ann Arbor #2176 and its white flags, prepare to pull one of this particular day's football extras south from Ferry Yard to Toledo. (Courtesy of the Benzie Area Historical Society.)

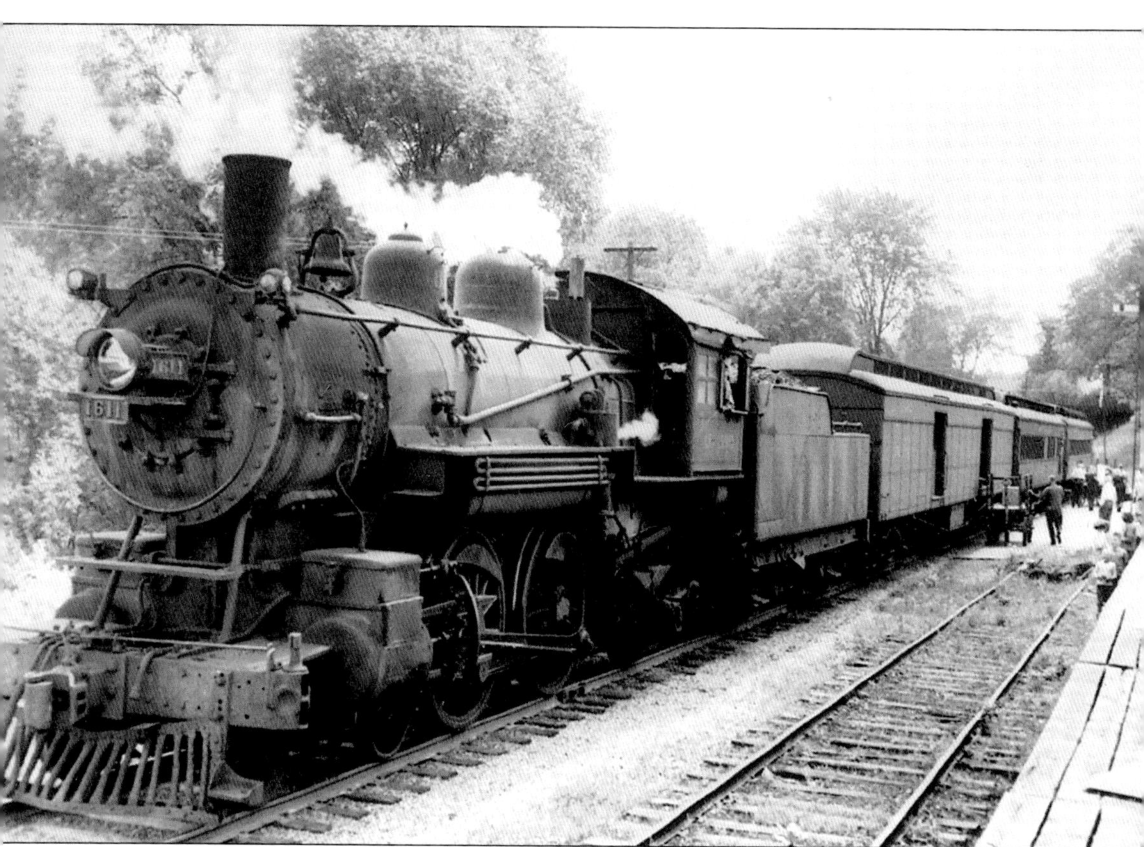

LAST TRAIN AT HOWELL. In this image, the last regular passenger train on the Ann Arbor Railroad prepares to leave the Howell, Michigan, station on July 19, 1950. After this train pulled away and reached its final destination, the era of passenger train service on the AA came to an end. Rock musician and Ann Arbor native Bob Seger reflected on this unwelcome milestone in his late 1960s song, "Railroad Days": *Yesterday, I heard they shut the trains down/The ones that ran by the field where I would play/They said the folks want new and faster transportation/It's just like me, I'll be obsolete one day.* (Courtesy of the Claude T. Stoner Collection, Bentley Historical Library, University of Michigan.)

Three

Tracks on the Water
The Carferry Fleet

Three rugged crewmen reveled in tales of their many Lake Michigan crossings; of the heritage of an America seemingly slipping away. Standing on the deck with them, gazing out at the waves, I could read the gleam of joy and pride in their eyes. They carried a sailing history in their souls.

—D. C. Jesse Burkhardt, journal entry, July 14, 1977

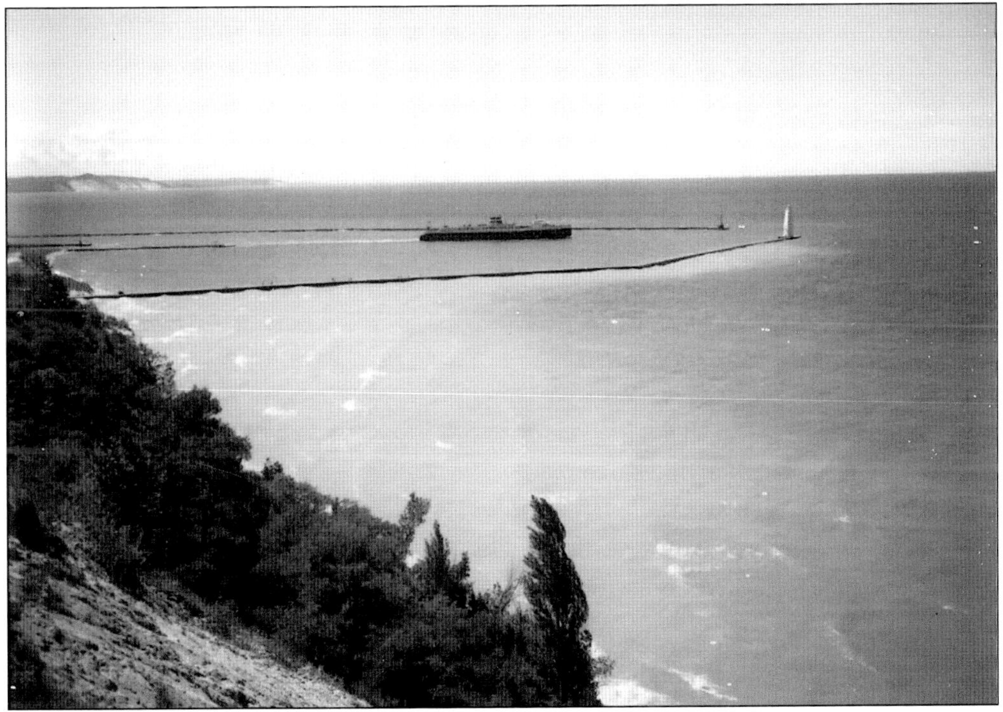

Headed To Wisconsin. Ann Arbor carferry *Arthur K. Atkinson* steams westward out of the harbor at Frankfort, bound for Kewaunee in August 1970. The Lake Michigan crossing took approximately four hours. (Photo by D. C. Jesse Burkhardt.)

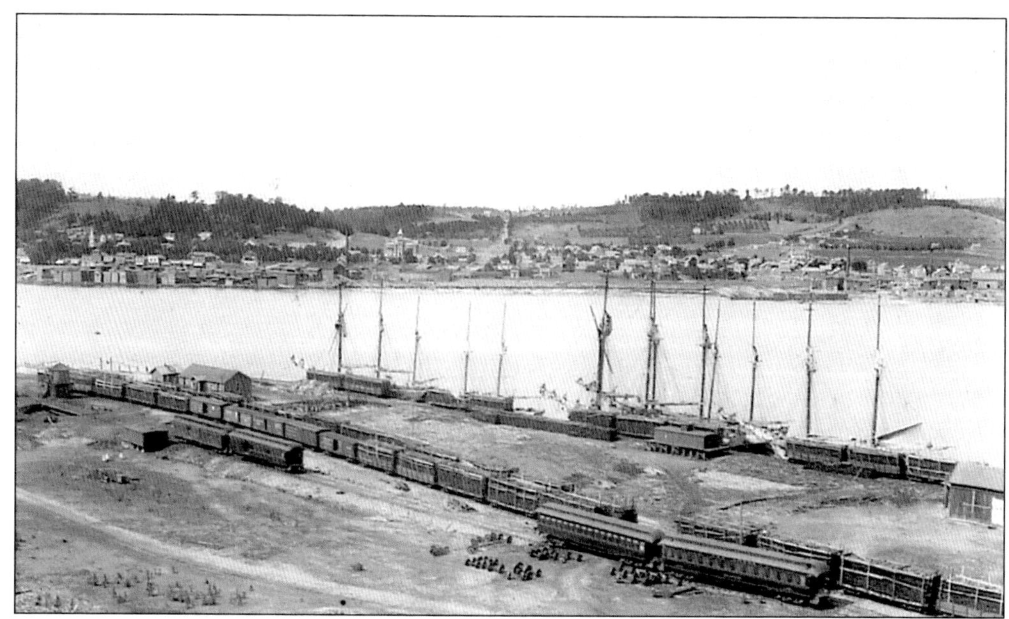

YARD WORK. This is an early view (looking north) of the Toledo, Ann Arbor & North Michigan Railway's freight yard at Elberta, *c.* 1890. The city of Frankfort is directly across Betsie Bay. In this scene, the yard is clearly still a work in progress, and it does not appear that ferry slips have yet been constructed. (Collection of the Benzie Area Historical Society.)

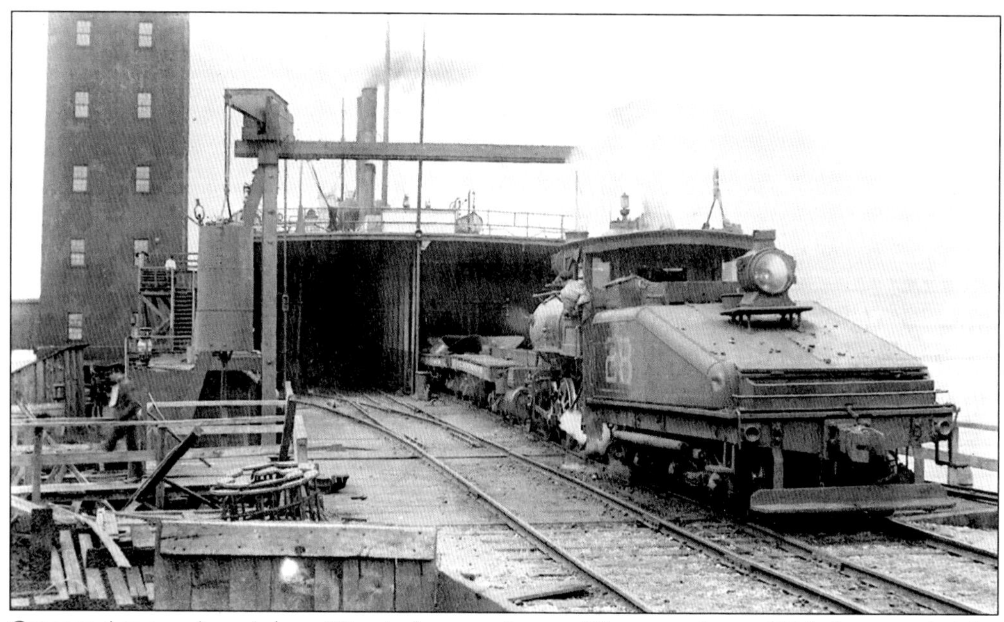

ON THE APRON. Ann Arbor #28 switches a carferry at Elberta in this *c.* 1905 photograph. The structure to the left of the ferry is a nine-story-tall grain elevator. Faintly visible to the right is the massive Royal Frontenac Hotel, built by the Ann Arbor Railroad in 1899. (It burned down in 1912). This locomotive went into service in November 1887, about five years before the first carferry sailed across Lake Michigan to Kewaunee, Wisconsin. (Courtesy of the Claude T. Stoner Collection, Bentley Historical Library, University of Michigan.)

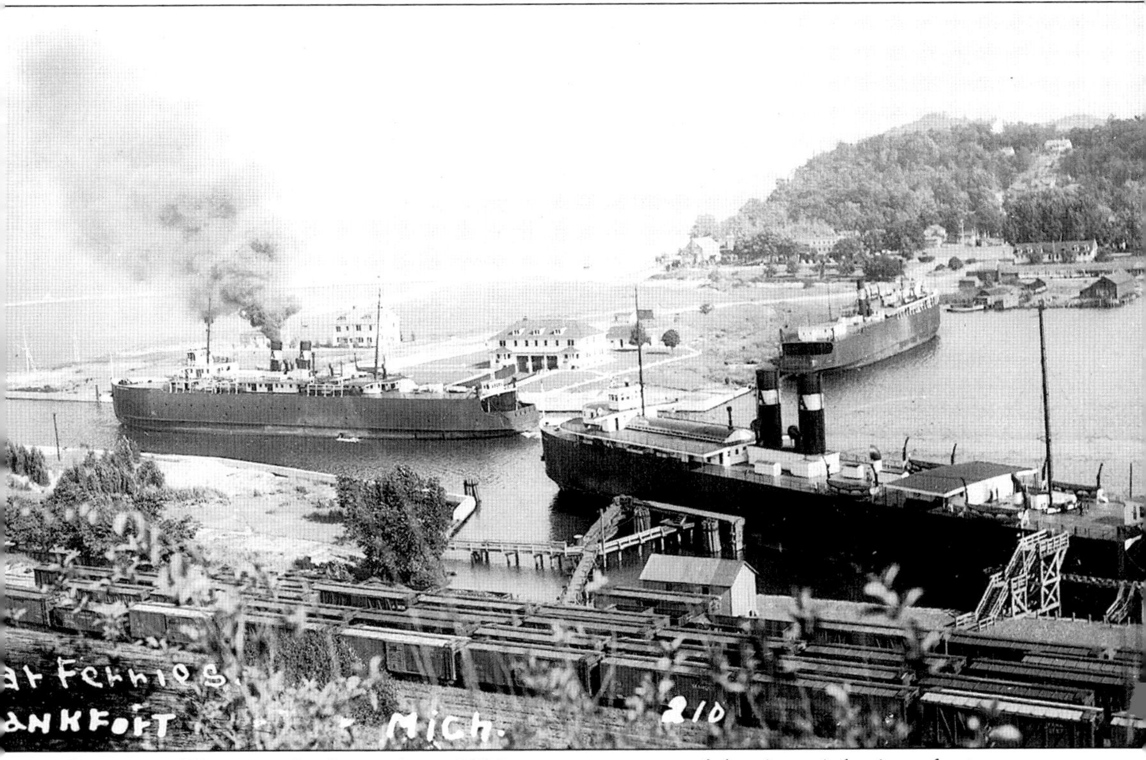

CROWDED HARBOR. In this striking 1920s panorama, one of the Ann Arbor's carferries pours out thick coal smoke as it heads away from Elberta and toward the open water of Lake Michigan after taking on freight cars at the harbor's east slip. Another AA carferry is being loaded at the harbor's west slip, while a third carferry is parked on the Frankfort side of Betsie Bay. In the foreground is a long string of Pere Marquette Railway boxcars. The Pere Marquette, a competitor of the Ann Arbor, also operated cross-lake carferry service to Wisconsin; its ferry terminal was at Ludington, Michigan, approximately 50 miles south of Frankfort. (Collection of D. C. Jesse Burkhardt.)

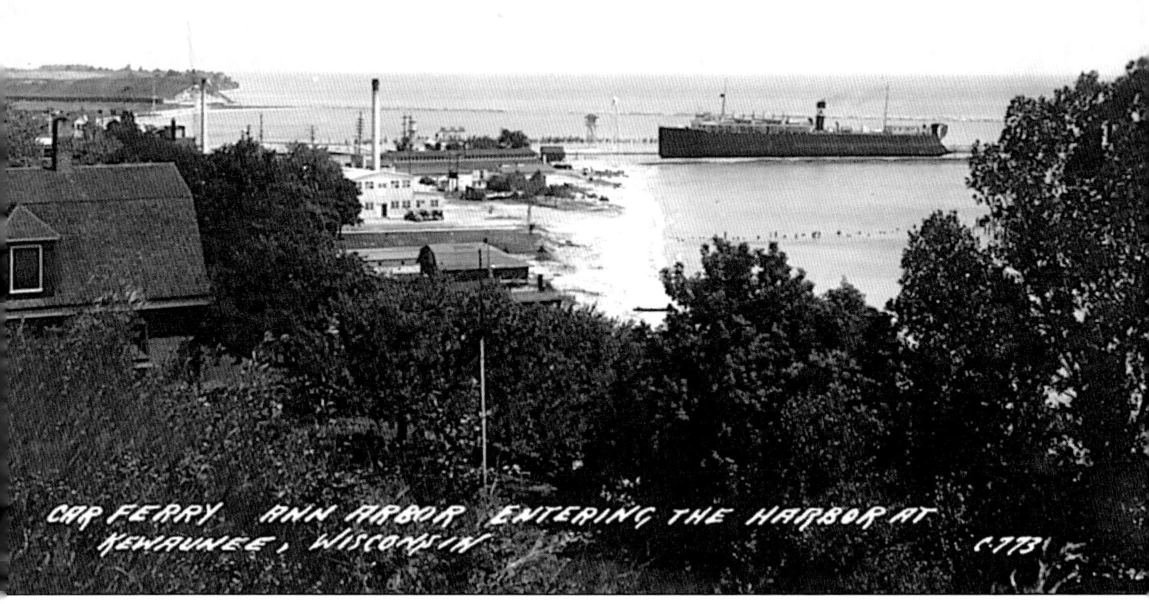

SLIPPING INTO KEWAUNEE. The Ann Arbor's first steel-hulled carferry, *Ann Arbor #3*, was launched in 1898. In this scene from the 1920s, the boat glides into the harbor at Kewaunee at the end of its westward journey from Elberta. *Ann Arbor #1* and *Ann Arbor #2*, the railroad's earliest carferries, had been built with wooden hulls. In 1892, Kewaunee became the first port to be called on by the Ann Arbor's fleet, and Kewaunee survived to be the last as well: the Ann Arbor Railroad moved rail traffic to and from the Wisconsin town until carferry service ended in 1982. Note the long cut of freight cars north of the harbor in this sharp photo. (Collection of D.C. Jesse Burkhardt.)

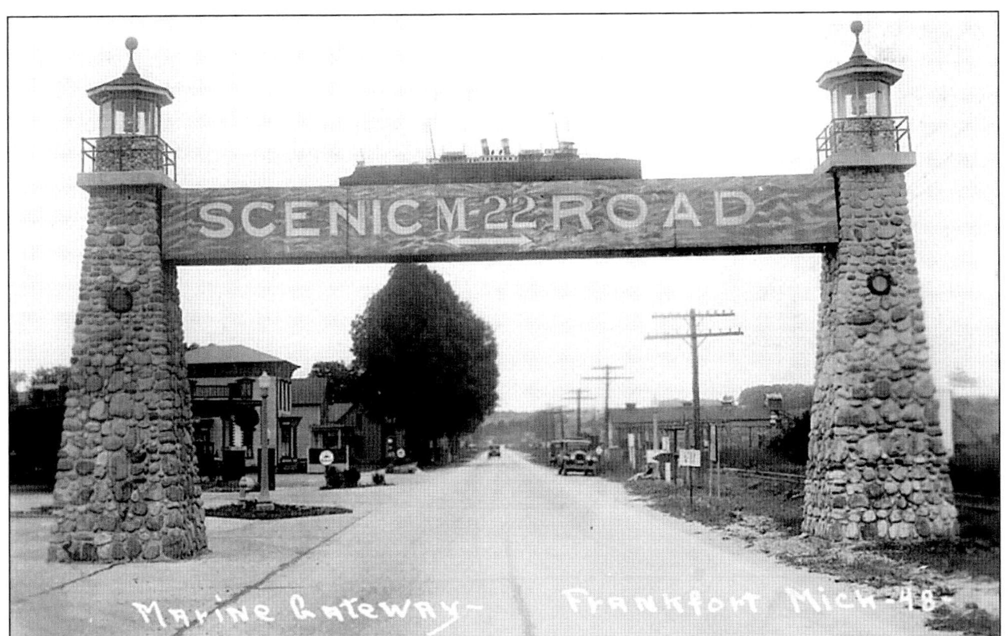

GATEWAY TO TOURISM. A stone archway celebrating the town's carferry operations welcomes visitors to Frankfort in this 1920s-era image. The sign stood over Main Street in Frankfort. The Ann Arbor Railroad's tracks are visible to the right. Although this structure did not last, the community carried the theme forward and later placed a new archway over nearby M-115. (Collection of D. C. Jesse Burkhardt.)

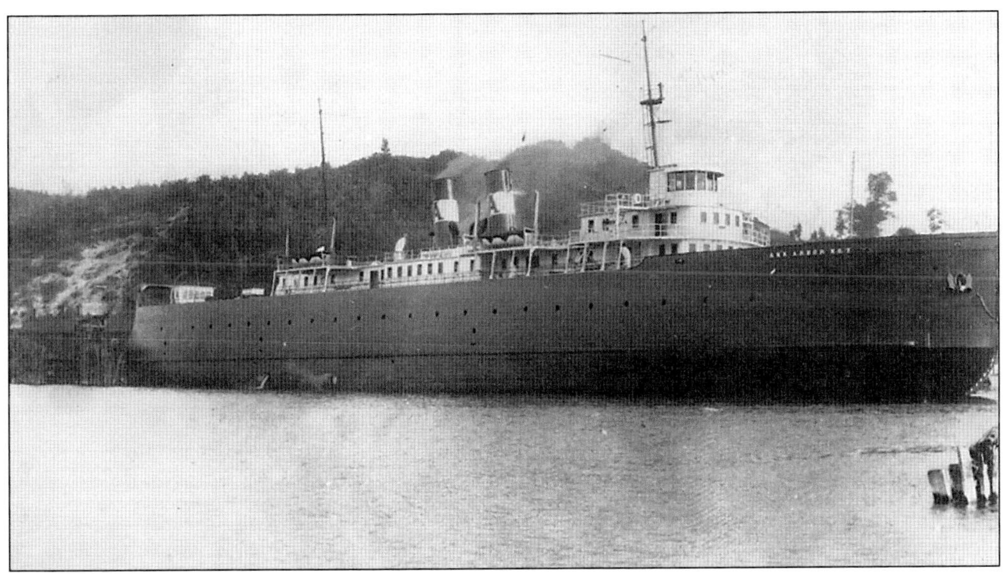

CAPACITY OF 30. *Ann Arbor #7*, seen here in the late 1920s docked at Elberta, was launched in 1925. Hauling freight cars on the carferries was clearly considered more important than moving passengers and automobiles, even by the 1950s. For example, the legend on the Ann Arbor's 1951 route map read as follows, in bold type: "ANN ARBOR CARFERRY #7—CAPACITY 30 FREIGHT CARS." Below that, in significantly smaller lettering, it continued: "With accommodations for handling passengers and automobiles." (Collection of D. C. Jesse Burkhardt.)

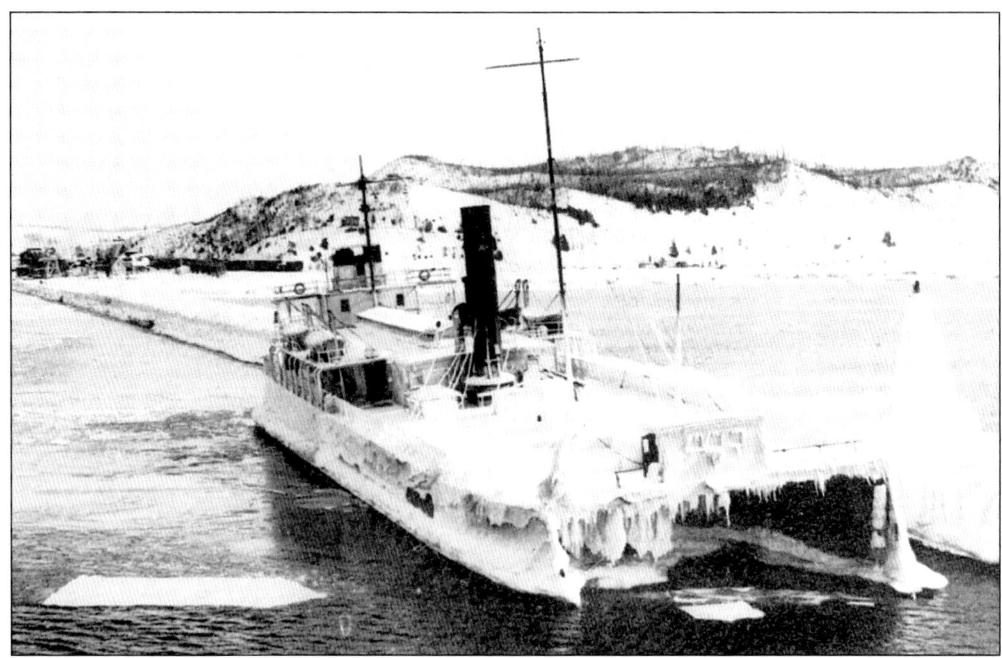

HEAVY WITH ICE. *Ann Arbor #4* founders against the Frankfort breakwater, February 14, 1923, after the gale depicted in Henry Bernstein's brilliant mural (opposite page). A thick coating of ice covers the entire boat in this photo, which was apparently taken from the lighthouse at the end of the north pier of the breakwater. A huge wave swamped the boat as it tried to get back to the dock in Betsie Bay. (Courtesy of the Claude T. Stoner Collection, Bentley Historical Library, University of Michigan.)

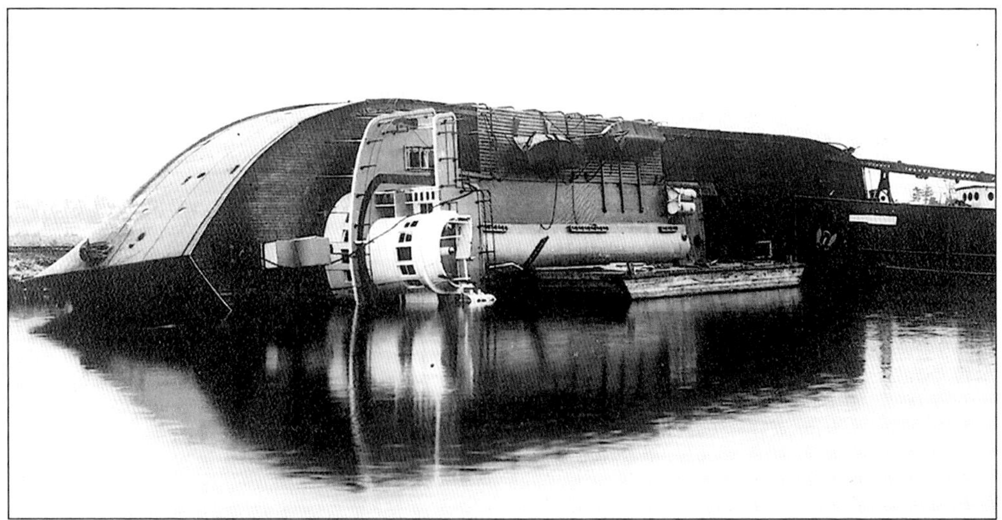

HAZARDS OF UNBALANCED LOADING. *Ann Arbor #4* is pictured half-submerged in the Manistique harbor after the boat capsized during the improper loading of ore cars on May 29, 1909. In this incident, too many cars were shoved onto one of the wing tracks, and over it rolled. No lives were lost in the mishap, but the carferry was out of service for four months while it was being repaired. (Courtesy of the Claude T. Stoner Collection, Bentley Historical Library, University of Michigan.)

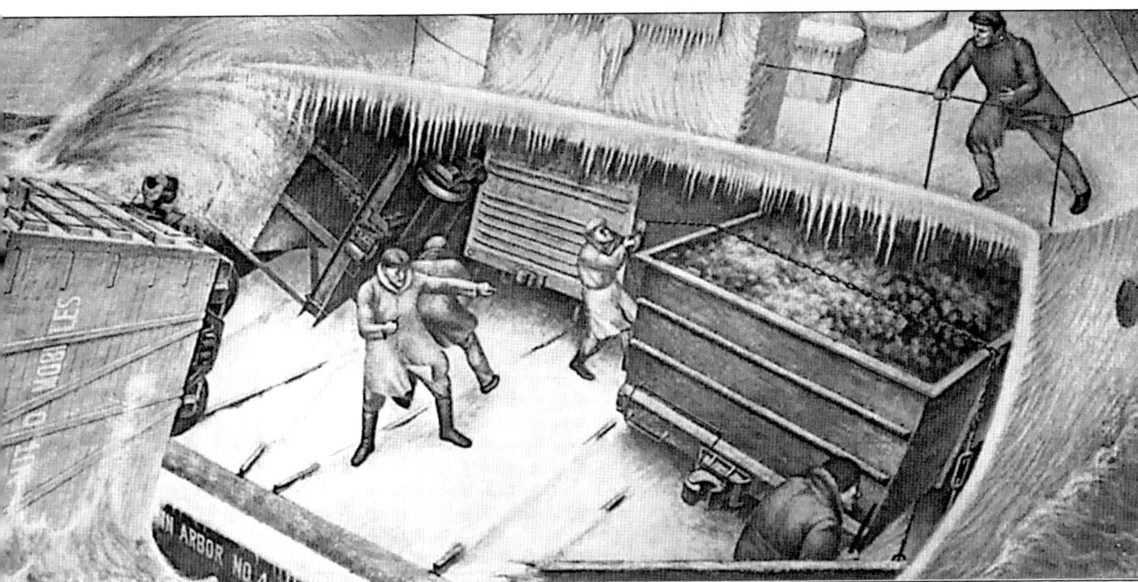

GALES OF FEBRUARY. This postcard depicts an incident that occurred on February 14, 1923. The carferry *Ann Arbor #4* encountered a gale soon after leaving Frankfort, and turned around to try to get safely back to the harbor. Boxcars and coal gondolas broke loose in the storm, and as the ship entered the breakwater, a big wave crashed over the boat and it sank beside the south pier of the harbor. No one perished, but some crewmembers were injured in the incident. This mural, which is featured on the western wall of the Frankfort post office, was created by artist Henry Bernstein in 1941. (Collection of D. C. Jesse Burkhardt.)

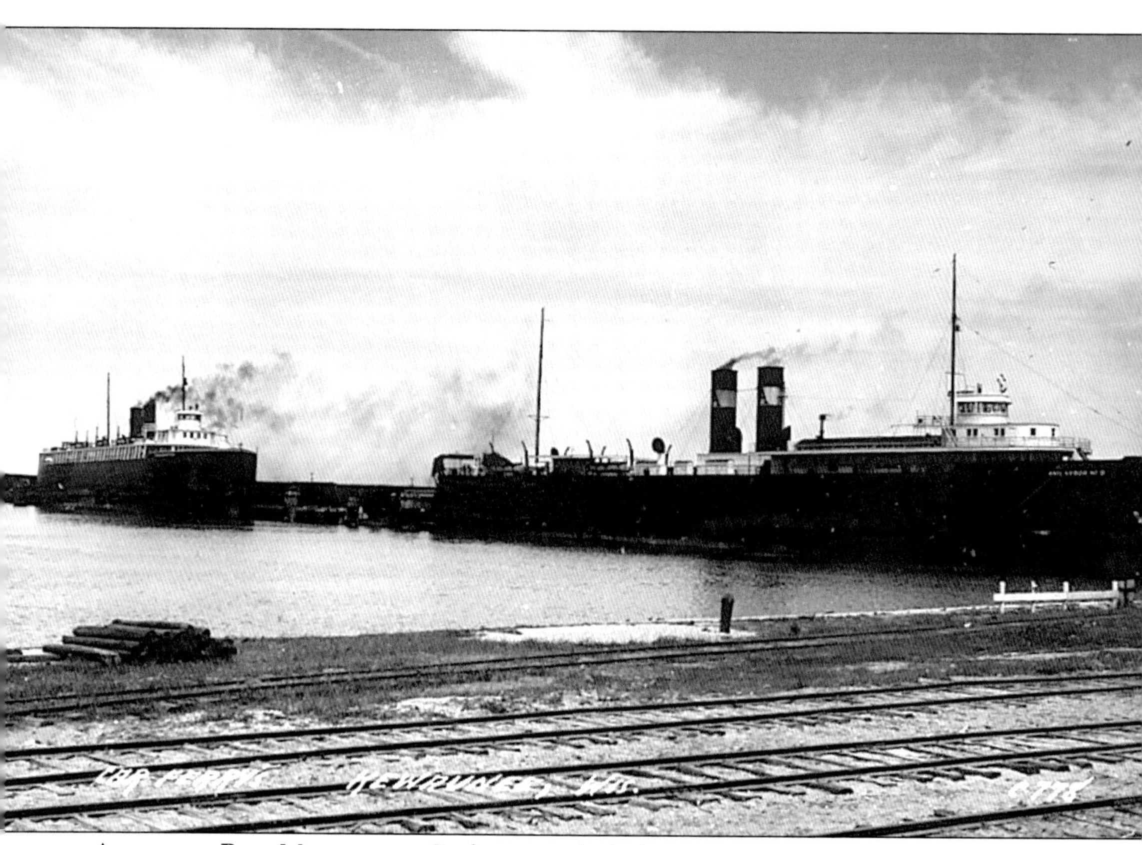

ANNIE AND PERE MARQUETTE. Carferries are docked at the Kewaunee, Green Bay & Western's two ferry slips at Kewaunee in this late 1920s scene. *Ann Arbor #5*, built in 1910 and considered the best icebreaker in the Ann Arbor's fleet, is in the foreground loading up for its return to Elberta, while a Pere Marquette boat out of Ludington (it appears to be *Pere Marquette #22*, which was built in 1924), is in the background. This shot looks north across the Kewaunee River harbor, with the KGB&W's yard tracks in the commercial district of Kewaunee in the foreground. Typically, one boat from the Ann Arbor and one from the Pere Marquette arrived in Kewaunee during the daylight hours, and another boat from each railroad came in during the night. (Collection of D. C. Jesse Burkhardt.)

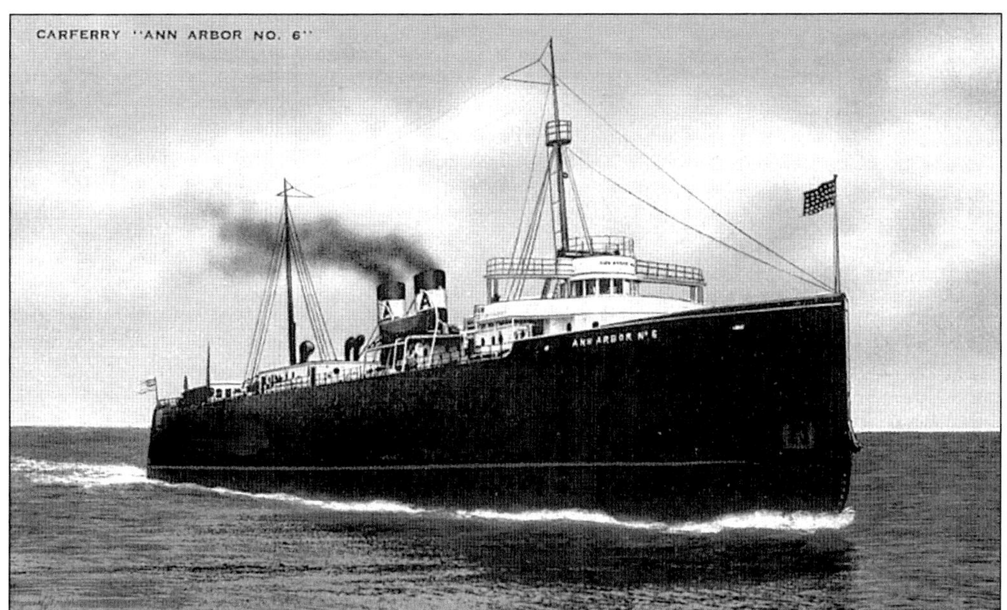

NUMBER 6. This is one of an extensive series of postcards featuring the carferry fleet of the Ann Arbor Railroad. This card, from the E. C. Kropp Company of Milwaukee, Wisconsin, displays *Ann Arbor #6*, which was built in 1917 by the Great Lakes Engineering Works of Ecorse, Michigan. In 1959, after an extensive refitting, *Ann Arbor #6* was renamed the *Arthur K. Atkinson*, for a president of the Wabash Railroad. (Collection of D. C. Jesse Burkhardt.)

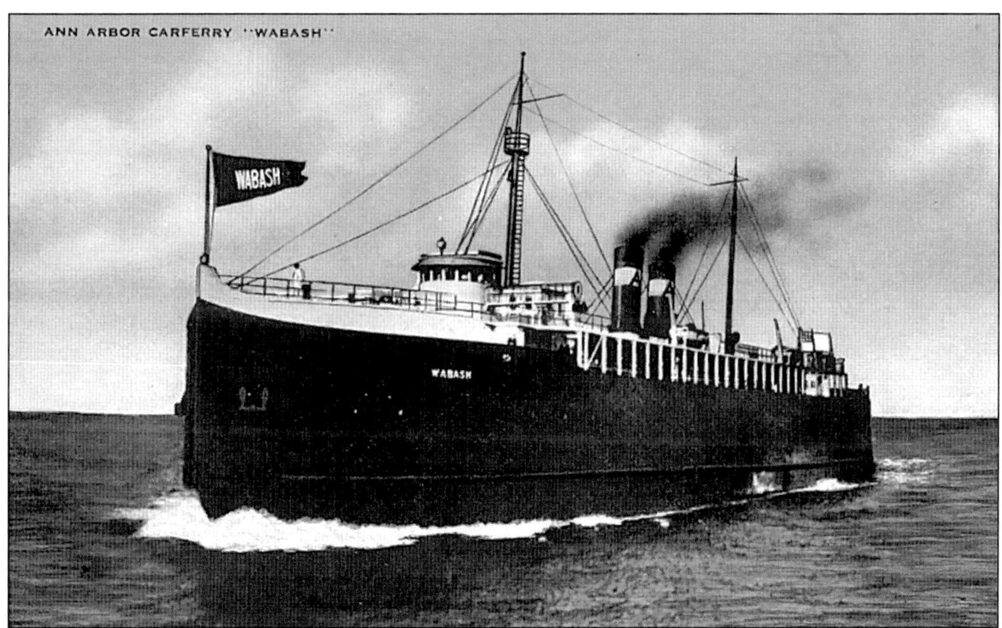

FLAGSHIP. The Ann Arbor carferry *Wabash* is shown steaming across the waters of Lake Michigan in this "antique" postcard also from the E. C. Kropp Company. The 366-foot *Wabash*, built by the Toledo Shipbuilding Company, was launched in 1927 and was the last new carferry ordered by the Ann Arbor Railroad. The ferry was renamed the *City of Green Bay* in 1962. (Collection of D. C. Jesse Burkhardt.)

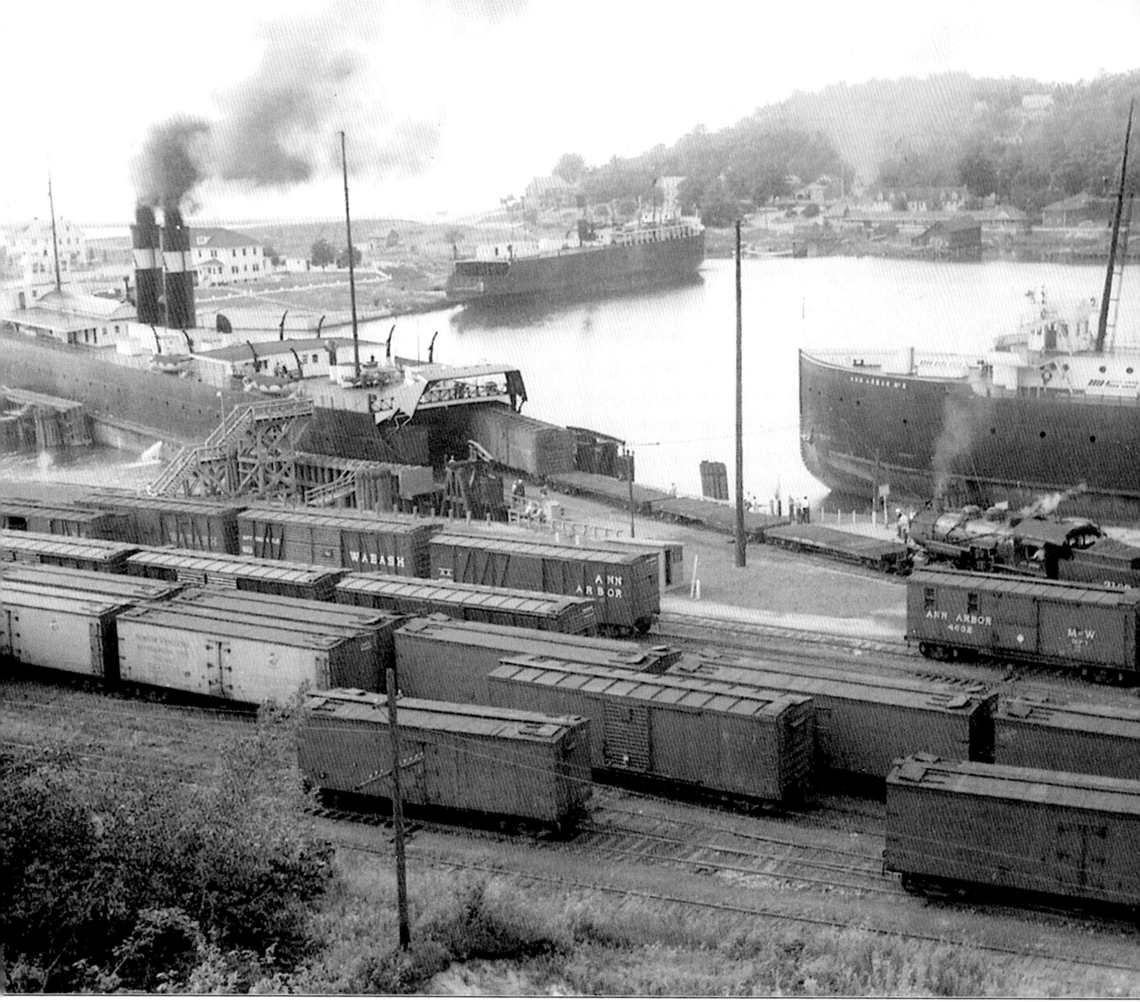

BOAT LANDING. The tracks of Elberta's Boat Landing Yard are jammed with boxcars and reefers, while a switching locomotive loads railroad cars into one of the Ann Arbor carferries in this dramatic view captured in 1938. Carferries backed up to one of the harbor's two ferry slips, and the rails in the dock "apron" were lined up with the rails on the ferries. The dock and boat would then be locked together, allowing freight cars to be rolled into and out of the ferries. This photograph was taken from the sand bluffs directly south of the Ann Arbor's freight yard. (Courtesy of the Claude T. Stoner Collection, Bentley Historical Library, University of Michigan.)

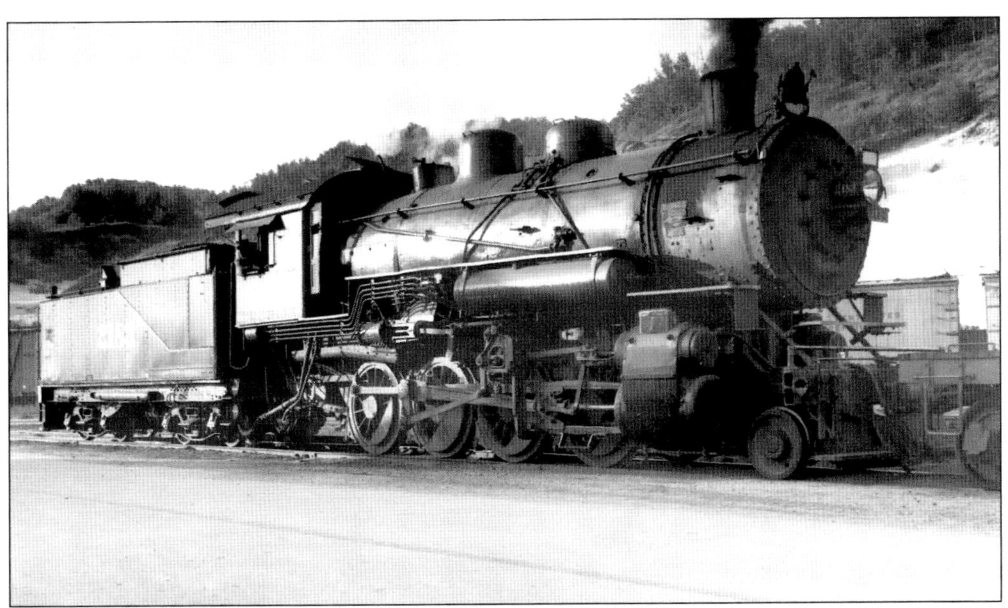

DUTY AT THE DOCKS. Ann Arbor #2183 is on the job loading one of the Ann Arbor's carferries in this July 1940 scene from Boat Landing Yard. Crews were instructed not to exceed five miles per hour when loading and unloading the boats. (Collection of Harold K. Vollrath.)

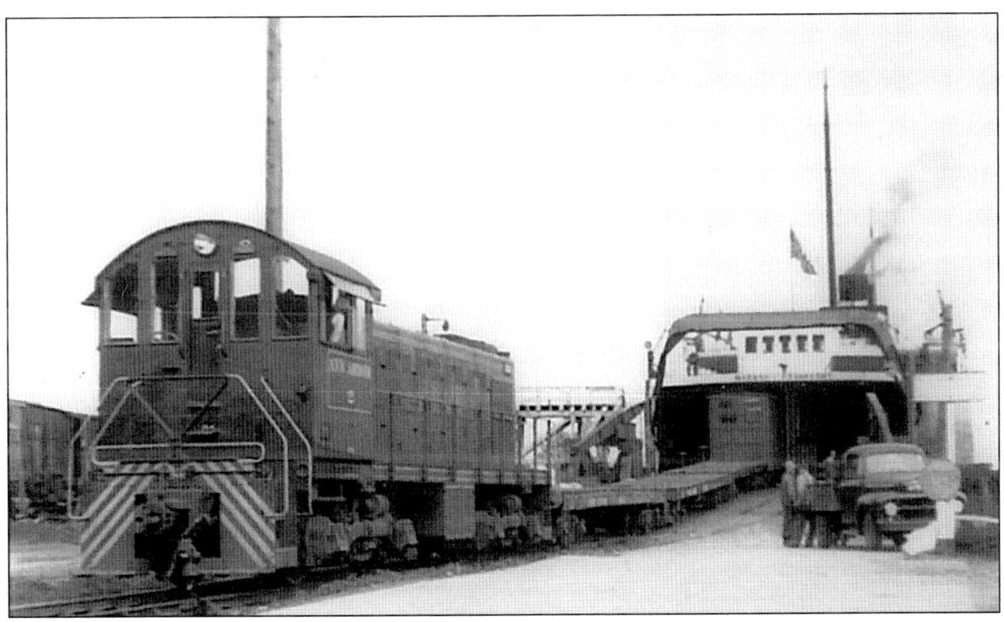

SWITCHING THE WABASH. In this photograph, Ann Arbor #2 works the ferry slip at Elberta in the 1950s. The Alco switcher is loading the *Wabash* in this scene. There are three idler cars in front of the locomotive; switching crews employed these cars to keep the relatively heavy locomotives off the boat and off the loading apron. Crews were further instructed that they "must stop and stretch slack to know cars are coupled before moving on to apron." (Courtesy of the Benzie Area Historical Society.)

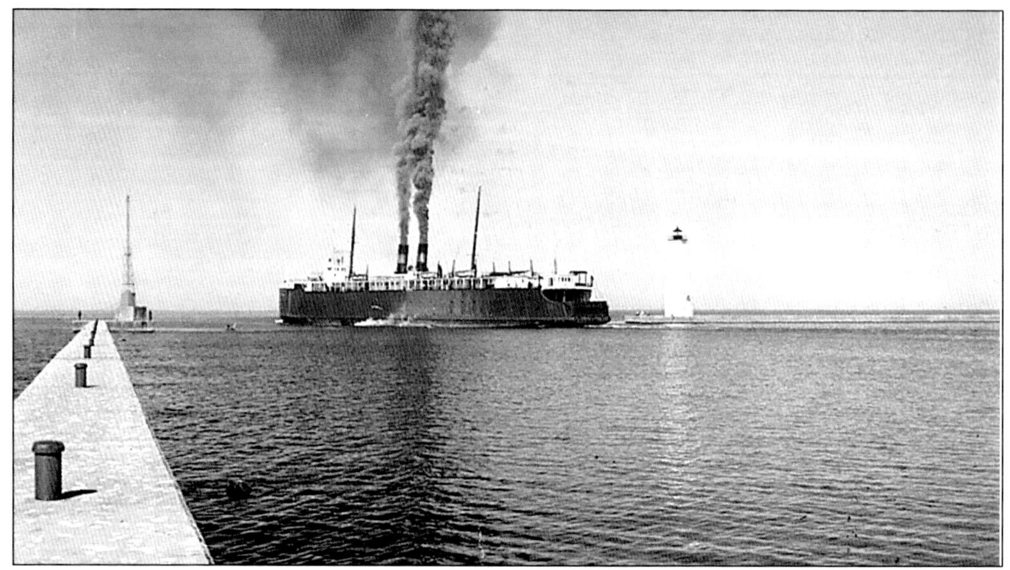

COAL SMOKE AT FRANKFORT. An Ann Arbor carferry splits through the piers of the breakwater at the mouth of Frankfort Harbor and heads out onto Lake Michigan. This postcard photo of the *Wabash*, with its twin funnels streaming coal smoke, is from 1957. The card was mailed from Beulah, Michigan, on July 14, 1959, and the writer's message to Mr. C. B. Miller in Owosso included the following: "The *Arthur K. Atkinson* was loading here when we arrived. So we've seen the best and fastest." (Collection of D. C. Jesse Burkhardt.)

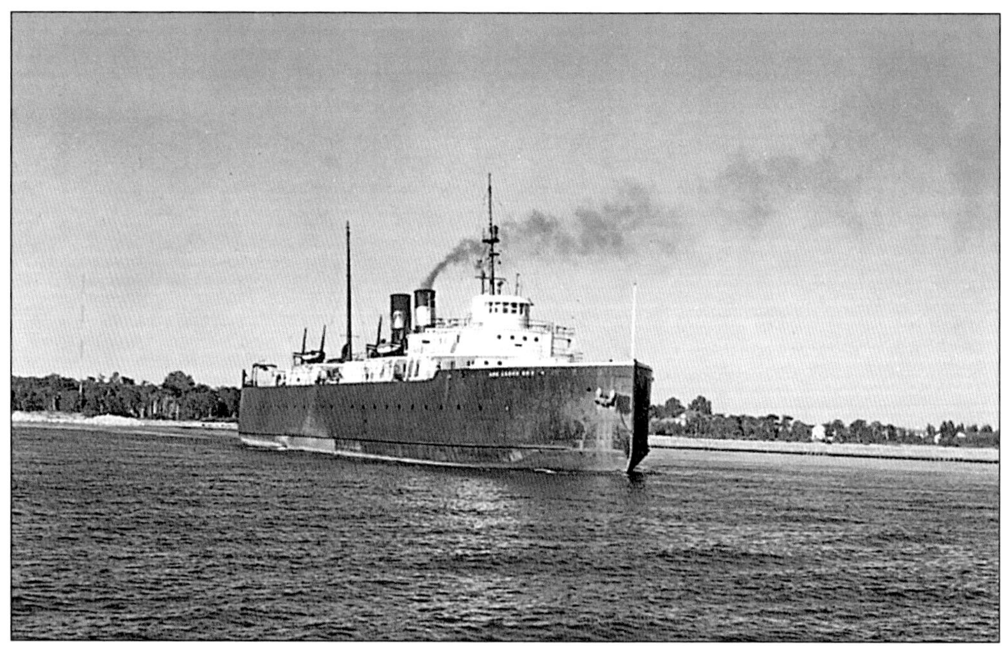

OFF THE SHORE OF MANISTIQUE. This color postcard depicts an Ann Arbor carferry pulling out of scenic Manistique, Michigan, on its run back to Elberta in the late 1950s. The caption on the reverse reads, "This ferry line maintains a daily schedule between Manistique and Frankfort, transporting passengers, automobiles and railway cars." The card was created by the Hiawatha Card Company of Ypsilanti, Michigan. (Collection of D. C. Jesse Burkhardt.)

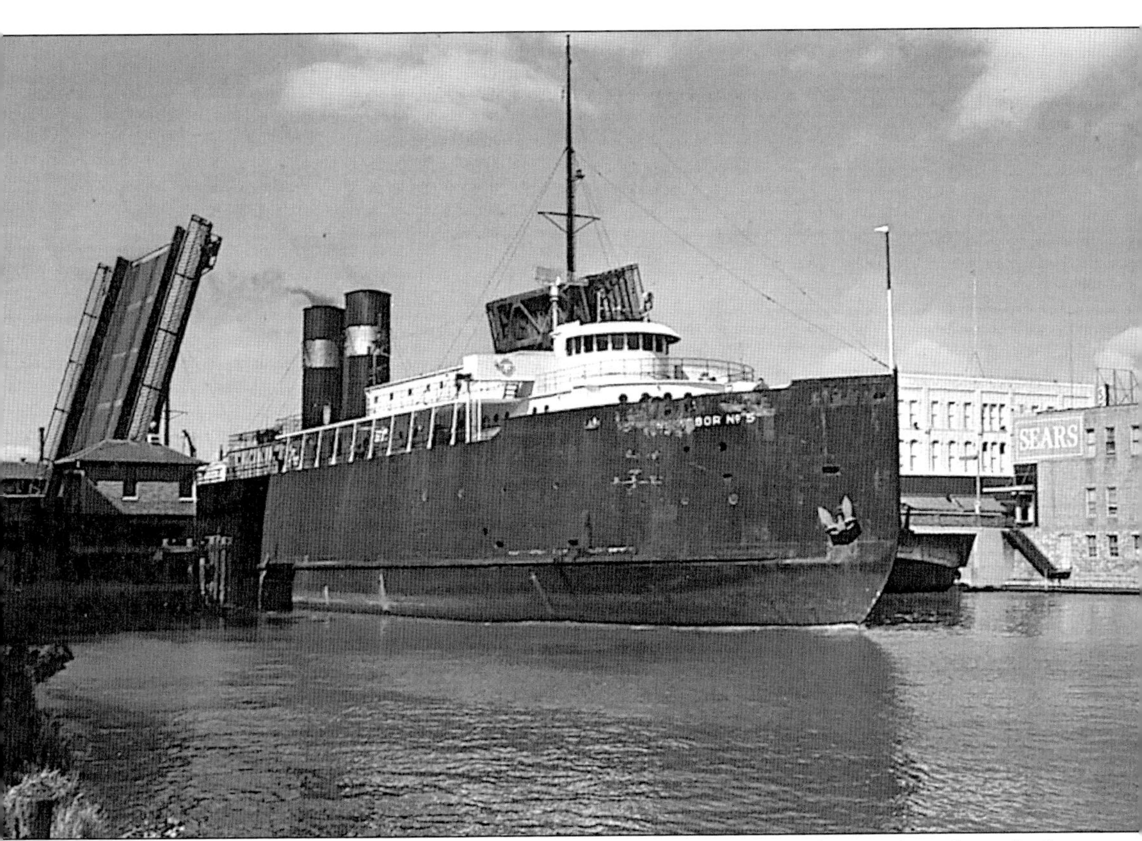

ON THE MANITOWOC RIVER. *Ann Arbor* #5 was the first Great Lakes carferry launched with a seagate, which was designed to keep high waves out of the otherwise open car deck at the stern. In this scene from the early 1960s, the boat cuts through the open Eighth Street drawbridge at Manitowoc, Wisconsin. The Ann Arbor Railroad served two separate ferry docks in Manitowoc. One connected with the Chicago & North Western and the other connected with the Soo Line. To reach the Soo Line's terminal, which was west of the harbor mouth and farther up the Manitowoc River channel, carferries had to pass through a series of drawbridges. The Ann Arbor's boats first docked in Manitowoc in 1896. (Collection of D. C. Jesse Burkhardt.)

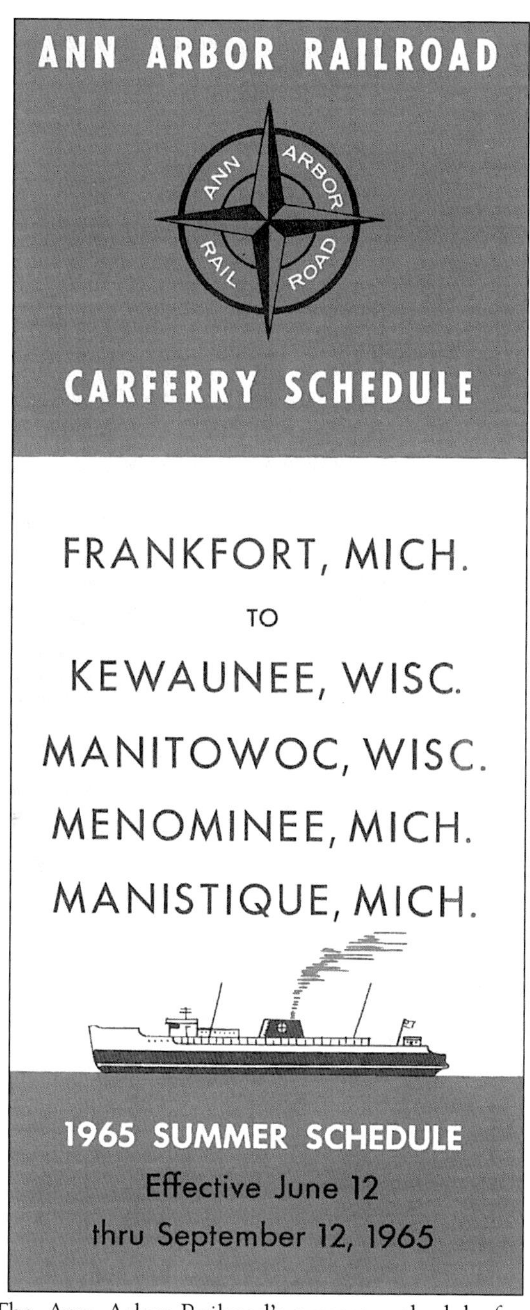

MULTIPLE SAILINGS. The Ann Arbor Railroad's summer schedule for 1965 shows sailings from Frankfort to four different Lake Michigan ports. At this time, the railroad offered two trips per day to Kewaunee and Manitowoc, and one per day to Menominee and Manistique. "This is an ideal route for motorists through the most picturesque and interesting sections of Wisconsin and Michigan," read an excerpt from one of the AA's brochures. "It eliminates the long drive around Lake Michigan and affords the traveler a cool and refreshing lake trip while vacationing." To handle all the work, four carferries operated at this time: *Arthur K. Atkinson*, *City of Green Bay*, *Viking*, and *Ann Arbor #5*. A one-way ticket to any of the ports served by the AA cost $4.50 per passenger and $8 for an automobile. (Collection of D. C. Jesse Burkhardt.)

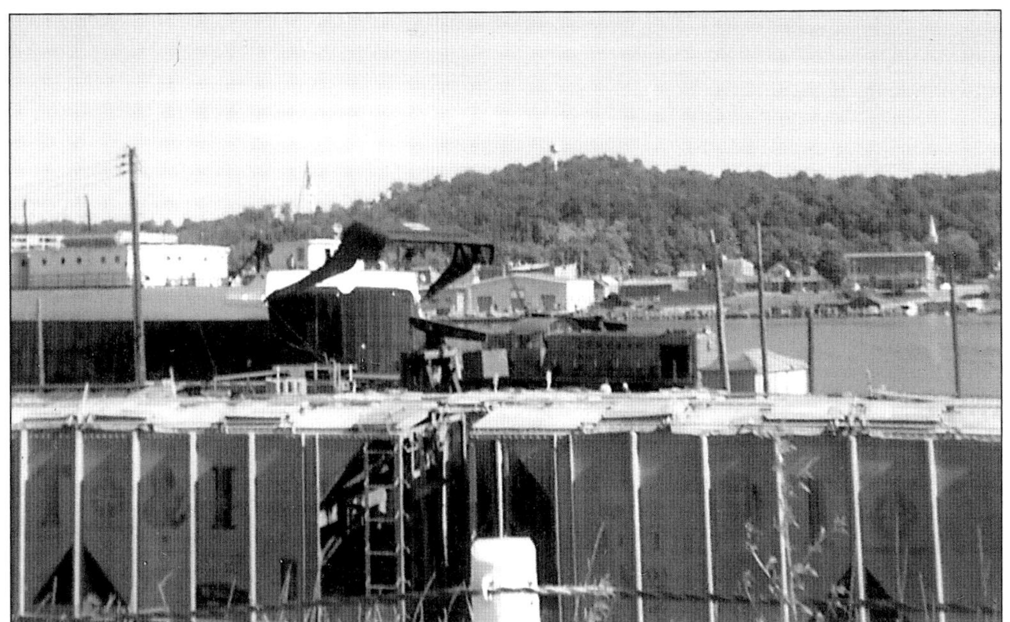

SWALLOWED WHOLE. In a shot taken from M-168, which came to a dead end at the Ann Arbor Railroad's Elberta ferry terminal, an Ann Arbor switching locomotive loads cars at the stern of a carferry in the summer of 1971. A cut of DT&I cement hoppers stands in the foreground. (Photo by D. C. Jesse Burkhardt.)

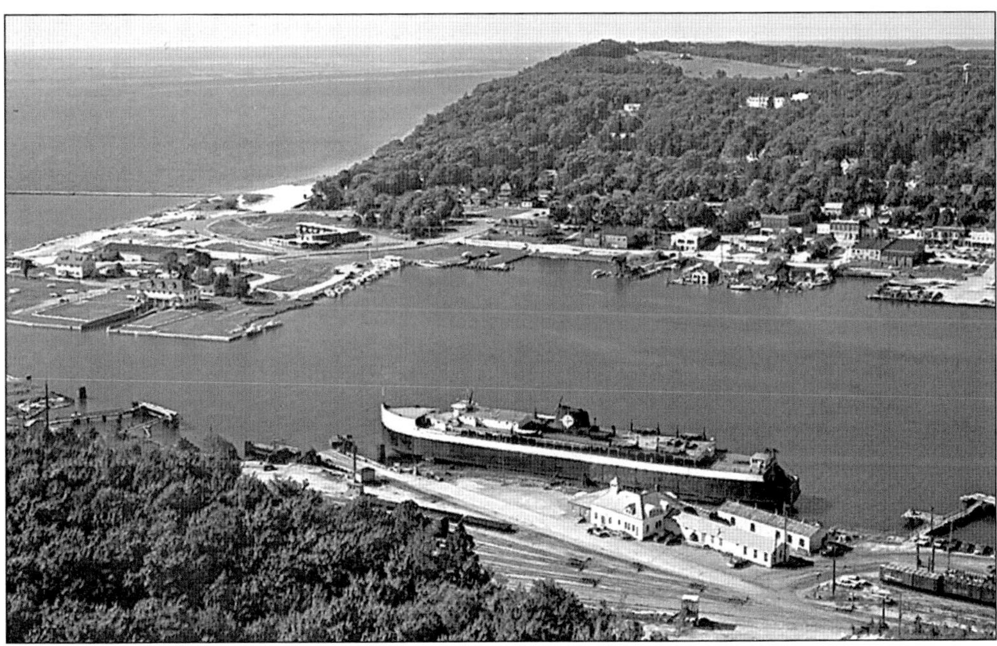

OVERVIEW. This is a postcard view of Betsie Bay, Boat Landing Yard, and the city of Frankfort in the 1970s, as operations began to decline. The scene, photographed by John Penrod, shows just one of the Ann Arbor's carferries in the harbor. The back of the postcard reads, "Frankfort, Michigan—A port and vacation city along the shores of Lake Michigan. Ferry boats carry passengers and railroad trains to Wisconsin on a daily schedule." (Collection of D. C. Jesse Burkhardt.)

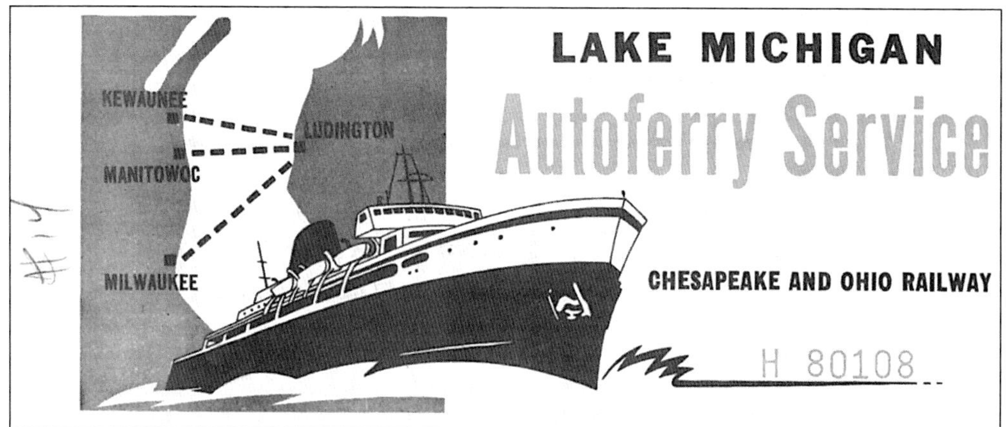

CROSS-LAKE COMPETITION. The Chesapeake & Ohio Railway was a vital connecting partner for the Ann Arbor in Michigan, but it was also a competitor in the freight-hauling business—especially on the Lake Michigan crossings, as this ticket cover from 1978 demonstrates. The C&O served Kewaunee and Manitowoc, two Wisconsin ports also called on by the Ann Arbor. The home terminal of the C&O carferries was at Ludington. (Collection of D. C. Jesse Burkhardt.)

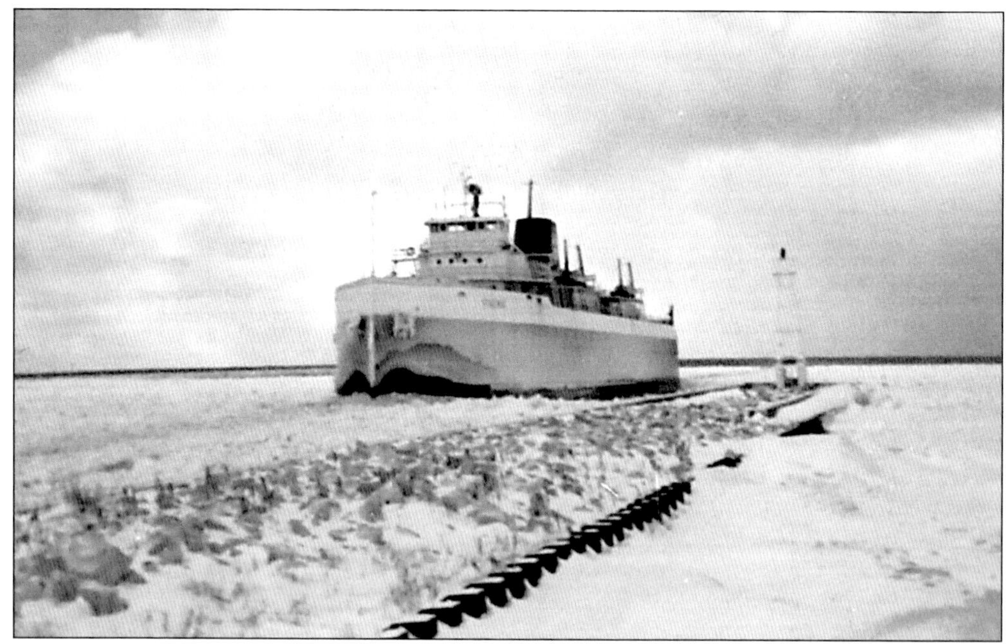

FROZEN FERRY. Coated in ice, the Ann Arbor carferry *Viking* creeps into snowbound Frankfort Harbor in February 1967. Despite brutal weather conditions at times, the railroad's ferries normally operated 365 days a year. This boat was built as *Ann Arbor #7* in 1925 by the Manitowoc Shipbuilding Company; it was renamed *Viking* after being rebuilt in 1965. (Photo by Scott Sparling.)

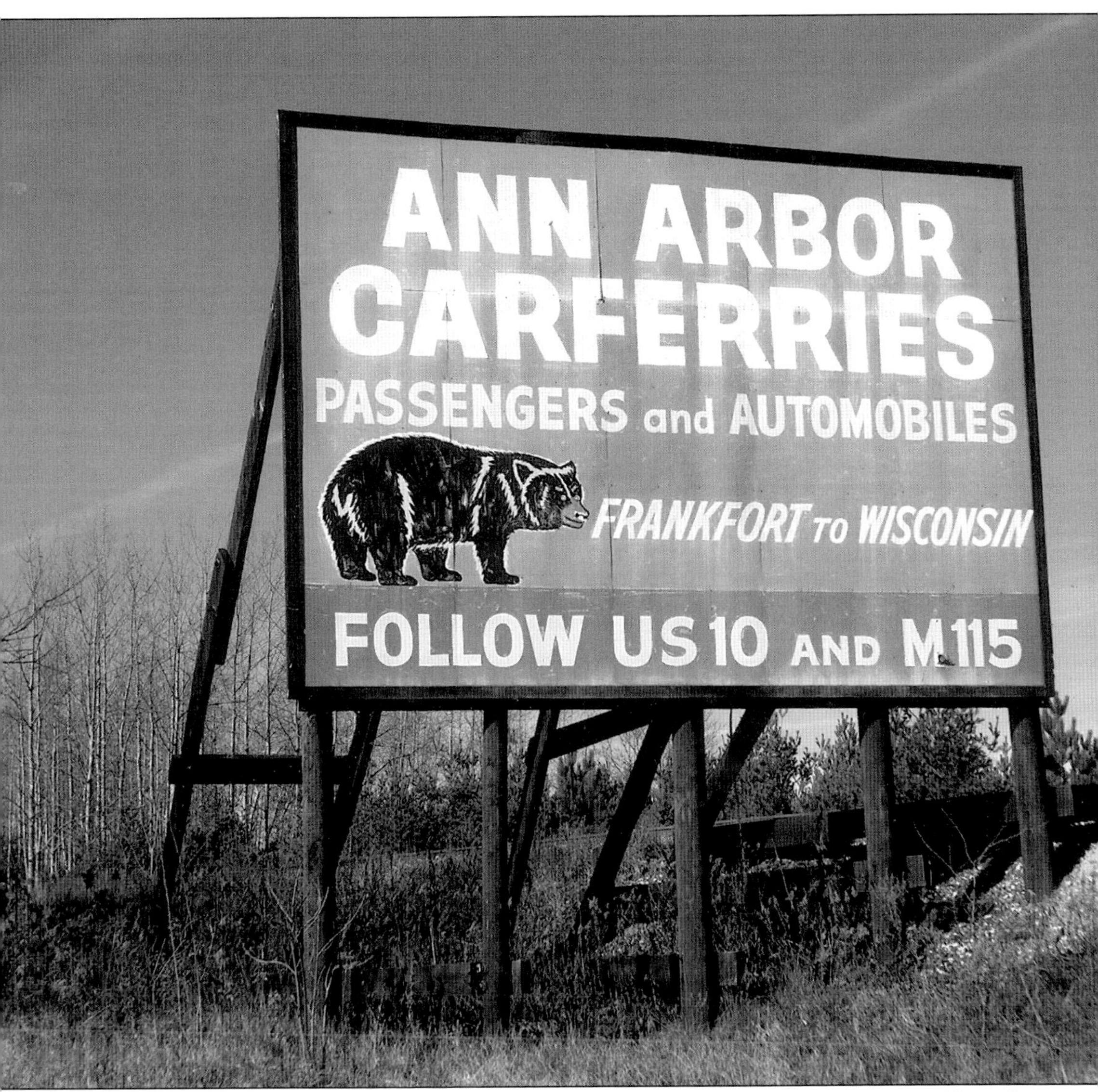

FOLLOW THE BEAR. With carferry service still going strong in the 1970s, this sweet billboard with the friendly bear—a symbol of northern Michigan tourism—greeted travelers heading out of Clare bound for points north. This was actually a strategic place for the sign, as a mile or so past this point was the junction of U.S. 10 and M-115. U.S. 10 led straight to Ludington, site of the Chesapeake & Ohio carferry docks, while M-115 led directly to Frankfort and the Ann Arbor's ferry landing. Contrast the condition of this sign as it appears here on November 19, 1977, with the photo that appears on Page 117, which was taken almost precisely 15 years later. (Photo by Dennis Schmidt.)

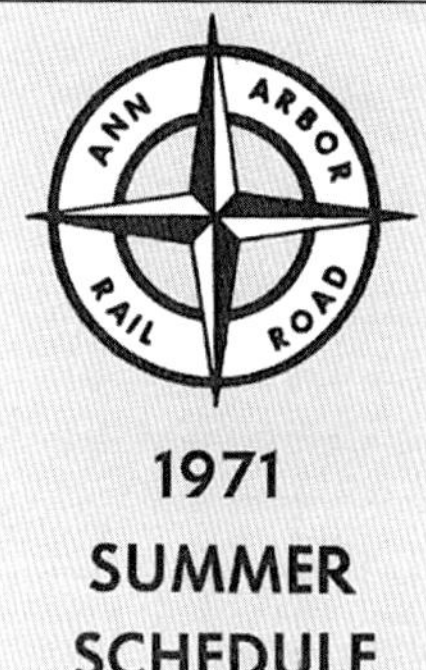

1971 SUMMER SCHEDULE

NOTE: Times shown are Central Standard (Daylight) Time. This is the same time as Michigan Unadvanced Time.

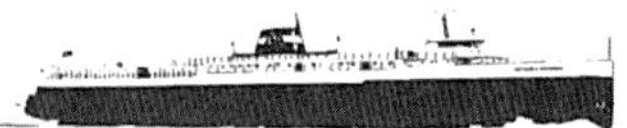

FRANKFORT (Elberta Boat Landing), MICH. — KEWAUNEE, WIS.

	Daily	Daily
Lv. Frankfort — Central Standard Time	9:30 AM	10:30 PM
Ar. Kewaunee — Central Standard Time	1:30 PM	2:30 AM
Lv. Kewaunee — Central Standard Time	3:00 PM	4:00 AM
Ar. Frankfort — Central Standard Time	7:00 PM	8:00 AM

FRANKFORT (Elberta Boat Landing), MICH. — MANITOWOC, WIS.

Carferries at Manitowoc may dock either at Chicago & Northwestern Dock or at Soo Line Dock. Consult ticket office Frankfort or Manitowoc.

	Daily	Daily
Lv. Frankfort — Central Standard Time	10:30 AM	8:00 PM
Ar. Manitowoc — Central Standard Time	3:30 PM	12:30 AM
Lv. Manitowoc — Central Standard Time	5:00 PM	3:00 AM
Ar. Frankfort — Central Standard Time	9:30 PM	8:00 AM

DOWN TO TWO. By summer 1971, the railroad was serving only two ports (Kewaunee and Manitowoc) and had reduced its fleet to three boats (the *Arthur K. Atkinson*, *Viking*, and *City of Green Bay*) from the four it operated in the early 1960s. The fleet was about to get smaller still; for seven years (1973–1980), the AKA was tied up and out of service due to a broken crankshaft. In this schedule, the one-way fare for passengers was $6, while the one-way cost per automobile was $11.50. (Collection of D. C. Jesse Burkhardt.)

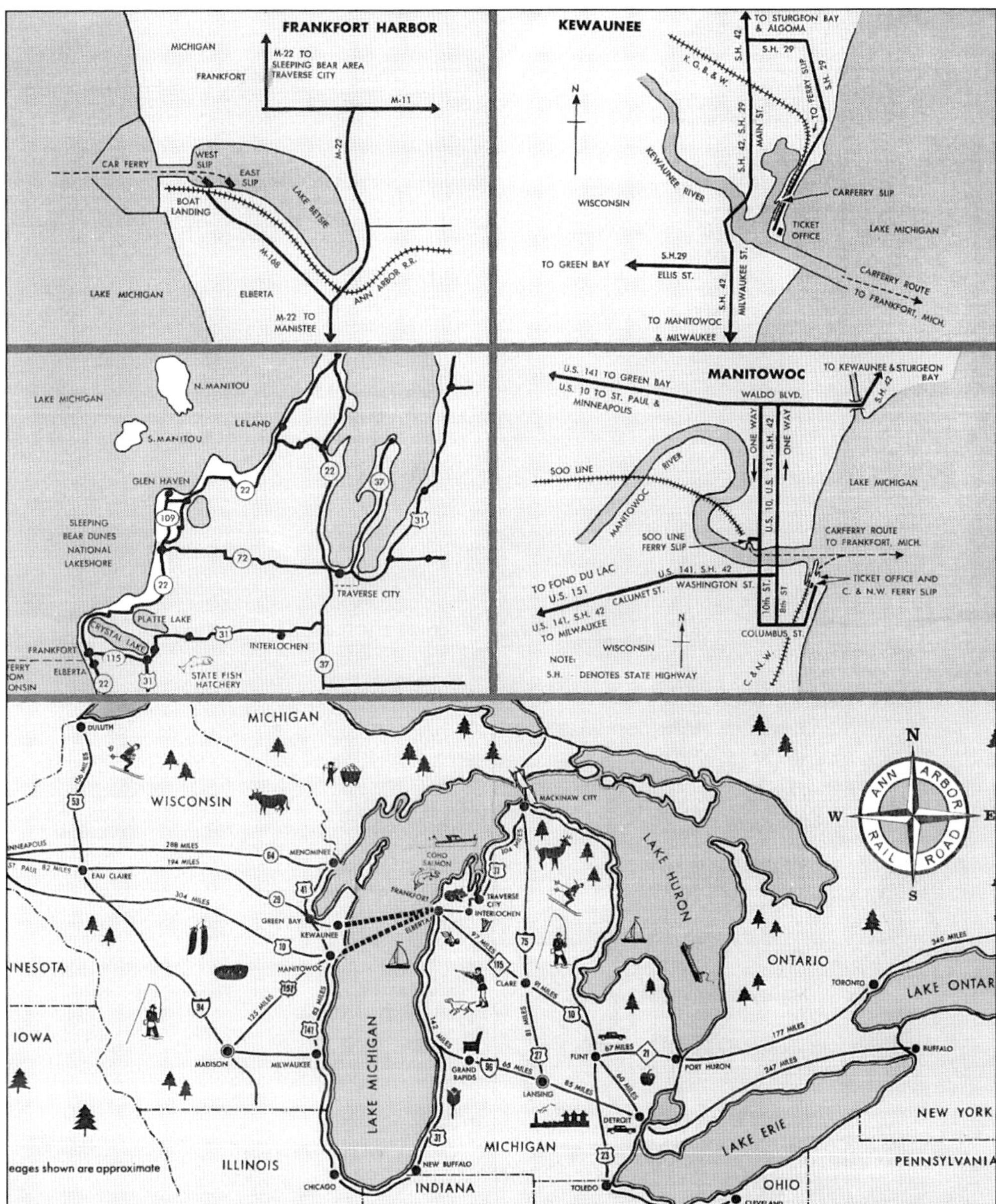

FRIENDLY MAPS. Note the vacationer-friendly schematic maps, complete with rail lines, of the towns the AA carferries served. "Sailings may be cancelled or delayed by Ann Arbor Railroad due to wind, weather, train connections or freight traffic conditions," read the disclaimer on the reverse side of the brochure. (Collection of D. C. Jesse Burkhardt.)

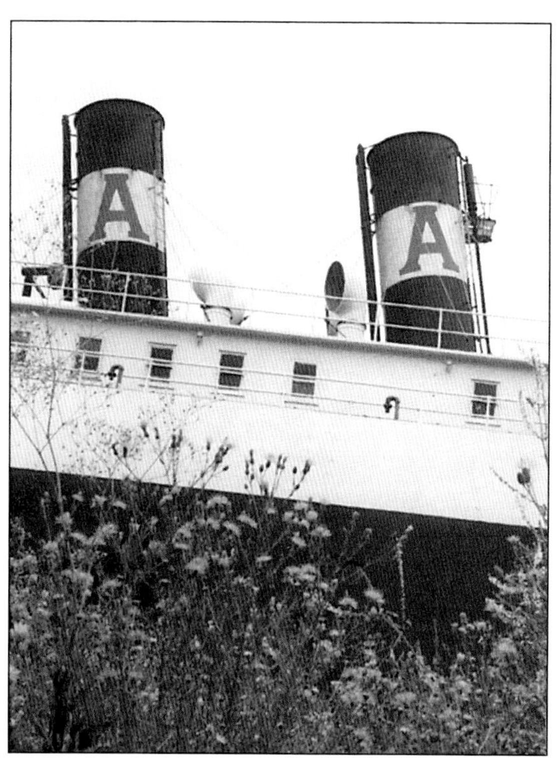

DOUBLE STACK. This image shows the "Double A" smokestacks of an Ann Arbor carferry. The steam whistle alongside the front funnel spoke in code to harbor personnel and the ship's crew. For instance, three long blasts were sounded one half hour prior to departure as a crew call, signaling all hands to return. One long and one short was the tie-up whistle once the boat was secured at the dock. In heavy fog or in other conditions of reduced visibility, one long blast would be sounded every two minutes. (Photo by Scott Sparling.)

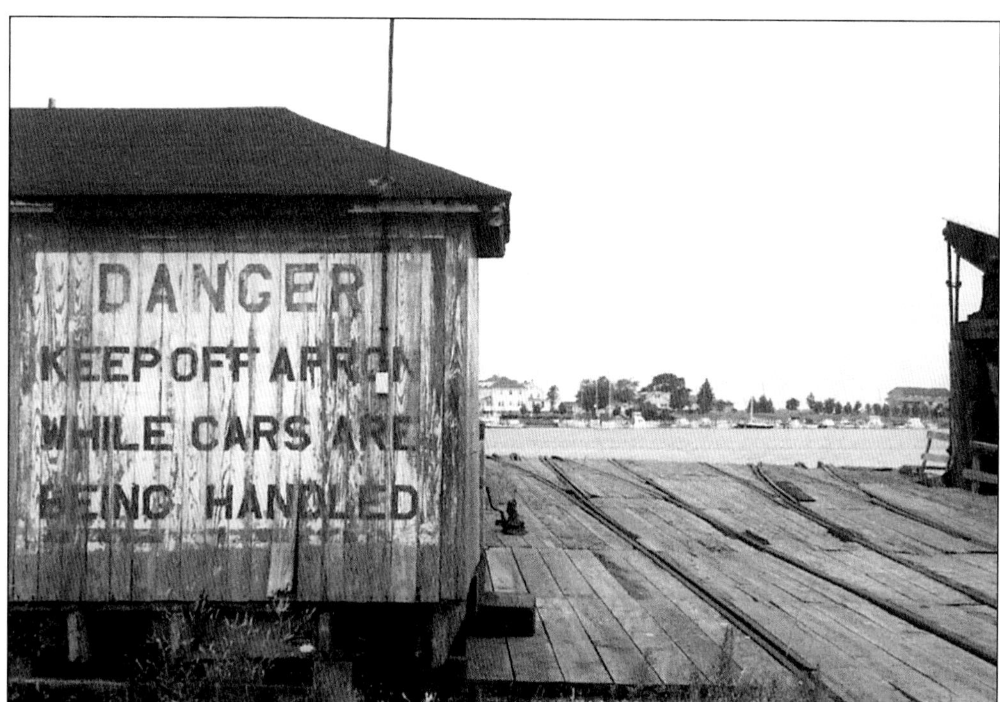

KEEP OFF THE APRON. A fading, obsolete sign on one of the sheds on the Elberta loading dock warns people to stay back during loading and unloading operations. This image was captured in the late 1980s, a few years after carferry service had ended. (Photo by Scott Sparling.)

Four

Terminals
Elberta, Cadillac, Owosso, Ann Arbor, and Toledo

A few miles out of Frankfort was the Betsie Bay campground. Now and then on summer nights I'd camp there under the endless stars, a few feet from the mainline of the Ann Arbor Railroad. One long train usually passed through in the night, heading in to Boat Landing Yard. Its baritone air horn sounding in the distance would wake me, then soon the train would come hissing and clanking and squealing out of the darkness, and I'd sit up and watch until the faint lights of the caboose passed by, disappearing into the trees.

—D. C. Jesse Burkhardt, journal entry, September 15, 1979

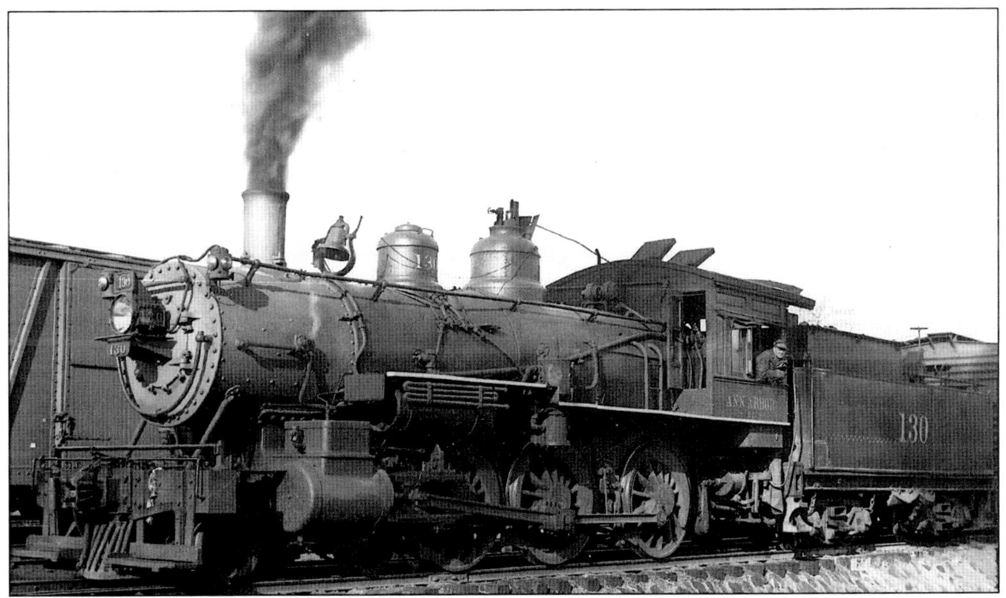

Yard Duty. With its smokestack churning, Ann Arbor #130, a 4-6-0 locomotive with a July 1898 birth date, works in the Ann Arbor's yard in Owosso in 1938. The hogger is taking a brief break from his train-building chores to eye the camera. (Collection of D. C. Jesse Burkhardt.)

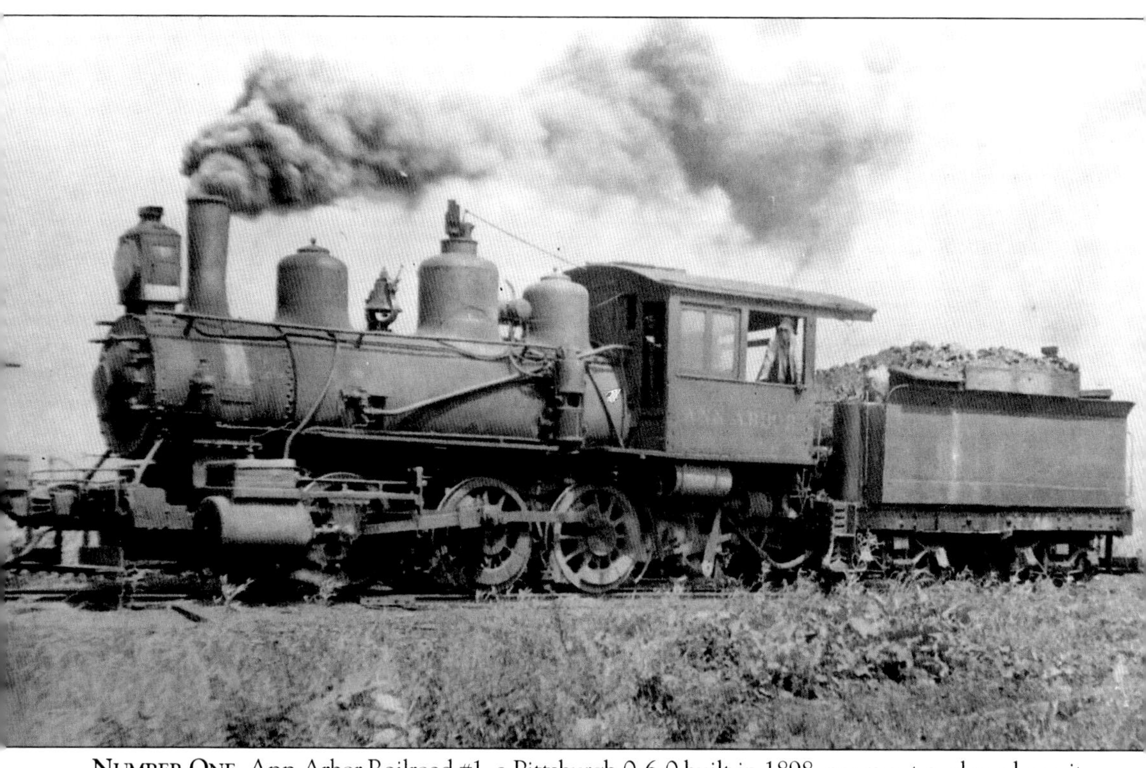

NUMBER ONE. Ann Arbor Railroad #1, a Pittsburgh 0-6-0 built in 1898, pours out coal smoke as it switches freight cars in the carrier's Toledo yard in 1921. (Collection of Harold K. Vollrath.)

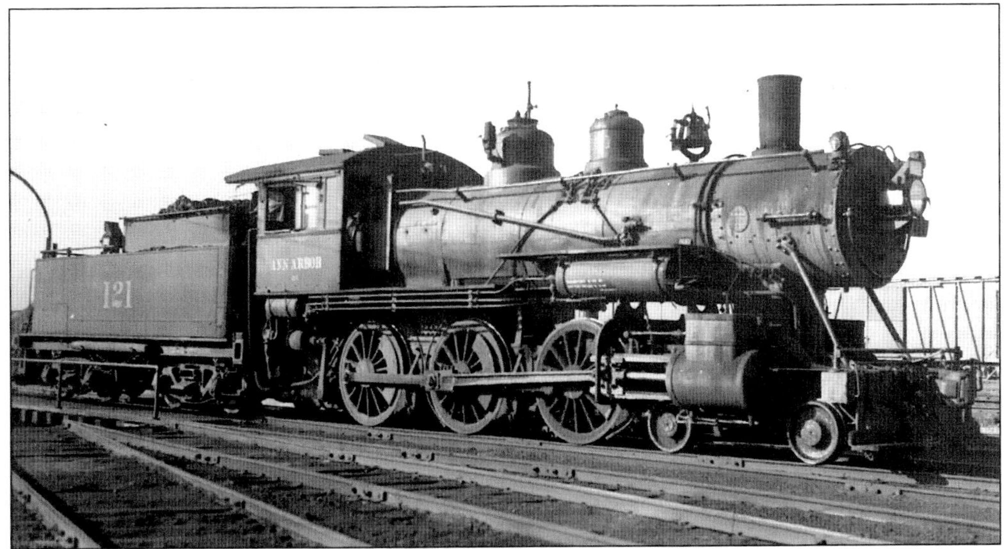

VINTAGE 1898. One of the Ann Arbor Railroad's earliest steam locomotives, AA 4-6-0 #121, is shown coming off the turntable in Ottawa Yard in Toledo in 1935. The Baldwin Locomotive Works built this machine in 1898; it ended up being converted into a static boiler at the AA's Elberta facility. (Collection of Harold K. Vollrath.)

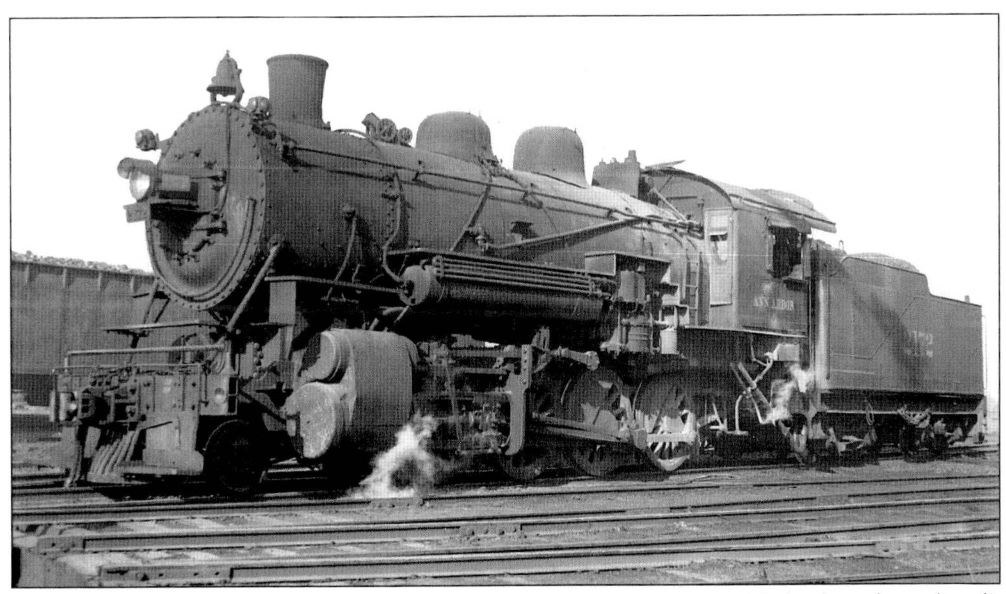

TURNTABLE LEAD. Ann Arbor #2172 is pictured on one of the turntable leads at the railroad's Toledo terminal in September 1949. (Collection of Harold K. Vollrath.)

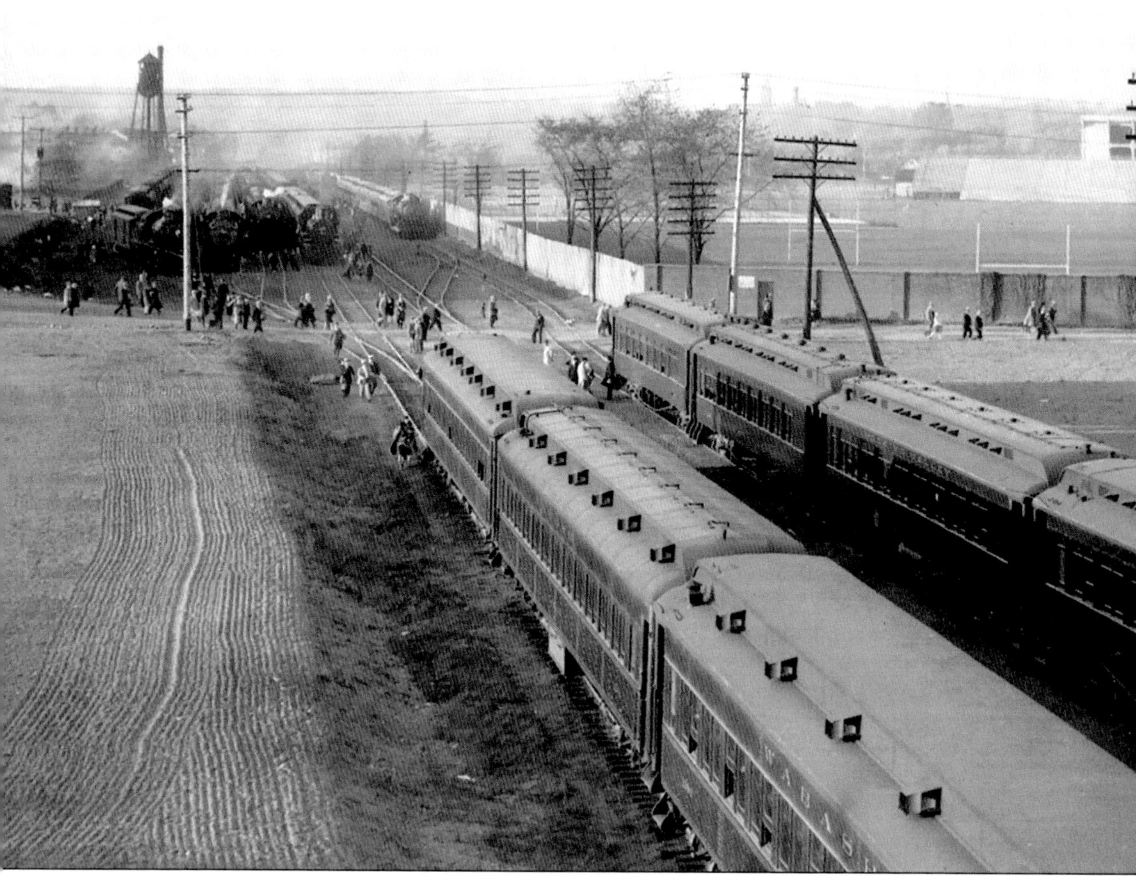

GAME DAY. Passenger extras bringing football fans to the University of Michigan crowd the Ann Arbor Railroad's Ferry Yard in Ann Arbor in the autumn of 1930. At least seven trains are visible in this north-looking view, and passengers appear to be headed back to their trains for the trip home. Take note of the variety of passenger equipment pressed into service to handle the popular football trains. In the foreground is a string of coaches from the Wabash Railroad, while several cars from the Hocking Valley Railway are waiting on the right. The Hocking Valley was a major Ohio railroad in this era, and its operations were centered at Columbus, Ohio—home of the Ohio State Buckeyes, a fierce rival of the Michigan Wolverines. (Courtesy of the Claude T. Stoner Collection, Bentley Historical Library, University of Michigan.)

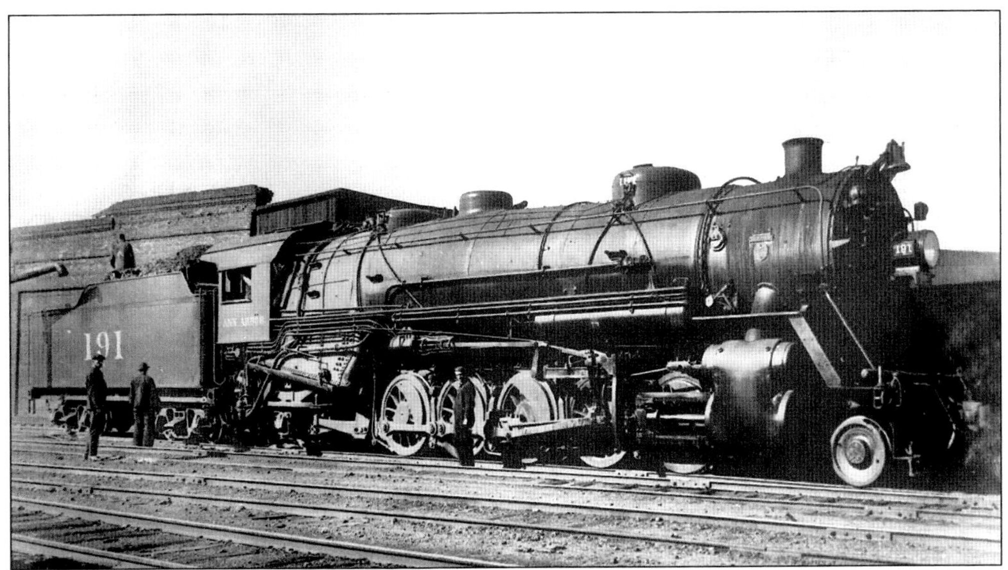

191 IN 1919. Ann Arbor #191, a 2-10-2 Baldwin, was among the largest locomotives in service on the Ann Arbor. The railroad owned four of the huge 2-10-2s (#190–#193). All four were built by Baldwin in 1919, and all four were sold to the Kansas City Southern in 1942. In this 1919 scene at the railroad's Owosso terminal, #191 appears to be taking on a load of coal. This unit was later renumbered as AA #2551. (Collection of Harold K. Vollrath.)

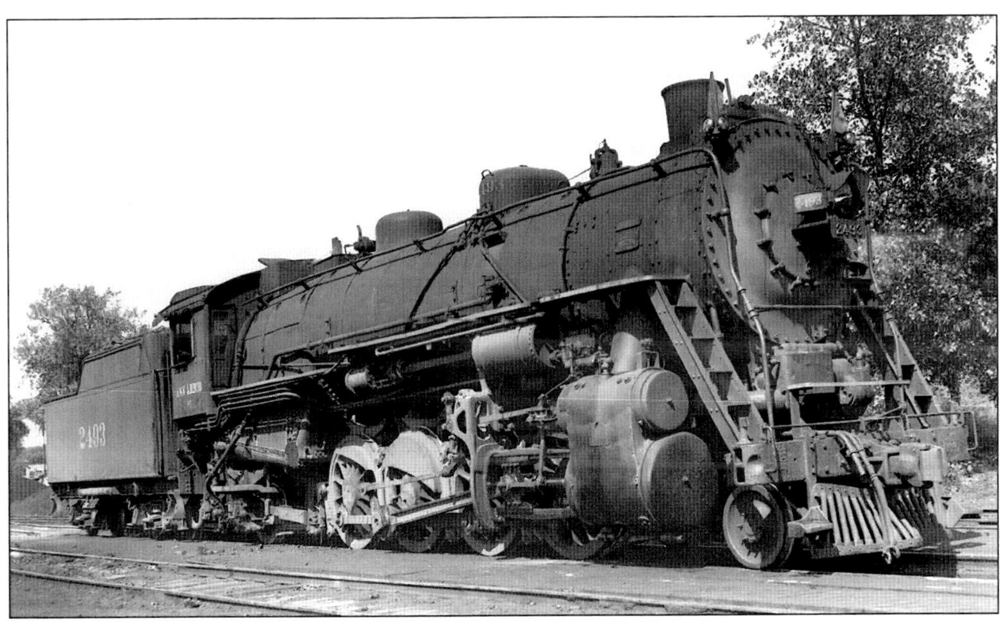

GREEN FLAGS HANGING. This is a September 1949 image of AA #2493 as it sits on a yard track in Owosso with green flags on the front, indicating that the locomotive will be on the head of a train of at least two sections. Displaying green flags told opposing trains and track maintenance crews that another section of the same train, running in roughly the same time slot, would be close behind. Less than two years after this photo was taken, #2493 was cut up by a scrapper's torch. (Collection of Harold K. Vollrath.)

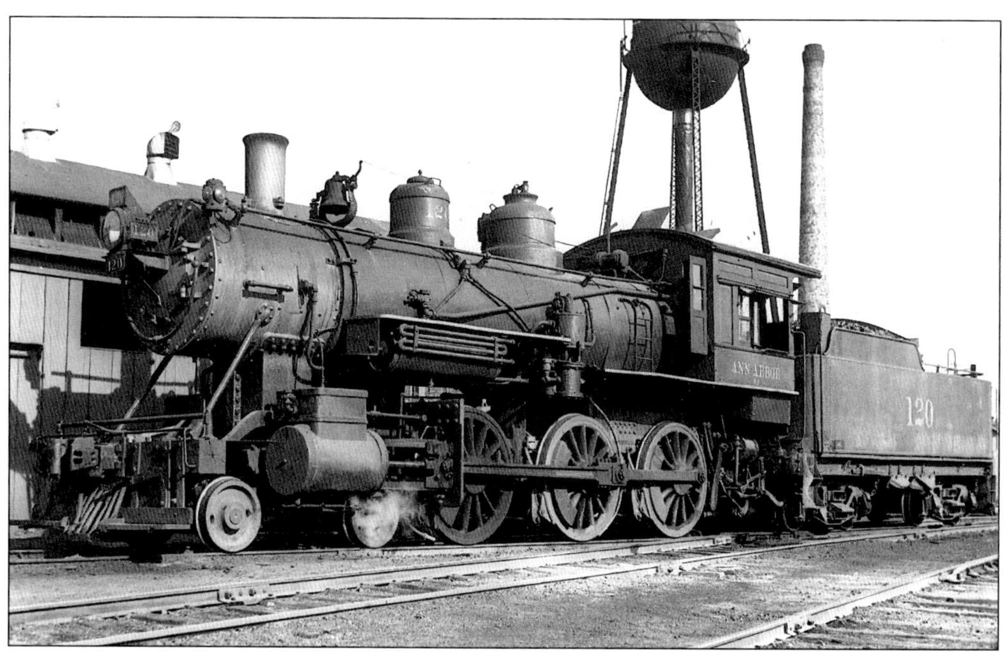

IDLE FOR NOW. Ann Arbor #120 rests between switching assignments at the railroad's freight yard in Owosso in the early 1940s. When this picture was taken, the locomotive had already been on the job for more than four decades: #120 was built by the Baldwin company in 1898. (Collection of D. C. Jesse Burkhardt.)

Made in U. S. A   Form 1347   5M Sets- 1 55

WABASH RAILROAD COMPANY

THE ANN ARBOR RAILROAD COMPANY

BAD ORDER

RETURN WHEN EMPTY TO .... R. R.

FOR REPAIRS ....

....

....

CAR NO. .... INITIALS ....

DATE .... 19 .... SIGNED ....

PER ....

DO NOT RELOAD THIS CAR

DO NOT RELOAD. Shown here is a "bad order" card from the era when the Wabash Railroad controlled the Ann Arbor. These cards were tacked to freight cars in need of repairs before they could again be used in freight service. Note the instruction on the right side of the card: "Do Not Reload This Car." This version of the Wabash bad order form was printed in January 1955. (Collection of D. C. Jesse Burkhardt.)

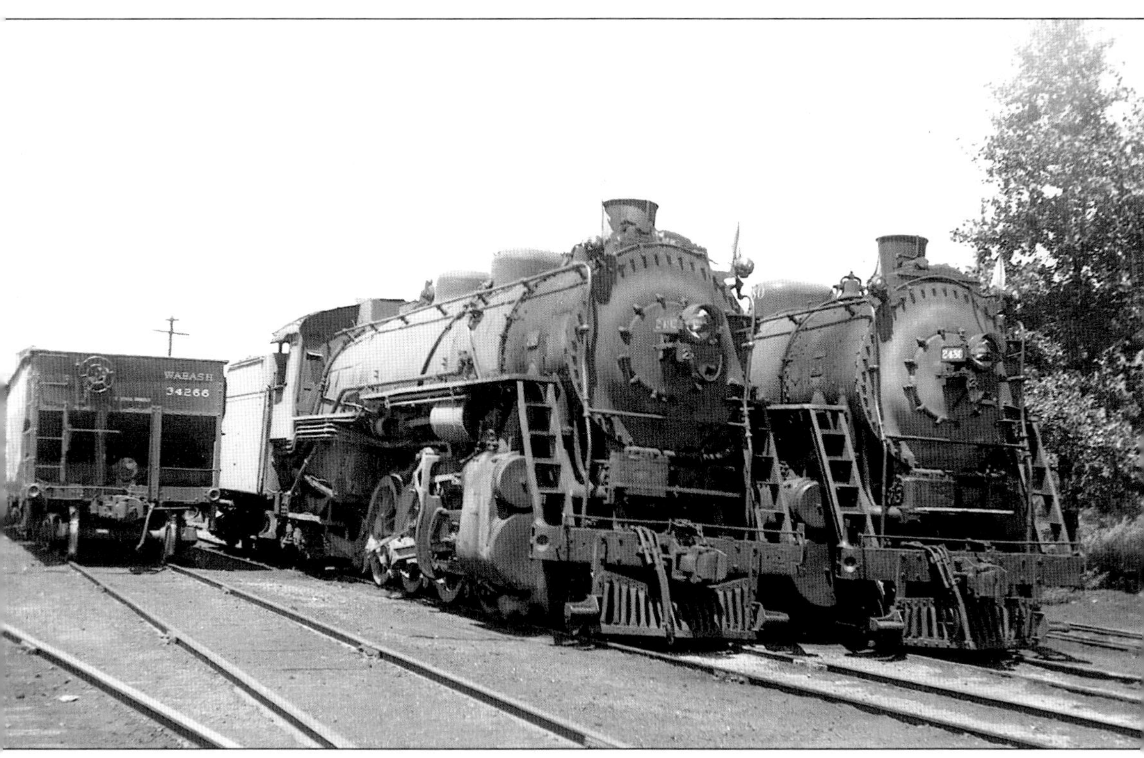

DOUBLE VISION. As if they were preparing for a race, two virtually identical Ann Arbor Railroad 2-8-2 locomotives (Brooks-built #2492 and #2480) line up before pulling trains out of the Ann Arbor's yard in Owosso in this gritty and wonderful scene from 1951. It was getting perilously close to the end of the line for #2492—it was scrapped later the same year. AA #2480 didn't last much longer; it was retired and disposed of in 1952. (Collection of Harold K. Vollrath.)

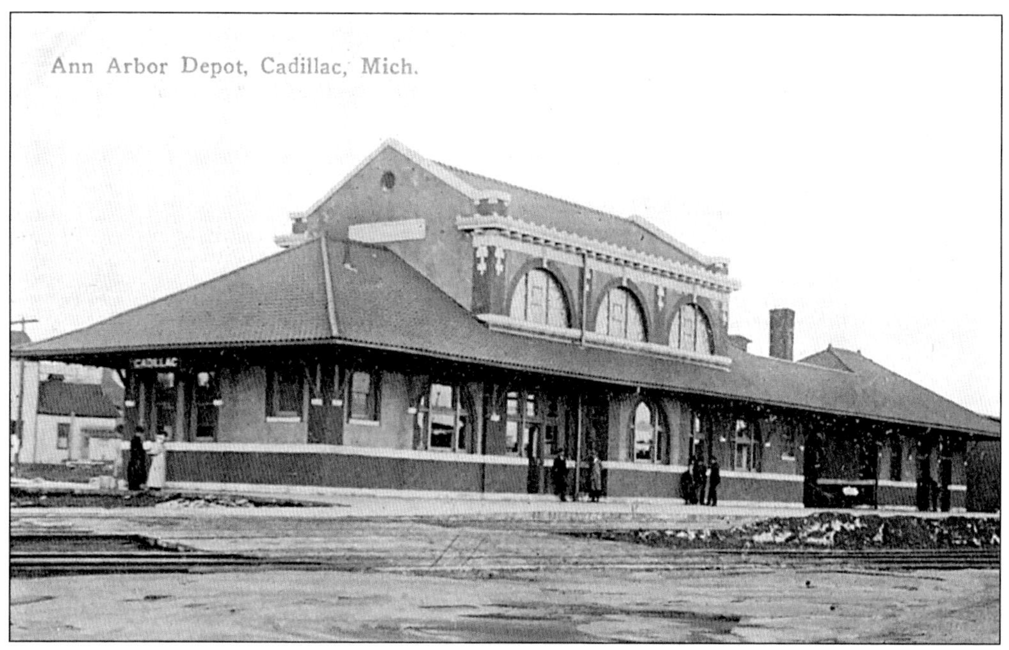

GRAND STRUCTURE. The Ann Arbor Railroad's depot at Cadillac, Michigan, is pictured in this undated postcard. Notice the intricate details of the stonework, on the second level in particular. The impressive station was built in 1911, and remains standing to this day. The structure has most recently been used as a headquarters for the local chapter of the VFW. (Collection of D. C. Jesse Burkhardt.)

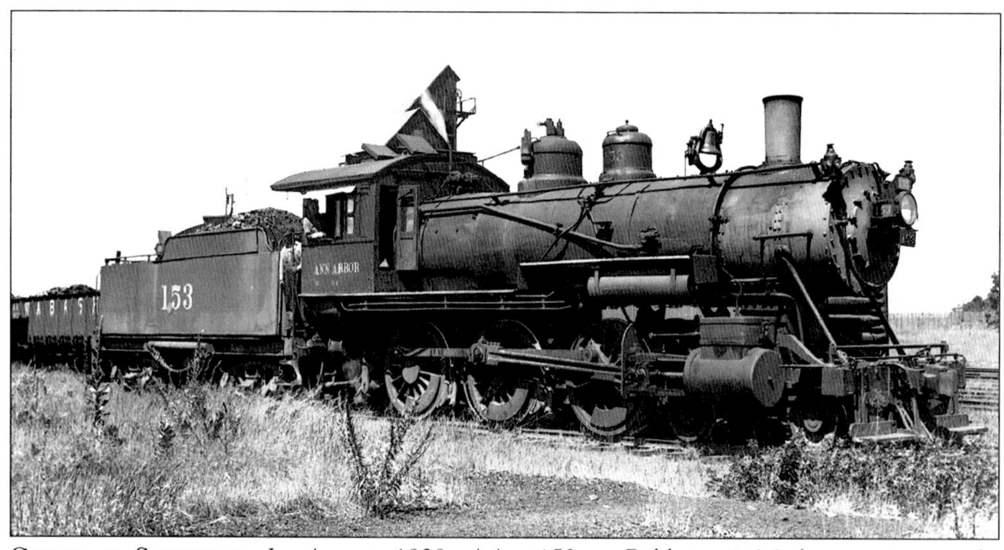

CADILLAC SWITCHER. In August 1938, AA #153, a Baldwin 4-6-0 locomotive, works around the Ann Arbor Railroad's Selma Yard in Cadillac. Note the Wabash gondola in the background. At this time, the Wabash Railroad controlled the Ann Arbor. (Collection of Harold K. Vollrath.)

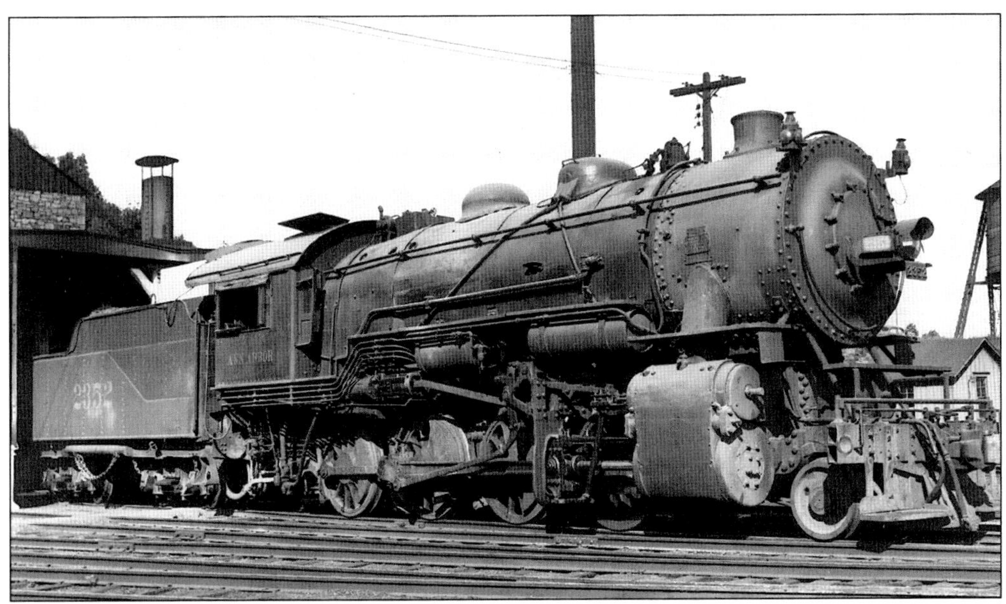

AT THE DOOR. Ann Arbor #2352, one of a total of twenty-nine 2-8-0 locomotives rostered by the Ann Arbor, rests just outside one of the roundhouse stalls at Elberta in July 1939. The Brooks Locomotive Works built this unit in 1912, and the Ann Arbor scrapped it in 1946. Over the years, the Ann Arbor also employed 2-8-0s manufactured by the Baldwin Locomotive Works and the Schenectady Locomotive Works. (Collection of Harold K. Vollrath.)

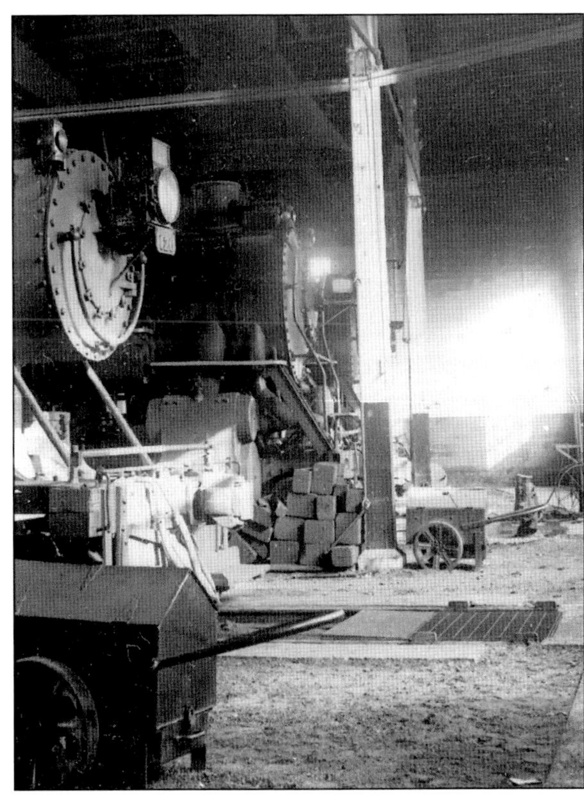

INSIDE THE ROUNDHOUSE. Locomotives rest in a row inside the dusty Elberta roundhouse in this image captured in 1940. The unit in the foreground is Ann Arbor #120, a Baldwin 4-6-0 built in 1898. (Courtesy of the Claude T. Stoner Collection, Bentley Historical Library, University of Michigan.)

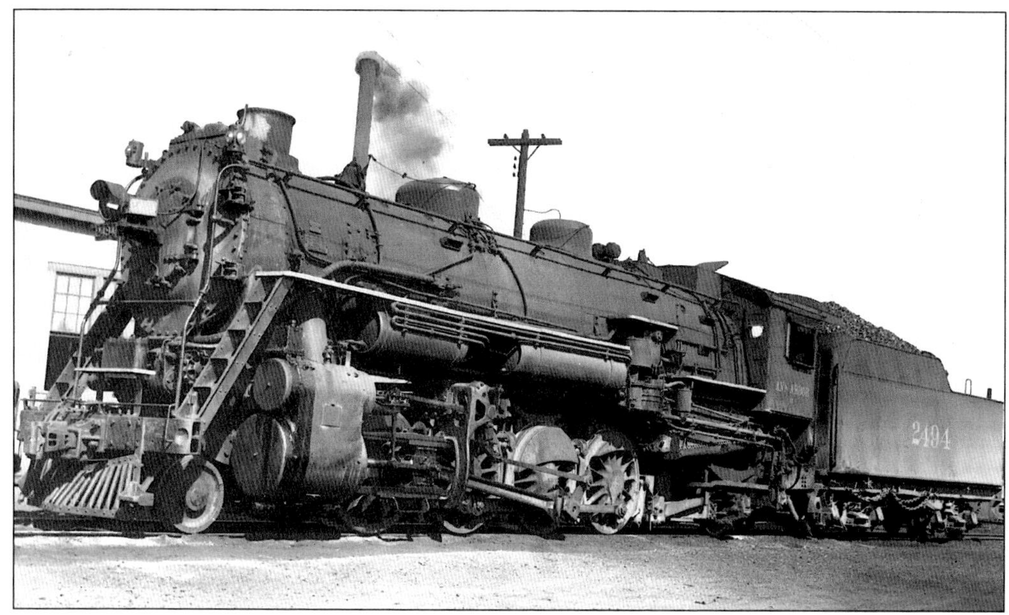

Power at the Ready. In July 1946, Brooks product #2494—a 2-8-2 locomotive built in 1923—awaits a call to work at Elberta's Boat Landing Yard. Note the tender, brimming with a full load of coal. The railroad's records show that this locomotive went to the scrapper in July 1951. Unfortunately, a trip to the scrap yard was to be the fate of every Ann Arbor steam locomotive—if they were not sold to another railroad first. No Ann Arbor steam engines have been preserved. (Collection of Harold K. Vollrath.)

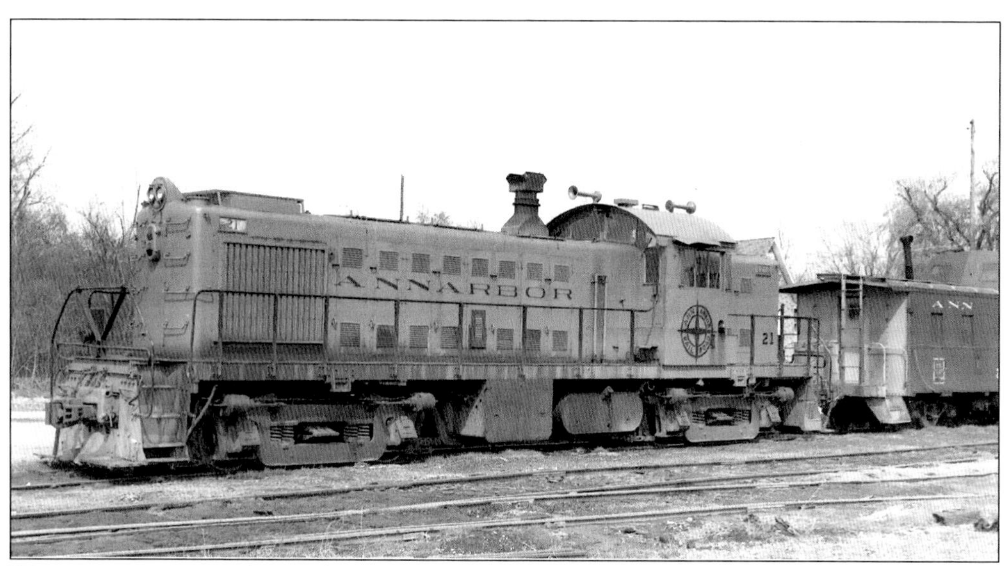

Workhorse. Ann Arbor Railroad Alco RS1 #21 lingers in the Owosso freight yard between assignments in April 1976. The AA rostered just two of these 1,000-horsepower diesels—#20 and #21—both built in 1950. (Collection of Harold K. Vollrath.)

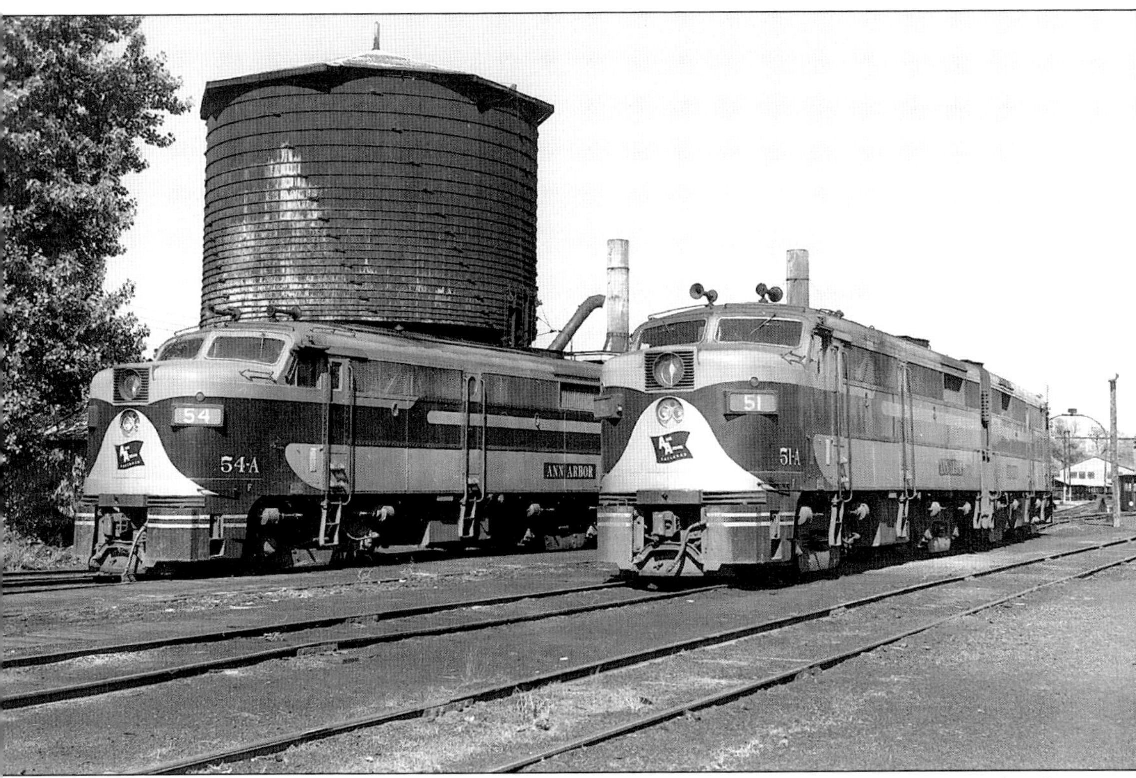

GATHERING PLACE. On the railroad's service track in Owosso Yard, Ann Arbor FA diesel engines wait for a call to lead freight trains to either Elberta or Toledo in this vintage 1953 scene. These FAs, built in 1950 in Schenectady, New York, made the Ann Arbor's steam locomotives obsolete, yet vestiges of the steam period remain—including the anachronistic water tank next to where these classic early diesel era units have gathered. The Ann Arbor once had 14 of these attractive FAs on the roster: #50–#56, and #50A–#56A. All of them were retired in 1964 in favor of GP35s. (Collection of D. C. Jesse Burkhardt.)

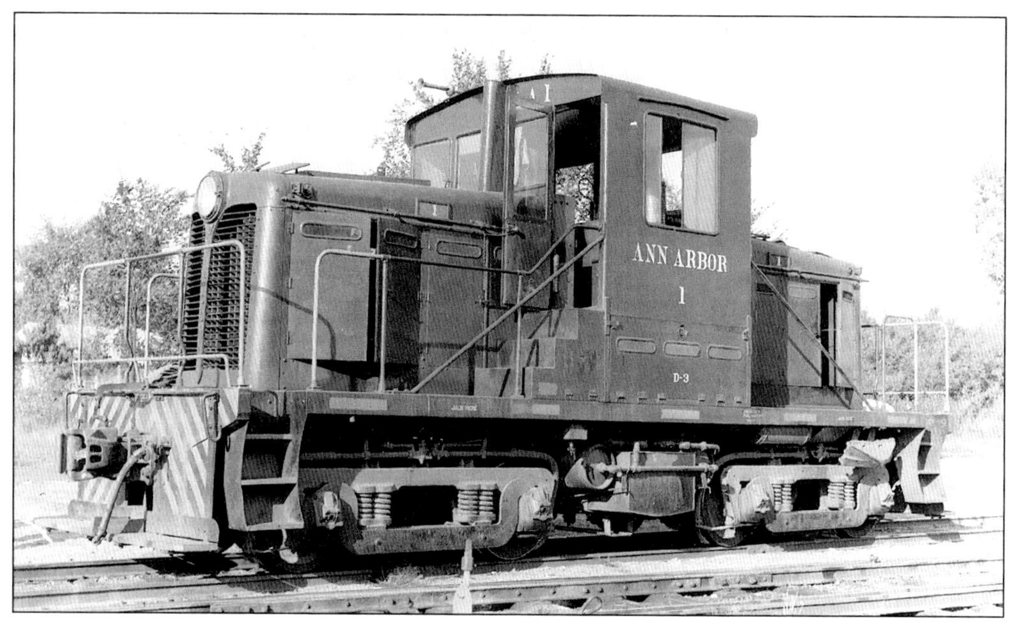

WHITCOMB SPECIAL. Two views show diminutive Ann Arbor #1, a Whitcomb 44-ton locomotive built in 1941, ready to shunt cars and cabooses around the Owosso freight yard in 1955. This locomotive, the only one of its type owned by the Ann Arbor Railroad, was sold to the Dundee Cement plant in Dundee, Michigan—a major shipper on the AA—in October 1985. The Whitcomb Locomotive Works, based in Rochelle, Illinois, was purchased by Baldwin Locomotive Works in 1931. Whitcomb survived as a separate division of Baldwin until 1940, after which it was submerged into the Baldwin company. (Both photos by Ron Morse.)

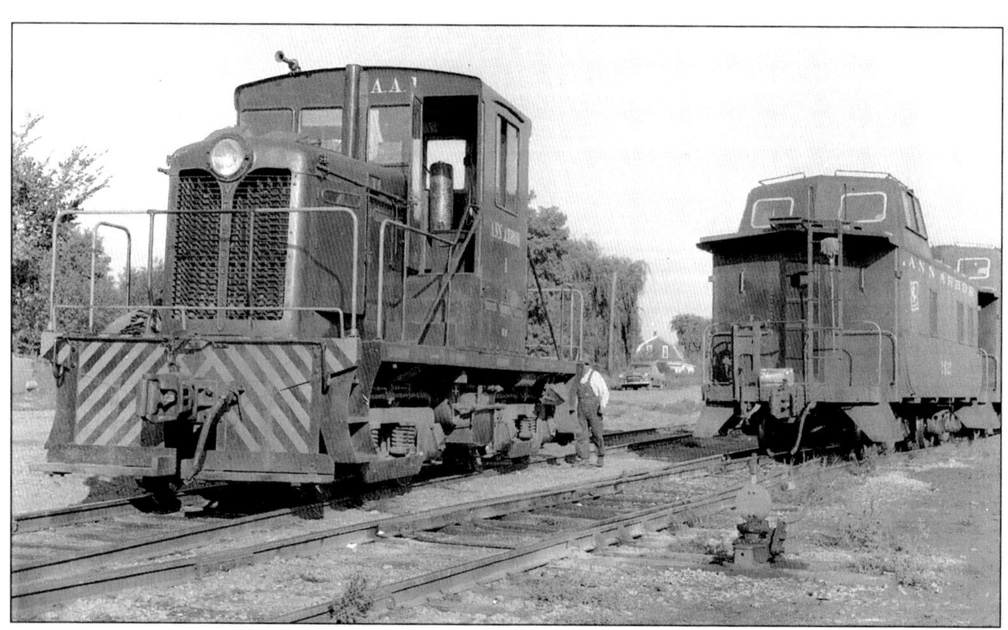

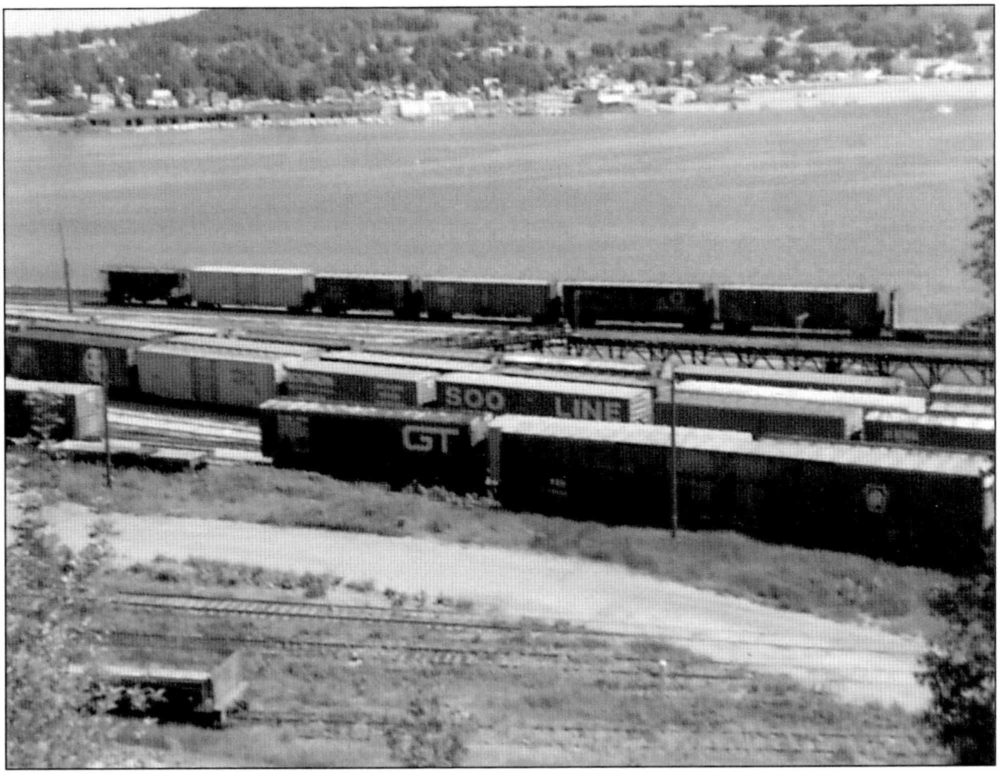

BUSY BY THE BAY. This image provides a glimpse of the Ann Arbor Railroad's Boat Landing Yard in Elberta, with Betsie Bay in the background. Virtually all of the freight cars seen in the yard—pictured here in the summer of 1971—had come into Elberta via eastbound carferries out of Wisconsin, or were bound for transport west across Lake Michigan to Wisconsin. With the ending of carferry traffic from Elberta in 1982, the once-congested yard became unnecessary. (Photo by D. C. Jesse Burkhardt.)

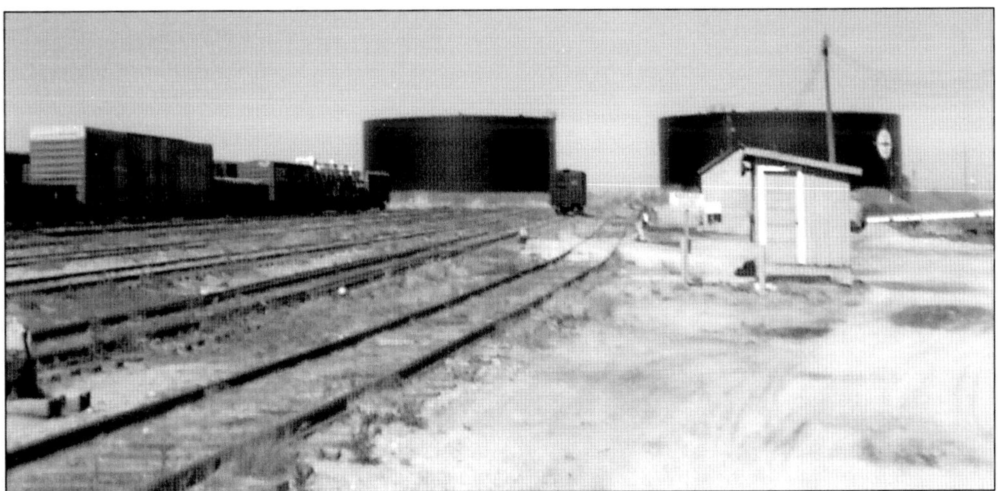

ENDS AT THE BIG LAKE. Tracks of the Ann Arbor Railroad's freight terminal in Elberta came to an end literally at the water's edge on Lake Michigan. This 1971 view looks west; the lake is directly beyond the railroad's huge fuel reservoirs. (Photo by D. C. Jesse Burkhardt.)

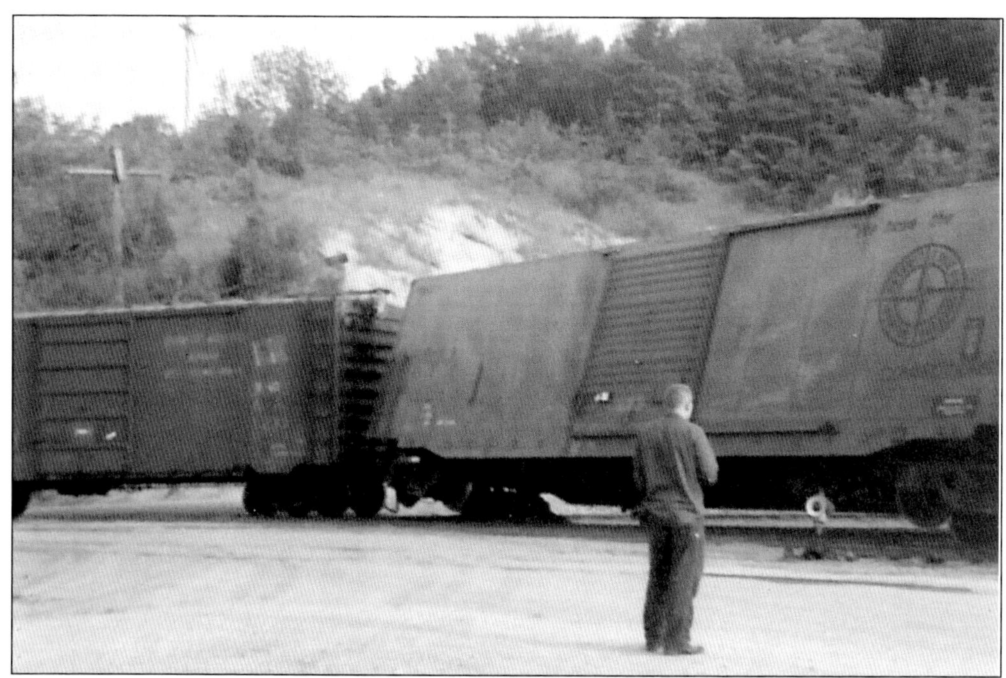

PUSHING TOO HARD. A switchman at Boat Landing Yard eyes a cut of boxcars that have jumped the tracks during switching operations in July 1971. Crackerjack crews had the cars re-railed within approximately half an hour, and work got under way again as if the mishap was just an everyday thing. (Photo by D. C. Jesse Burkhardt.)

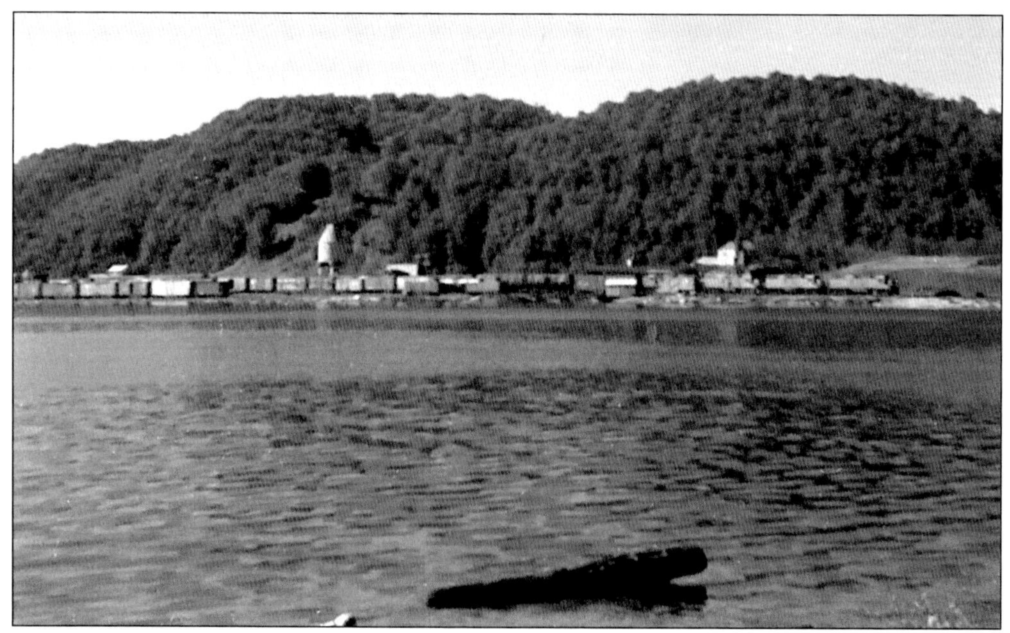

ACROSS THE HARBOR. Orange road locomotives and freight cars rest at the Ann Arbor's Elberta freight yard in this 1971 view taken from just across Betsie Bay in Frankfort. The concrete coaling tower rising above the freight cars is a fitting monument to the steam era. (Photo by D. C. Jesse Burkhardt.)

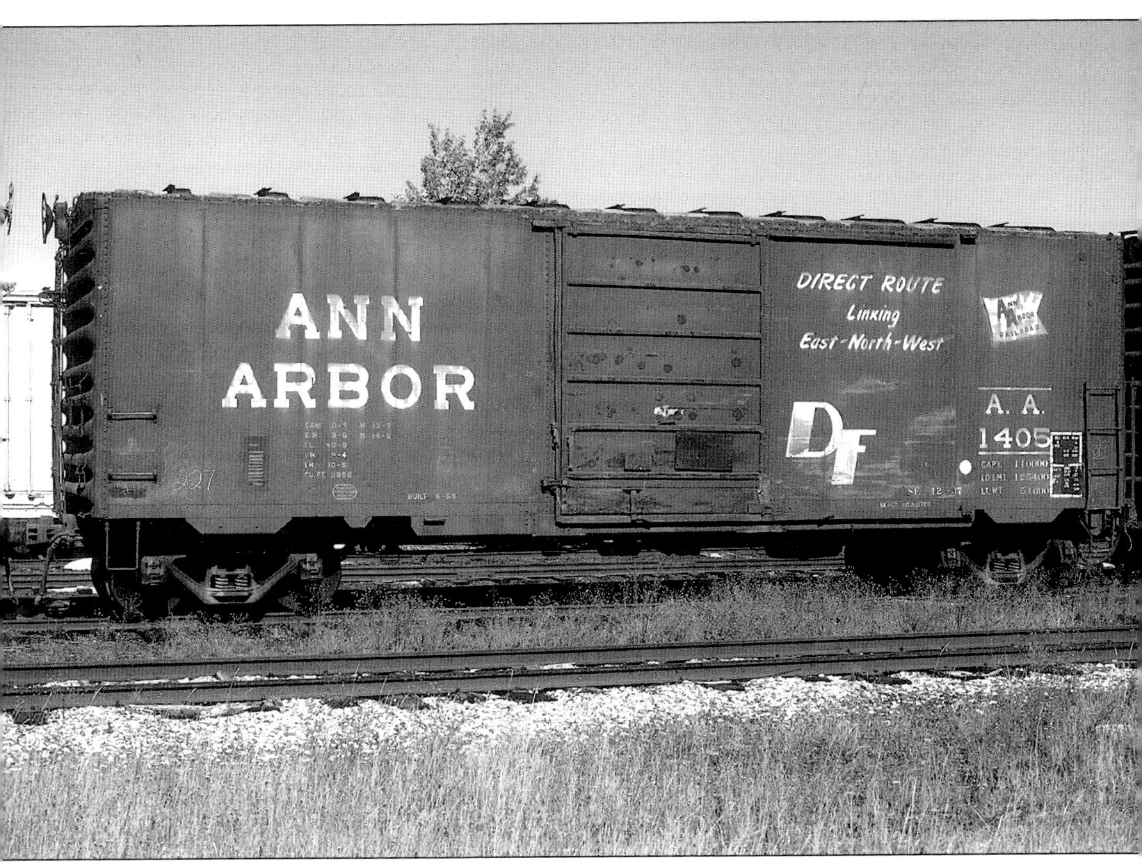

Direct Route. Ann Arbor Railroad boxcar #1405 rests in the Cadillac rail yard in September 1979, still sharply displaying the carrier's old slogan: "DIRECT ROUTE Linking East-North-West." The flag logo to the right is fashioned after the emblem employed by former parent Wabash Railroad, which owned the Ann Arbor from 1925 to 1963. The Wabash's motto, appropriately, was "Follow the Flag." The large "DF" symbol stands for "Damage Free," a claim made because these cars used interior bulkheads to secure goods being transported inside. Most of these boxcars were stenciled with the directive: "When Empty Return to Ann Arbor RR, Frankfort, Michigan." Thus, although the yard complex and carferry docks were in Elberta—not Frankfort—the railroad itself added to the ambiguity over which town was the railroad's true northern terminus. (Photo by Dennis Schmidt.)

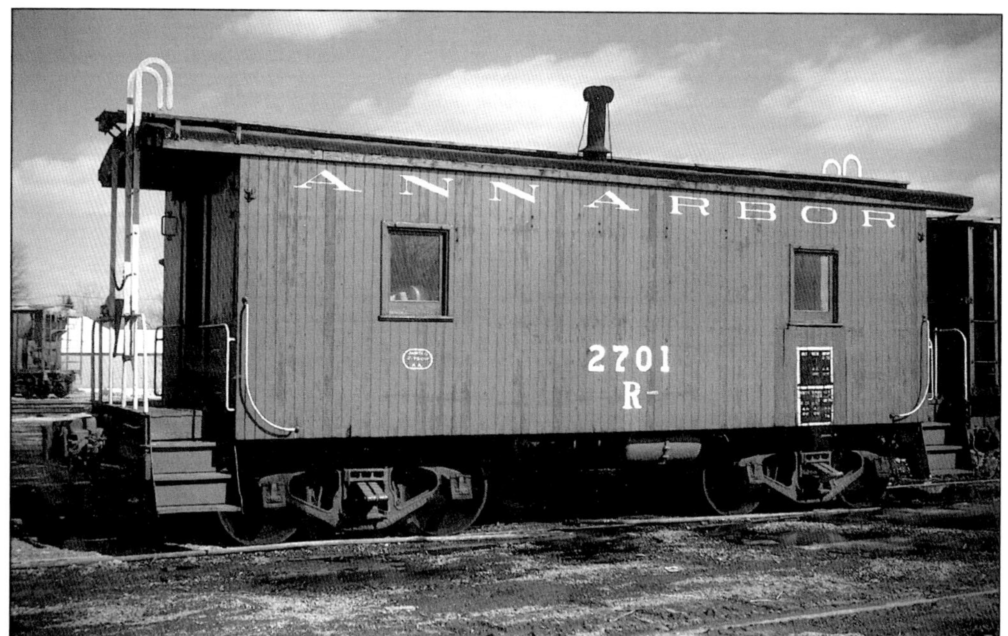

Wooden Sides. Ann Arbor caboose #2701 is pictured in Owosso on February 19, 1977 (above), and on November 22, 1980 (below). This 1925-era caboose has a body made of wood and a plywood roof. When these photos were taken, it was still in pretty good shape for being more than 50 years old, but it had been relegated to yard switching duty and rarely left Owosso. Notice the new lettering to "Ann Arbor Railroad System" in the 1980 photo, which reflects the Michigan Interstate Railway's late 1977 takeover of the AA's operations. It's a bit of a surprise they bothered to repaint it, as the caboose clearly was not long for the world. (Both photos by Dennis Schmidt.)

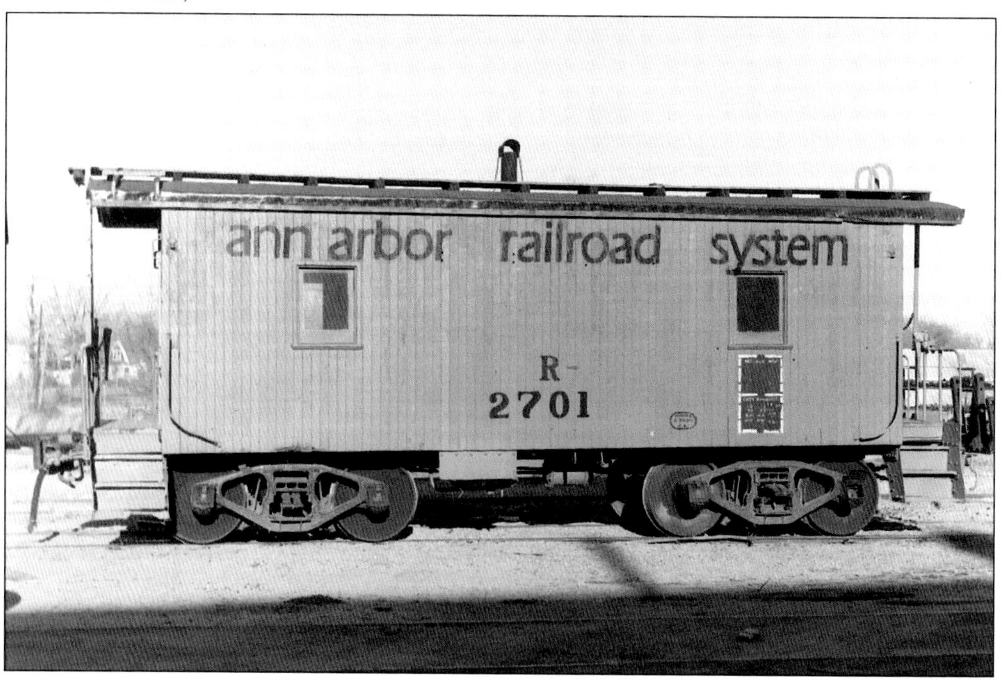

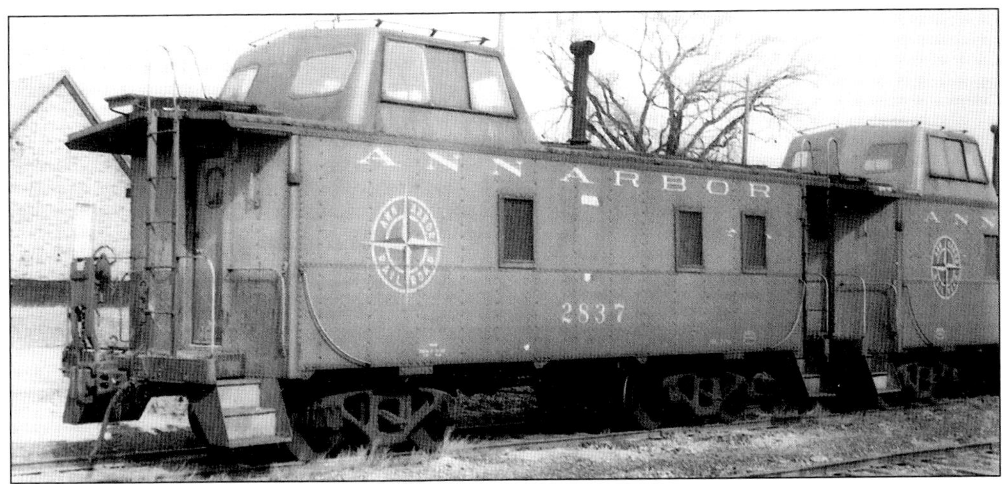

Streamlined Design. While the Ann Arbor Railroad was under the control of the Wabash Railroad, the Wabash shops built 10 AA cabooses with the Wabash's standard streamlined cupola. This caboose, Ann Arbor #2837, was built in February 1952 as part of an order that included AA road numbers 2830–2839. Resting in the caboose line in Owosso in January 1968, #2837 displays the compass herald of the railroad's new owner, the Detroit, Toledo & Ironton. (Collection of the Benzie Area Historical Society.)

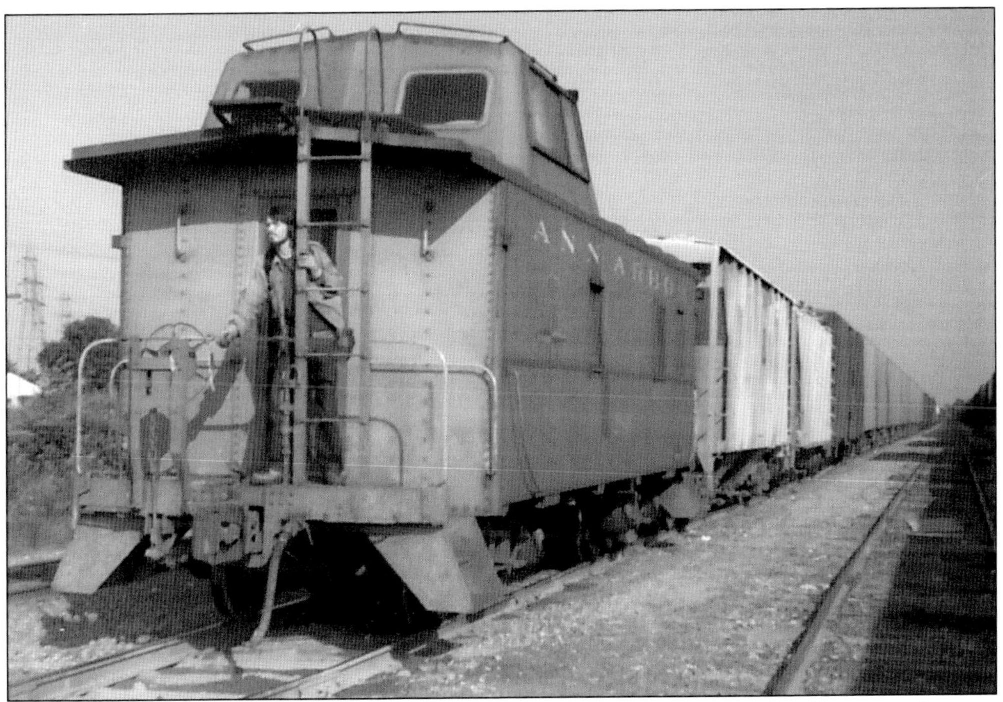

Summer Dreams. The author is pictured on an Ann Arbor Railroad caboose, at the rear of a northbound (westbound by timetable) train in Owosso in 1974. The AA classification yard in Owosso was situated at Milepost 107, near the center of the carrier's 292-mile line, and it was a natural crew-change point. Through trains arriving here from either direction were usually reconfigured, and a new crew came aboard before continuing the run. (Photo by Marie Groshans.)

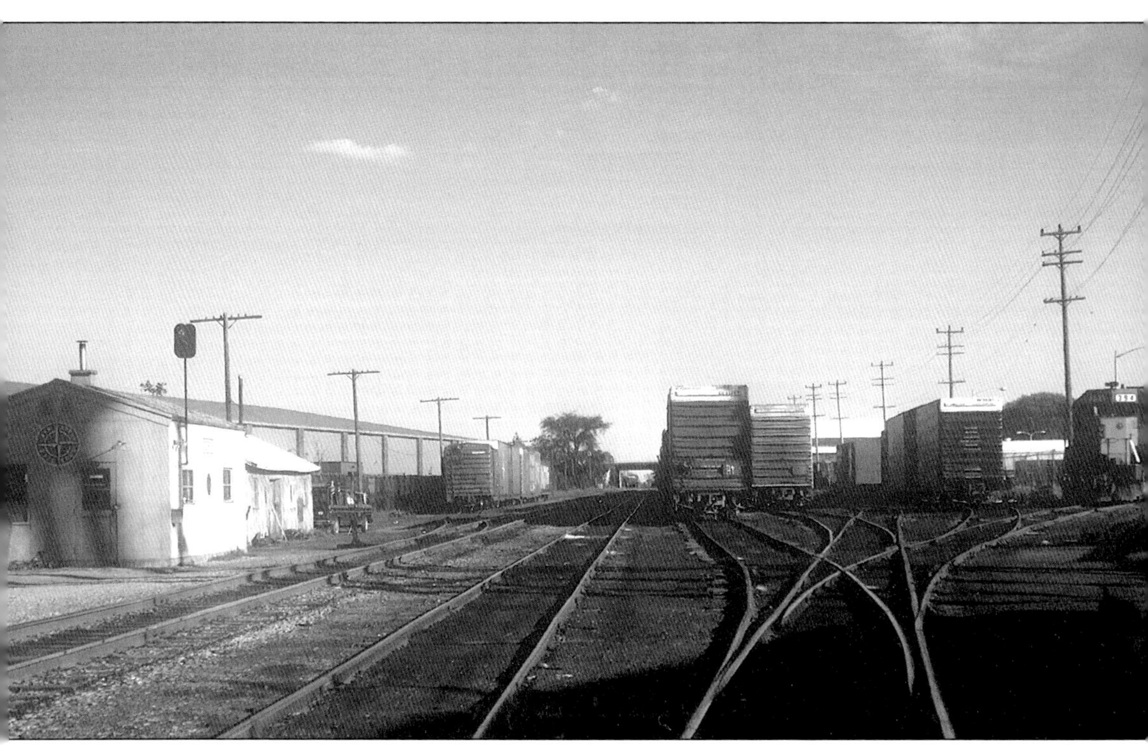

FERRY YARD, LOOKING SOUTH. High-cube auto parts boxcars and other freight cars fill the tracks at Ferry Yard in Ann Arbor in this scene captured on May 21, 1976. The signal mast attached to the side of the yard office is displaying a green light, which signifies a "proceed" indication for oncoming traffic. On the right, one of the railroad's GP35s sits on the engine spur track, awaiting its next assignment. A local switching crew and locomotive were based at Ferry Yard until the 1980s. (Photo by Dennis Schmidt.)

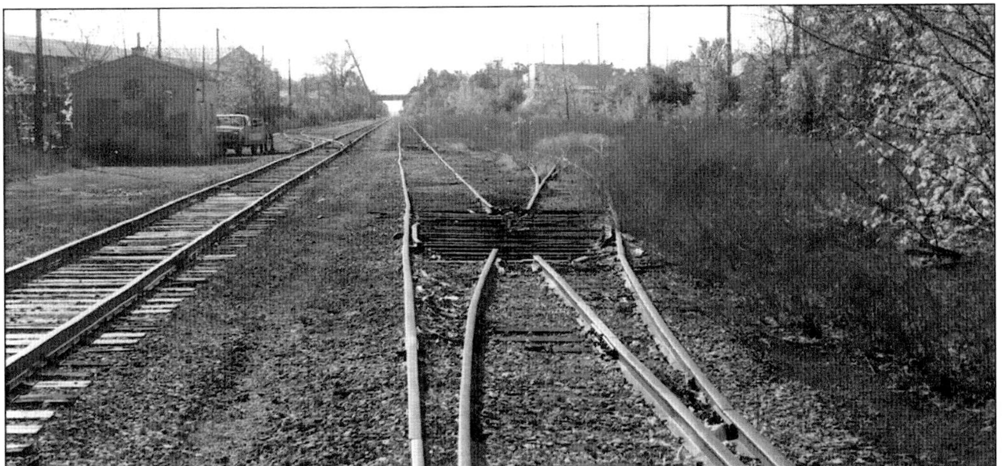

Expendable Trackage. This is the view looking south at an empty Ferry Yard, the Ann Arbor's once-busy terminal in the railroad's namesake city—quite a contrast with the scene on the opposite page. Although the main track was still getting daily traffic when this photo was taken in 1992, the yard tracks were obviously no longer needed. (Photo by D. C. Jesse Burkhardt.)

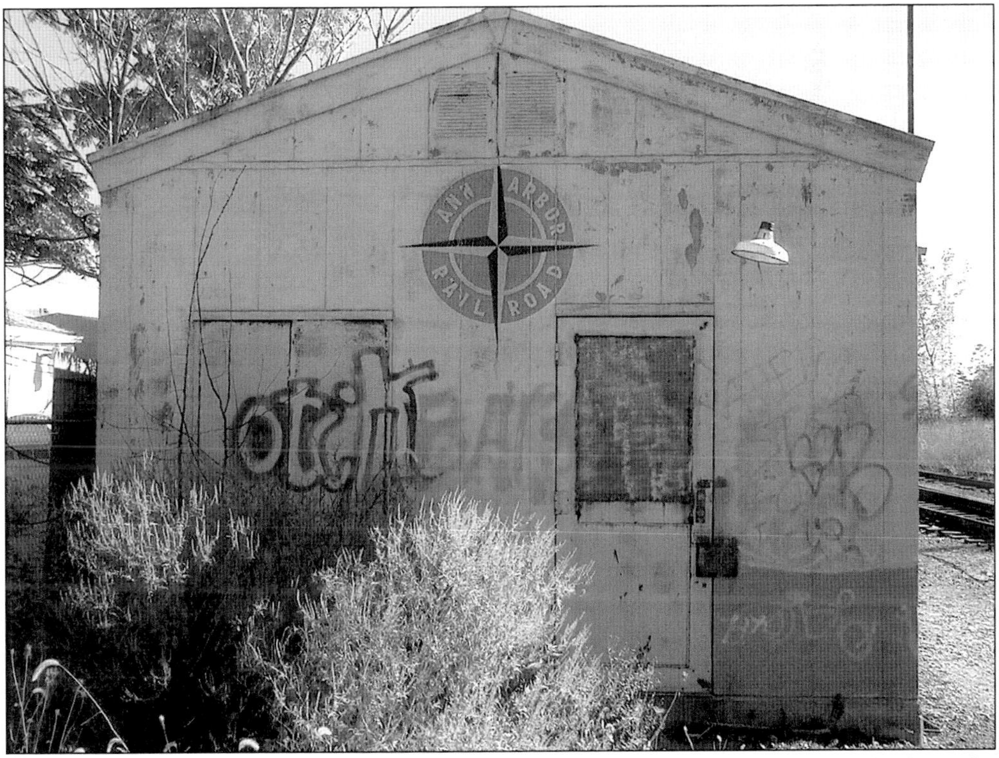

Office Closed. This is a late 1990s view of the Ann Arbor Railroad's Ferry Yard office. The Ann Arbor's compass logo, adopted from former parent DT&I, adorns this weathered and virtually abandoned structure, once the working headquarters for a relatively busy facility. The now useless post on the upper right of the building at one time held a blinking-light train order signal. Now the metal shack simply rests locked up and forlorn, attracting graffiti and providing shade for some very tall weeds. (Photo by Jim Rees.)

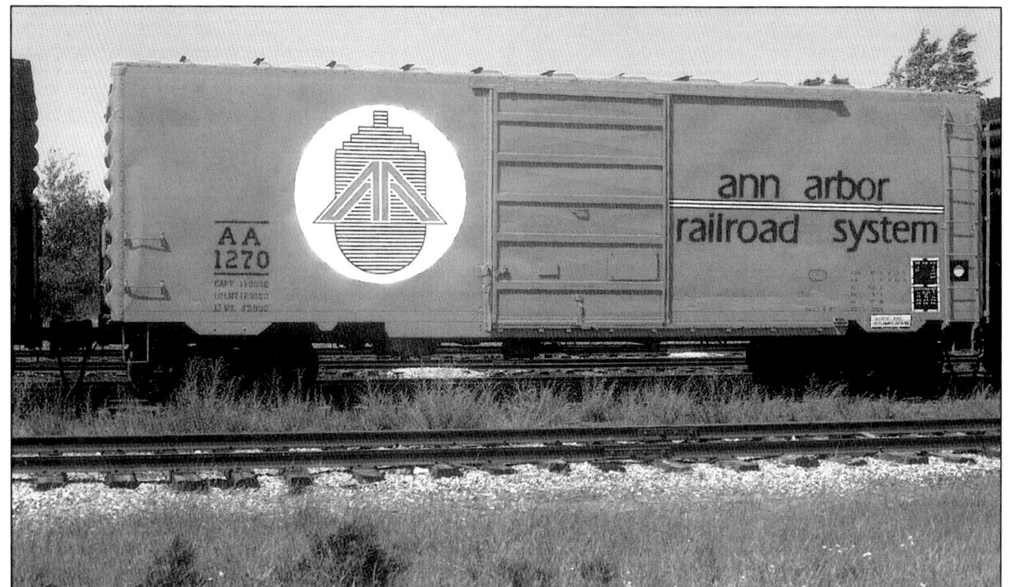

TRANSITION IN CADILLAC. Ann Arbor #1270, a standard, single-door boxcar, basks in the sun in the fresh, bright-red look of the "new" Ann Arbor Railroad as it evolved in the late 1970s. The ferry logo demonstrates that the railroad was still heavily invested in the carferry system in this era. This boxcar was in the railroad's Selma Yard in Cadillac on July 4, 1979. (Photo by Dennis Schmidt.)

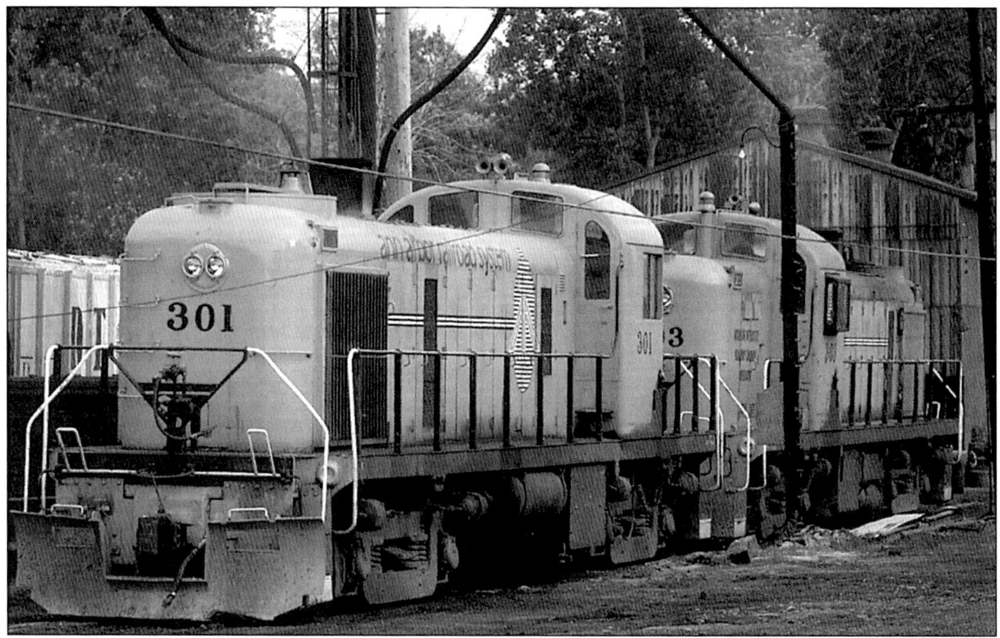

TOLEDO SERVICE TRACK. Ann Arbor Alco RS2 road-switchers #301 and #303 (ex-Green Bay & Western units) idle on the yard service track in Toledo, Ohio, in 1980. Observe the "ferry in the fog" logo visible on the lead unit. It was a new design created after the State of Michigan purchased the entire Ann Arbor line as a stopgap measure to prevent its abandonment in 1977. (Collection of D. C. Jesse Burkhardt.)

Five

THE WAR YEARS

In either direction, the Ann Arbor ferry is carrying materials essential to victory; taking them quickly and safely to points where Uncle Sam needs them. Ann Arbor is glad to be able to be helping win America's battle of transportation.

—Ad from *Traffic World*, September 1944

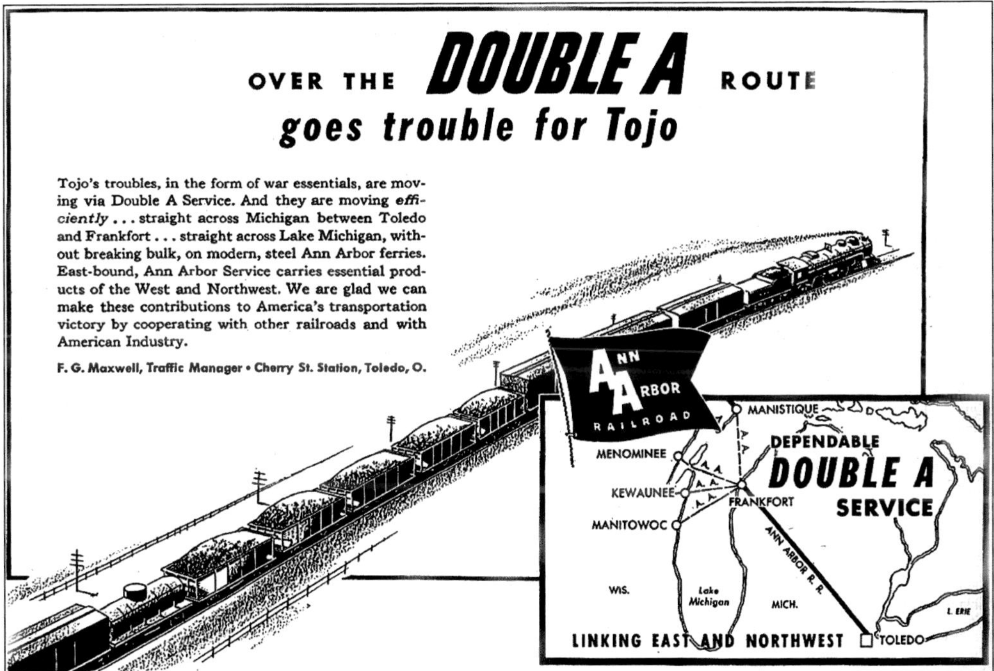

TROUBLE FOR TOJO. "Over the Double A route goes trouble for Tojo," blares the dramatic headline of this wartime advertisement from 1944. The text is similarly patriotic: "Tojo's troubles, in the form of war essentials . . . are moving efficiently, straight across Michigan between Toledo and Frankfort, straight across Lake Michigan—without breaking bulk—on modern, steel Ann Arbor ferries." (Collection of D. C. Jesse Burkhardt.)

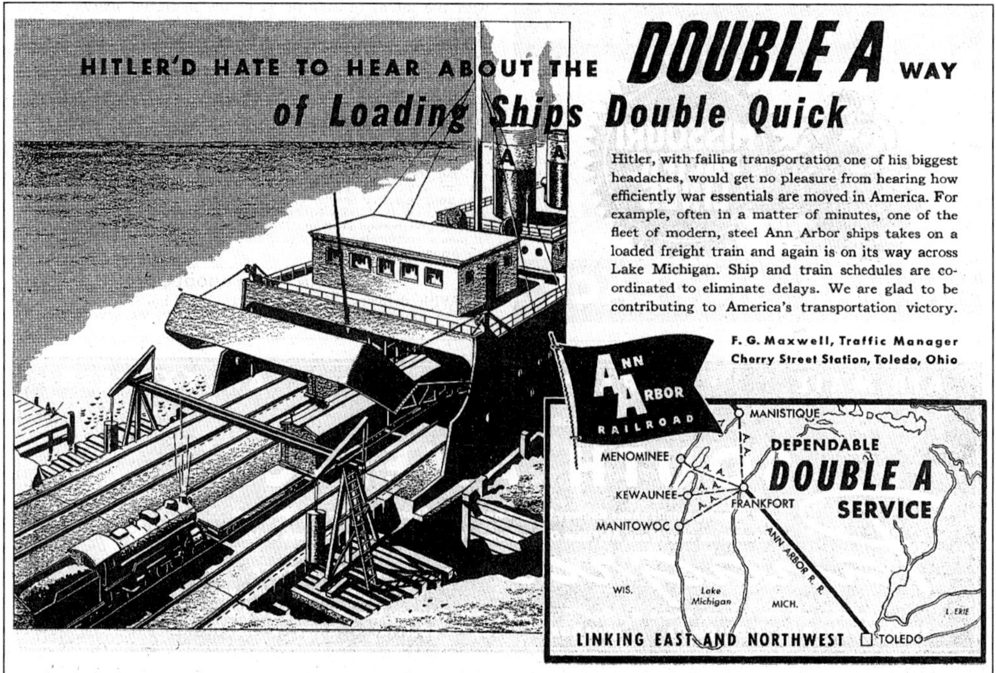

DOUBLE QUICK LOADING. This *Traffic World* advertisement, dated April 8, 1944, mocks Hitler's troubles as the Allied noose closes around him. "Hitler, with failing transportation one of his biggest headaches, would get no pleasure from hearing how efficiently war essentials are moved in America," reads the narrative. "For example, often in a matter of minutes, one of the fleet of modern, steel Ann Arbor ships takes on a loaded freight train and again is on its way across Lake Michigan." (Collection of D. C. Jesse Burkhardt.)

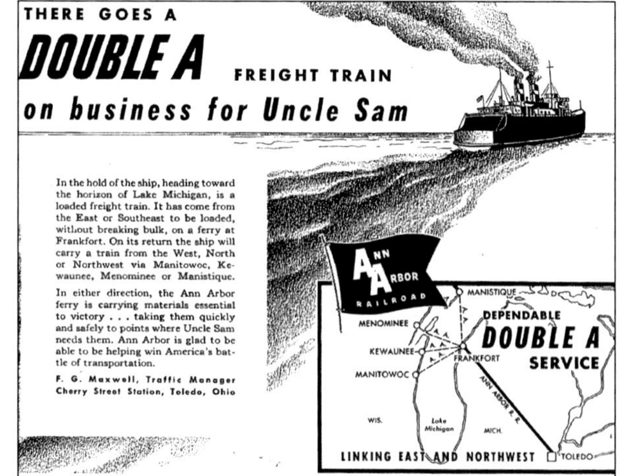

FREIGHT ON THE WATER. The writers of this 1944 advertisement managed to conjure up almost romantic imagery, despite the deadly serious nature of the wartime ad campaign. The artwork pictures a steaming carferry, with a confident headline and ad copy that reads: "In the hold of the ship, heading toward the horizon of Lake Michigan, is a loaded freight train. The Ann Arbor ferry is carrying materials essential to victory; taking them quickly and safely to points where Uncle Sam needs them." (Collection of D. C. Jesse Burkhardt.)

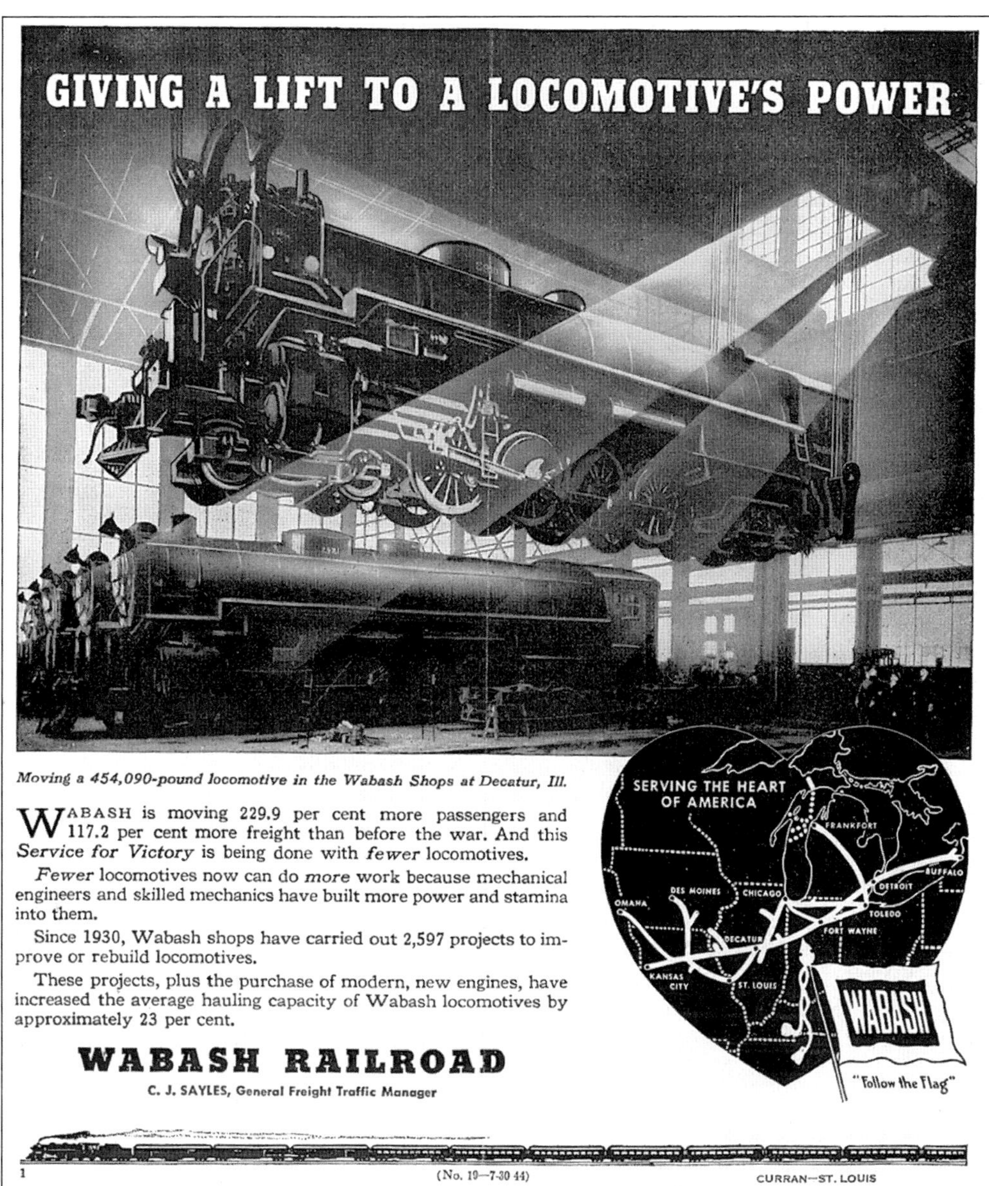

WABASH FOR VICTORY. The Ann Arbor Railroad's longtime parent company, the Wabash Railroad, put patriotic themes on the first page of its system timetable from July 1944. This promotional campaign tied the efficiency of the railroad's locomotive fleet directly to the war effort. Note the heart-shaped route map, the flag logo, and the great slogan, "Serving the Heart of America." The map prominently displays the Ann Arbor Railroad (as well as Ann Arbor subsidiary Manistique & Lake Superior) and the ferry system operating out of the harbor at Frankfort. (Collection of D. C. Jesse Burkhardt.)

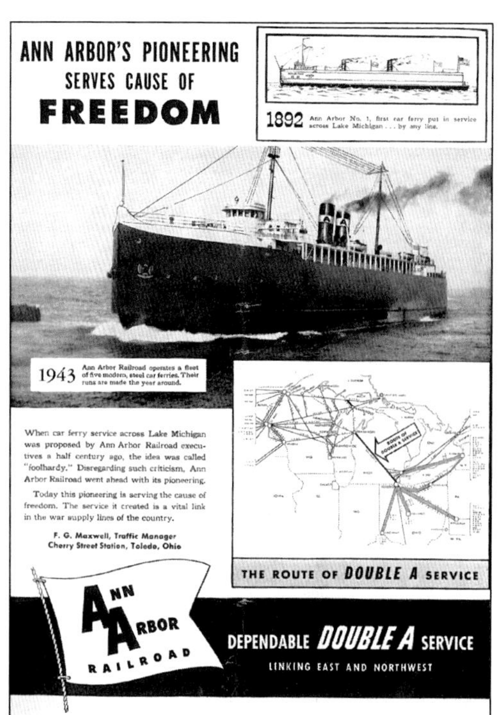

WAR EFFORT. This full-page advertisement, published in *Traffic World* in October 1943 while World War II was raging, put a patriotic spin on the Ann Arbor's cross-lake service: "Today this pioneering is serving the cause of freedom. The service it created is a vital link in the war supply lines of the country," the ad copy reads. The inset map of "The Route of Double A Service" highlighted the many transportation connections the Ann Arbor Railroad enjoyed across the region. (Collection of D. C. Jesse Burkhardt.)

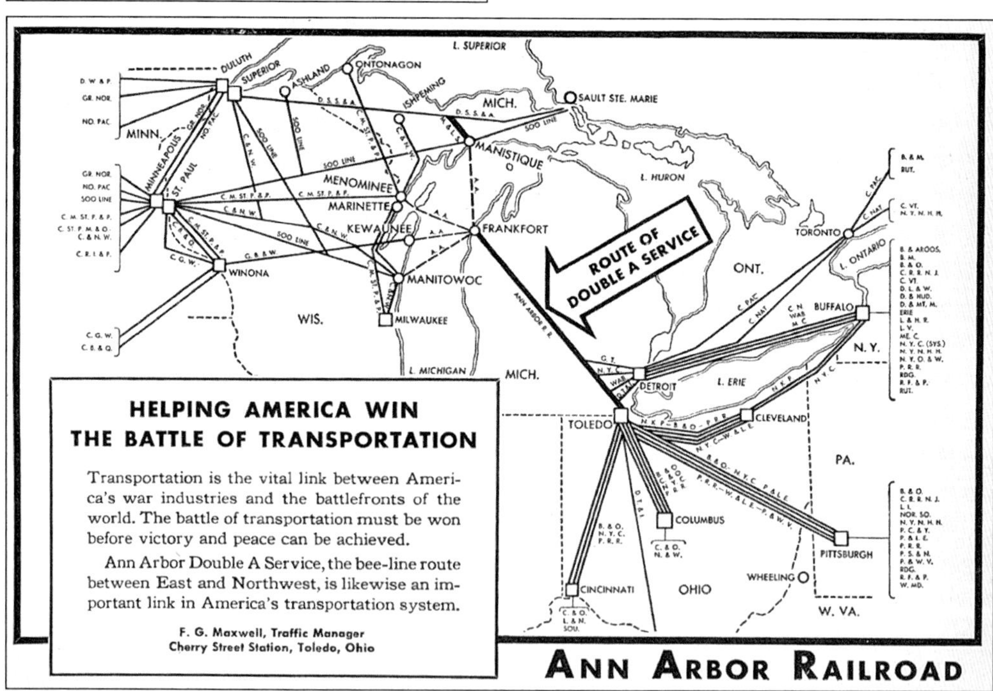

THE BATTLE OF TRANSPORTATION. A schematic map of the Ann Arbor's routes and its connections published in the August 26, 1944, issue of *Traffic World* stresses the role of the railroad in the war effort. "Transportation is the vital link between America's war industries and the battlefronts of the world," the ad reads. "The battle of transportation must be won before victory and peace can be achieved." (Collection of D. C. Jesse Burkhardt.)

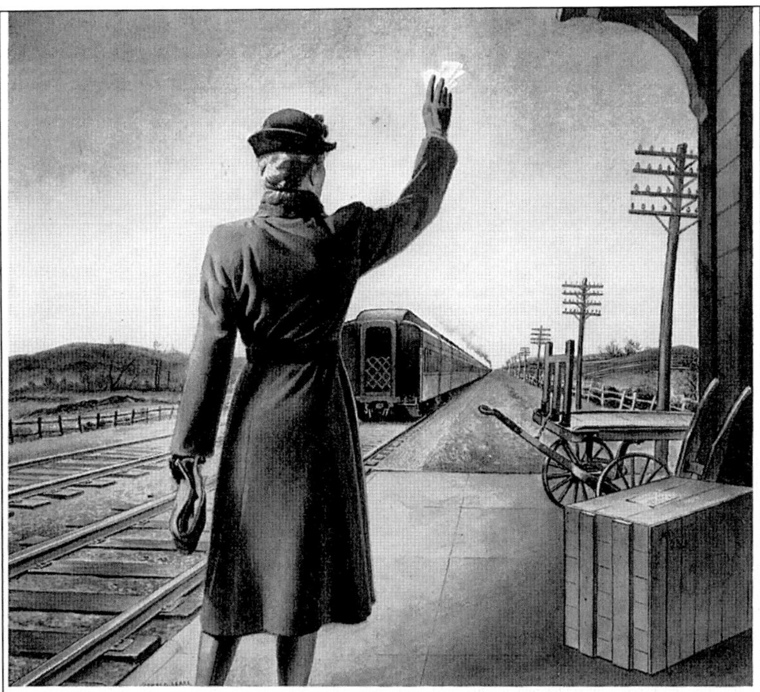

TO EVERY MOTHER IN AMERICA

Somewhere in America, tonight, a young man sits in a railroad car . . . bound for a destination unknown. He wears the olive drab of the Army, the blue of the Navy, or the forest green of the Marines.

He may be your son.

We know how you feel about that boy. We know what was in your heart when you said goodbye.

We know . . . because that boy is our son, too. And wherever he's going, we promise you this:

That to the very limit of our abilities, where he's concerned, it will never be "too little and too late." Because...it can blow or storm or sleet or rain . . . we'll get the supplies through. The guns he needs to do the job. The food to sustain him and give him strength. The medical equipment, the winter clothing, the mail from home...

That every hour of every passing day will see a million freight cars rumbling across the land ... carrying raw materials to factories, steel mills and refineries . . . rushing the finished cargoes of war to the ships waiting in the harbors...

And that with us, the men of the railroads, *your son will always come first!*

For he is the hope of America.

Tonight, mothers of America, remember these things, and listen for the whistle of the trains as they go thundering in the dark. Listen . . . and you'll hear the voice of a nation's fury . . . the battle-hymn of free men working together, fighting together, until Victory is ours.

NEW YORK CENTRAL

INVEST IN VICTORY... BUY UNITED STATES WAR BONDS AND STAMPS

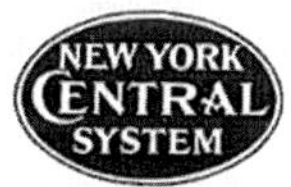

TO EVERY MOTHER IN AMERICA. The Ann Arbor Railroad's freight connection partners were also active in the war effort, as demonstrated by this poignant material from the "golden age" of advertising. A touching New York Central advertisement from 1943 depicts a mother waving as her son's train leaves the station, carrying him off to duty in World War II. "Somewhere in America, tonight, a young man sits in a railroad car . . . bound for a destination unknown," the text reads. The New York Central interchanged with the AA in Toledo, Ohio, as well as in Owosso and Ann Arbor in Michigan. (Collection of D. C. Jesse Burkhardt.)

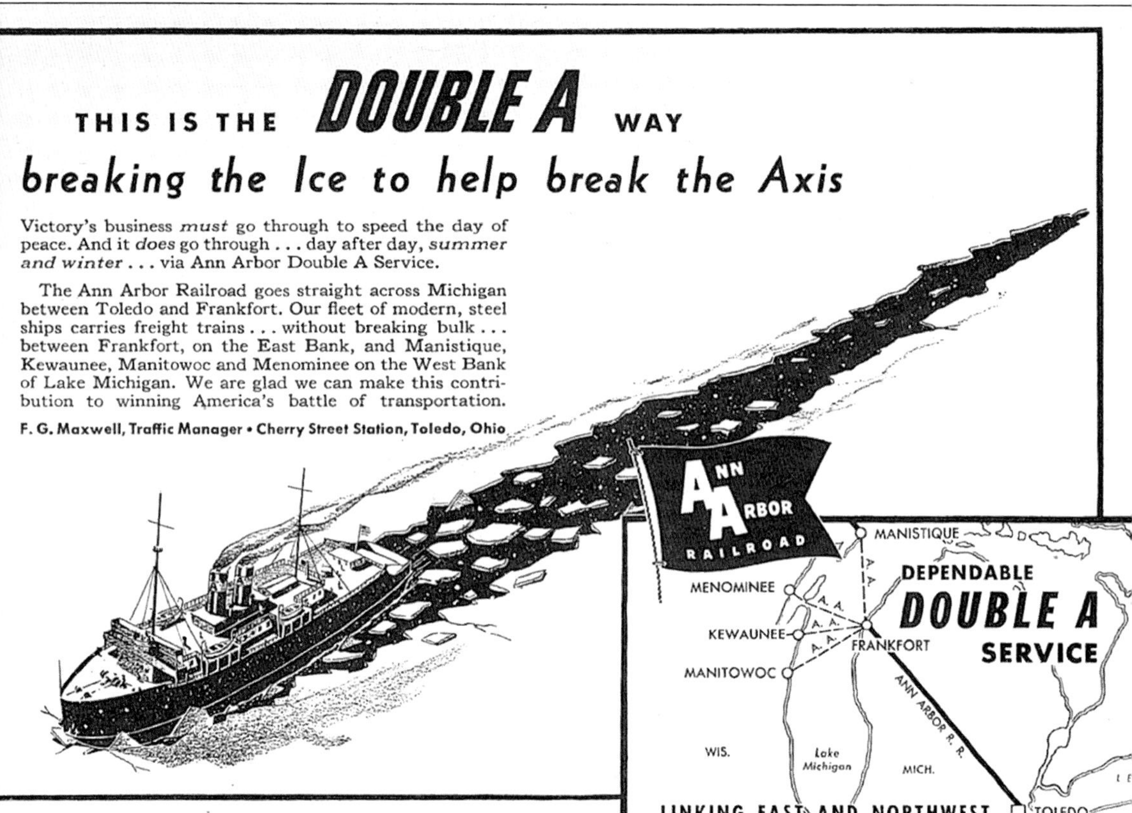

BREAKING THE AXIS. Another advertisement produced for the Ann Arbor Railroad during World War II—this one from the February 12, 1944, issue of *Traffic World*—touts the fact that the Ann Arbor's ice-breaking carferry fleet keeps the freight moving every day of the year, regardless of the season. "Victory's business must go through to speed the day of peace," reads an excerpt of the text. "And it does go through—day after day, summer and winter, via Ann Arbor Double A Service." (Collection of D. C. Jesse Burkhardt.)

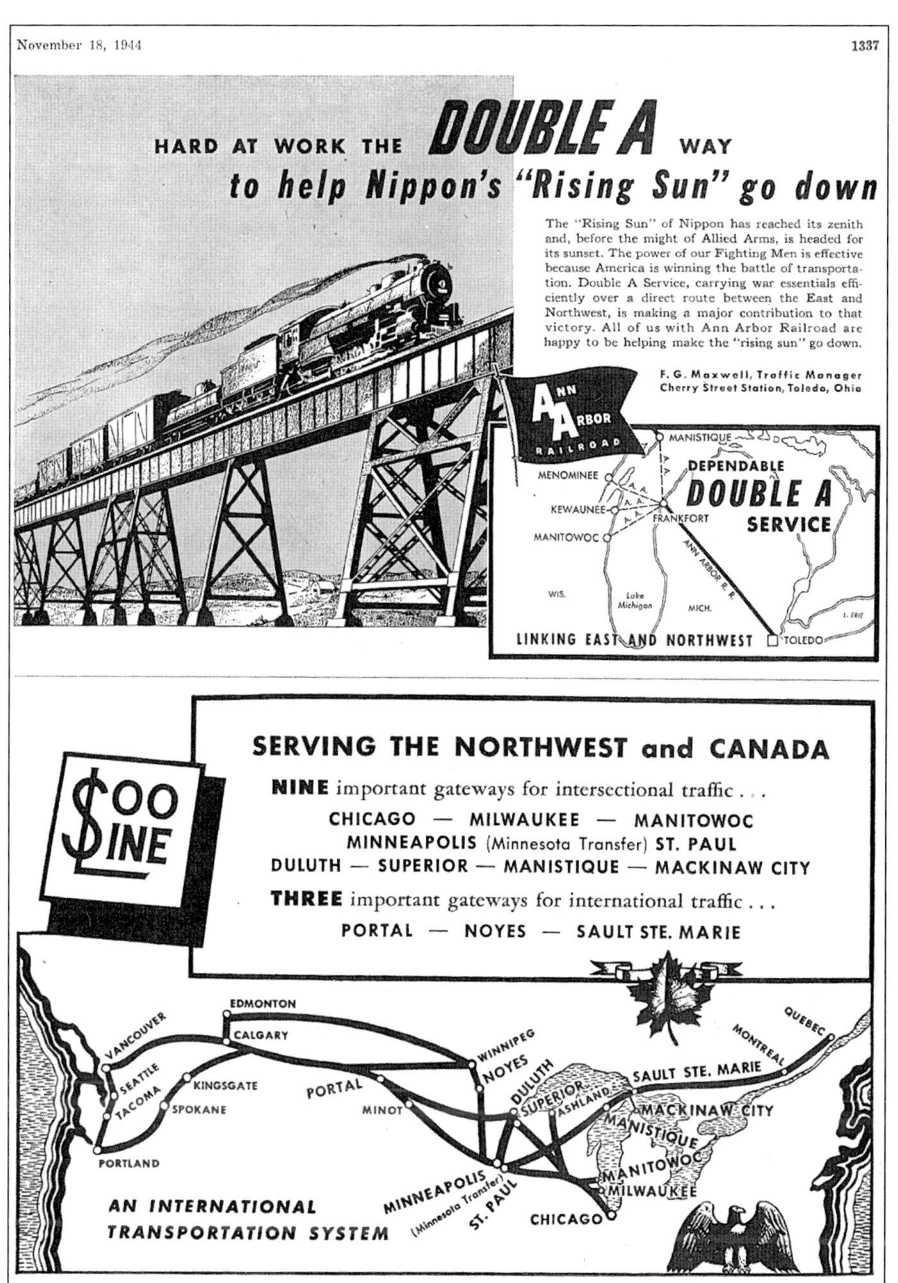

THE SUN GOES DOWN. This ad, which appeared in November 1944, shows a speeding freight on a high bridge and employs patriotic themes to promote the railroad's service. "The Rising Sun of Nippon has reached its zenith and, before the might of Allied Arms, is headed for its sunset. . . . Double A Service, carrying war essentials efficiently . . . is making a major contribution to that victory," a portion of the ad reads. On the same page, one of the Ann Arbor's connecting railroads, the Soo Line—which linked with the Ann Arbor's carferries at Manistique, Michigan, and Manitowoc, Wisconsin—uses a war-like eagle as part of its World War II ad campaign. (Collection of D. C. Jesse Burkhardt.)

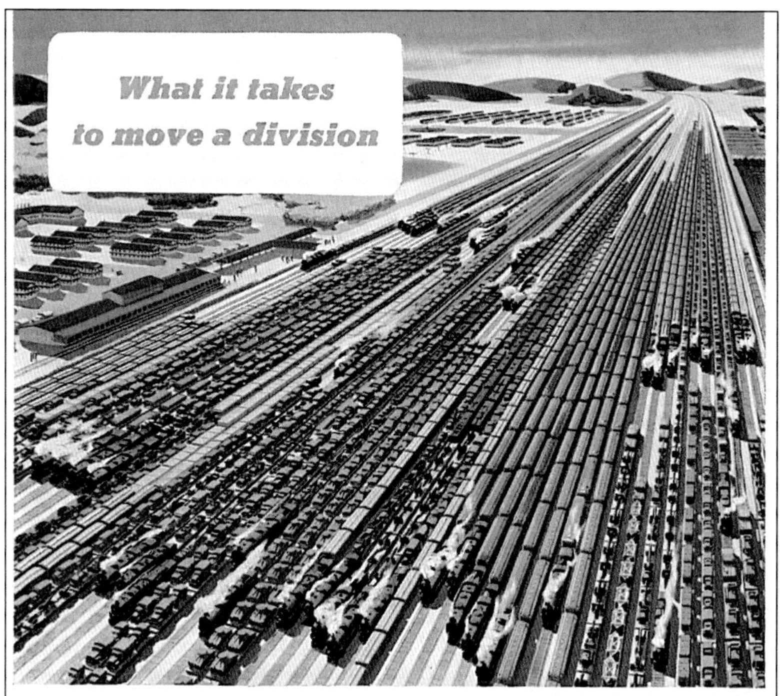

IF, like the eagle, you could look down on the amount of railroad equipment it takes to move a single armored division, here is what you would see . . . *75 trains!*

For a division takes all its equipment with it — tanks, jeeps, armored cars, supply trucks, tractors, anti-aircraft guns, many things. And its men, numbering about 12,000, need berths in which to sleep!

Those 75 trains *taken out* of civilian service and *put into military service*, are *about equal to* the number of passenger trains running daily over the Pennsylvania Railroad between *two of the busiest places on the face of the globe*—New York and Washington.

Multiply this one division by the many moving in this country and you can understand why . . . you may have difficulty getting a berth . . . or be obliged to stand in a coach . . . or arrive at your destination late. In fact, demand for equipment is now so great that on arriving at terminals cars must be put right back into service, so you may find them not quite so spic and span as we would like. Housekeeping facilities are adequate but there's not always time.

But Americans are taking all this like good soldiers. For they know this is a war of movement, and that movement begins right here—*in America, on the rails.*

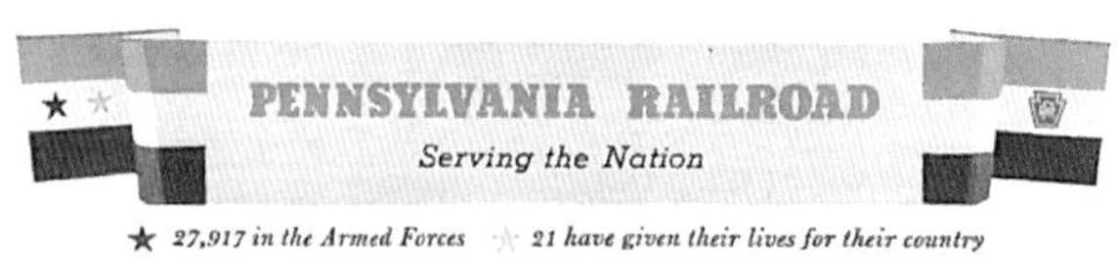

BUY UNITED STATES
WAR BONDS AND STAMPS

★ *27,917 in the Armed Forces* ☆ *21 have given their lives for their country*

MOVING A DIVISION. Railroads played a major role in winning World War II, as freight trains hauled war materials from coast to coast while troop trains moved armies. This 1943 advertisement from the Pennsylvania Railroad noted that it required approximately 75 trains to move the men and material of one military division. In the small type at the bottom of the ad, the railroad notes that 27,917 PRR employees were serving in the nation's armed forces at the time, and further points out that "21 have given their lives for their country." The Pennsylvania Railroad connected with the Ann Arbor in two different cities in two different states: Toledo, Ohio, and Cadillac, Michigan. (Collection of D. C. Jesse Burkhardt.)

Six

We have the Connections

The orange locomotives of the Ann Arbor Railroad were a landmark of Michigan's north country. The tracks cut through some of the sweetest landscapes Michigan has to offer. Its rails wound through the sand dunes near Yuma and the forests around Mesick; crossed the Chesapeake & Ohio diamond at Thompsonville; rolled over the Betsie River on a low trestle just outside of Frankfort. Finally the rails butted up against the ferry docks at Elberta's Lake Michigan harbor, literally heading off over the water.

—D. C. Jesse Burkhardt, journal entry, August 16, 1981

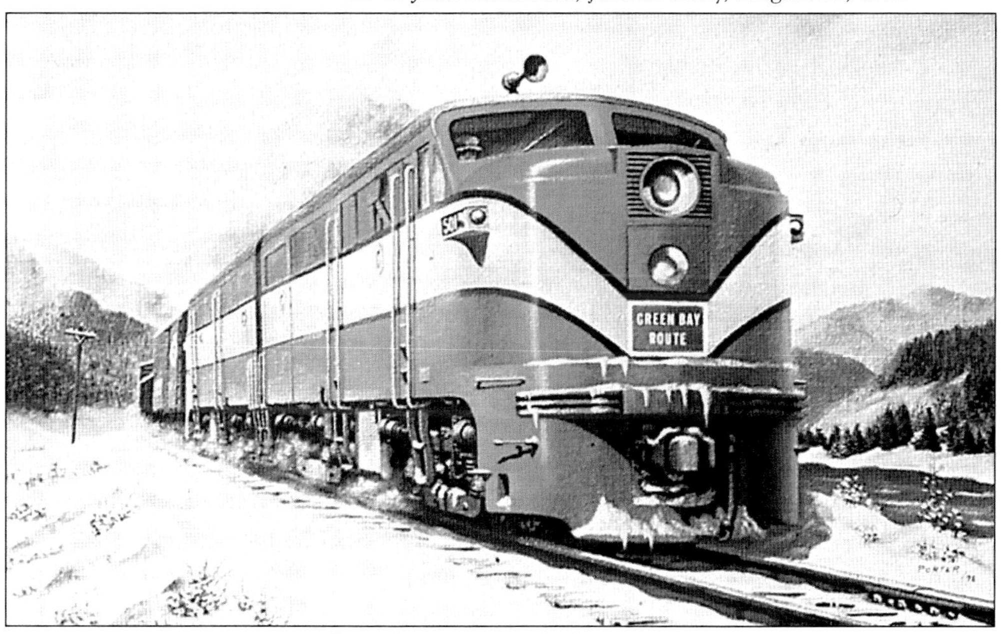

The Green Bay Route. Pulling freight through the icy cold of Wisconsin in January, a Green Bay & Western train heads eastward toward Green Bay in this postcard scene of 1959 from classy painter Russ Porter. The GB&W was a key Ann Arbor partner. (Collection of D. C. Jesse Burkhardt.)

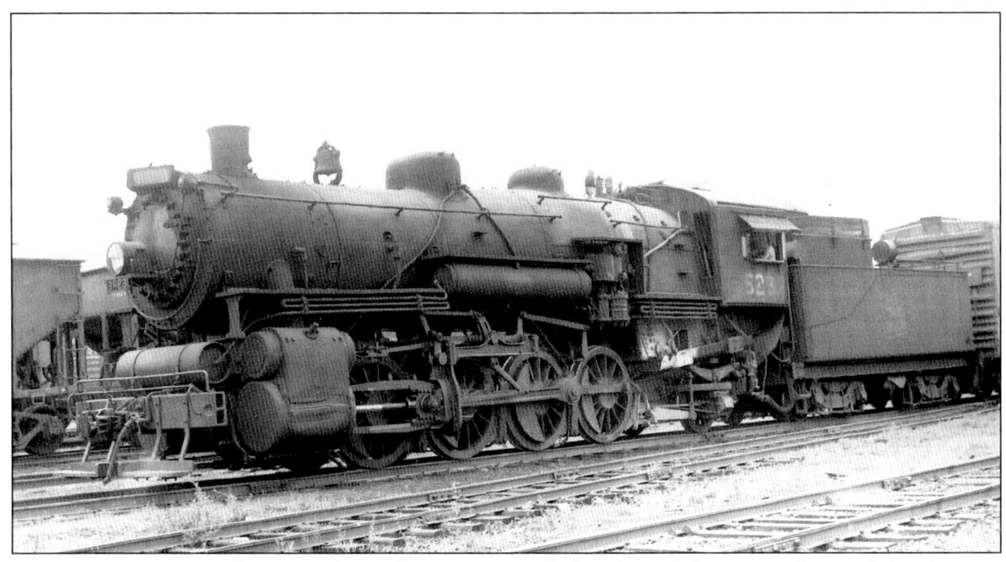

DURAND IN 1956. The Grand Trunk Western and the Ann Arbor interchanged freight cars at four Michigan stations: Lakeland, Durand, Ashley, and Owosso. In this image from July 1956, GTW #3523 prepares to pull a long freight eastward from the railroad's yard in Durand. Besides being a connecting point with the Ann Arbor, Durand was a key GTW terminal with rails stretching in five directions and carrying its trains to Detroit, Port Huron, Saginaw, Grand Rapids, and Battle Creek. (Collection of Harold K. Vollrath.)

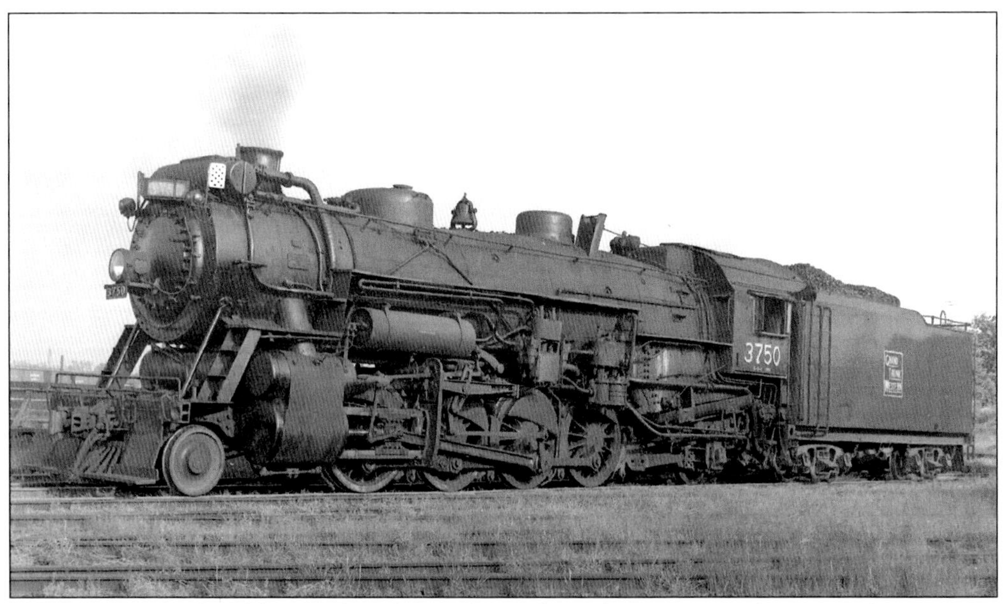

PONTIAC. Five railroad lines radiated out of Grand Trunk Western's Johnson Yard in Pontiac, Michigan; it was a hub that sent trains north to Caseville, northeast to Port Huron, northwest to Grand Rapids and Greenville, south to Detroit, and southwest to Jackson. On the route to Jackson, the GTW interchanged traffic with the Ann Arbor Railroad at Lakeland; GTW's line to the northwest reached three additional AA connections. In this scene from July 1956, GTW #3750 waits for a road freight to pull. (Collection of Harold K. Vollrath.)

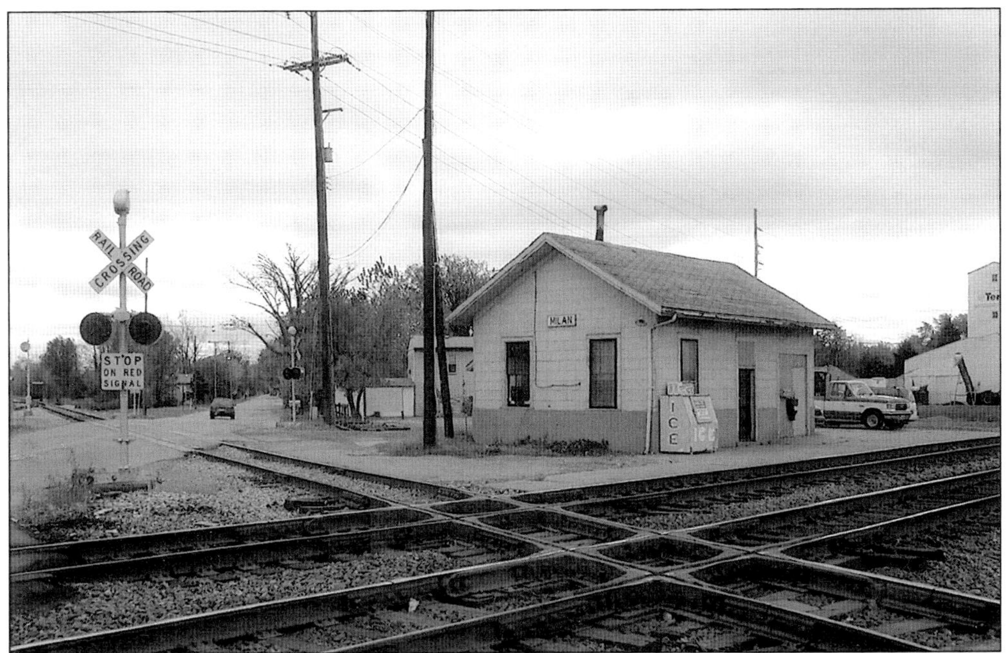

MILAN CROSSING. This view looks south from where the former Wabash Railroad tracks cross the Ann Arbor at Milan, Michigan. The AA owns the single north-south track, while the dual tracks of the Wabash run east-west. The Wabash, which was merged into the Norfolk & Western in 1963, built the small depot pictured here; it is now used as a section house. Milan remains an important interchange point between the two carriers, although the N&W is now known as Norfolk Southern. (Photo by Jim Rees.)

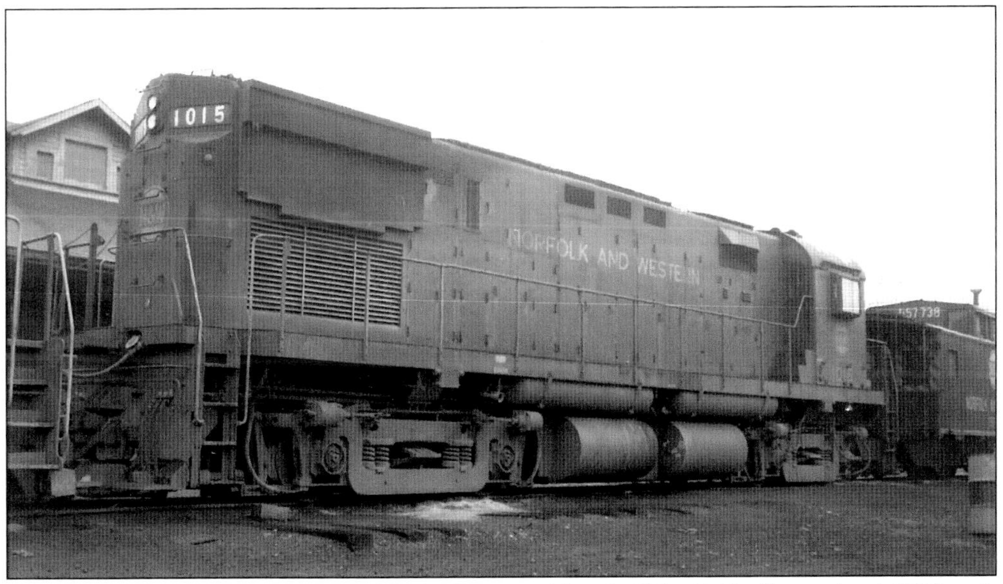

ON THE OLD WABASH LINE. Norfolk & Western Alco C-425 #1015 idles in April 1970 with N&W caboose #557738. The N&W interchanged traffic with the Ann Arbor at Toledo, Ohio, and Milan, Michigan. The N&W also had trackage rights on the Ann Arbor mainline between Toledo and Milan. (Collection of Harold K. Vollrath.)

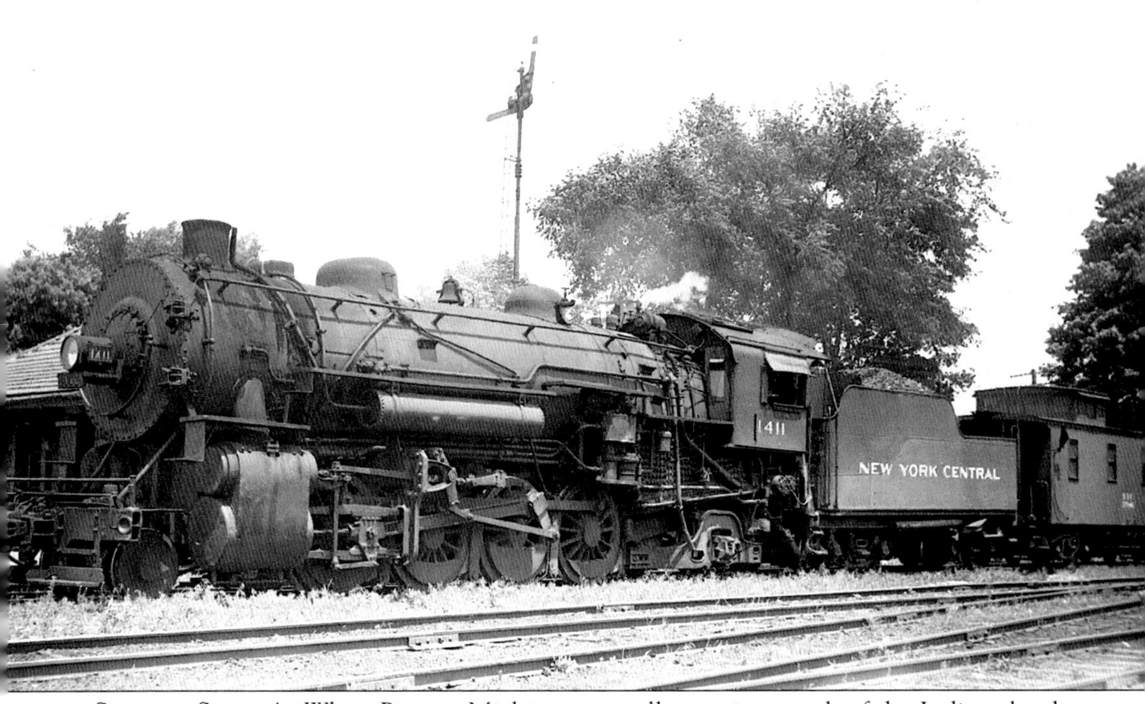

STATION STOP. At White Pigeon, Michigan, a small town just north of the Indiana border, New York Central #1411, with a wood-sheathed caboose in tow, pauses at the depot in a scene from June 1954. The NYC connected with the Ann Arbor at three stations, and coincidentally, all three were where the "Double A" operated major terminals: Toledo, Ann Arbor, and Owosso. Note the unusually high semaphore signal tower at this station. (Collection of Harold K. Vollrath.)

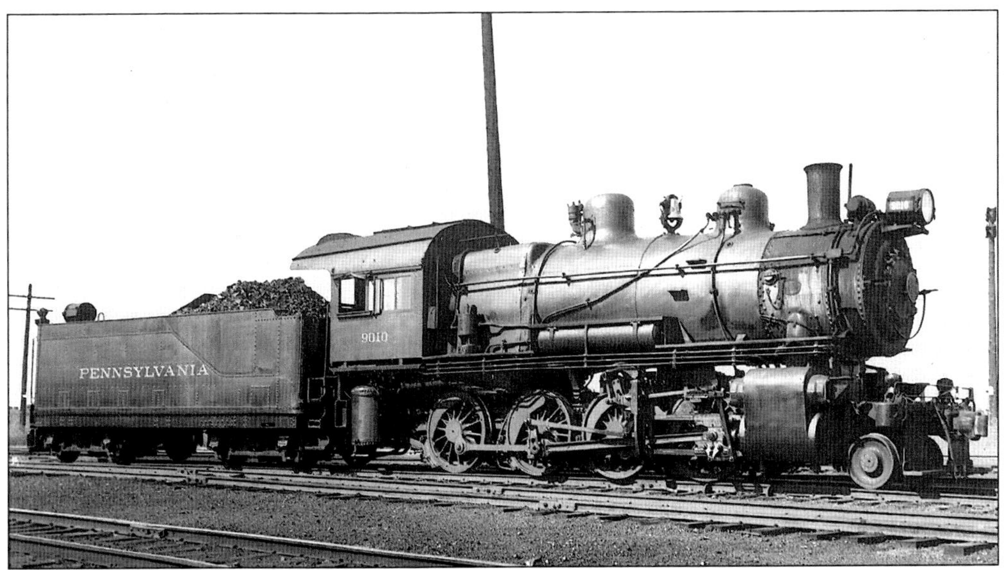

CADILLAC CONNECTION. At its northernmost point, the storied Pennsylvania Railroad reached as far as Mackinaw City, Michigan, at the northern tip of the state's Lower Peninsula. On the way to and from that station, the Pennsylvania's tracks crossed the Ann Arbor at Cadillac, where this scene of PRR #9010 was captured in June of 1938. The Pennsylvania, which had a modest freight yard at Cadillac known as North Yard, also directly interchanged traffic with the Ann Arbor at Toledo. (Collection of Harold K. Vollrath.)

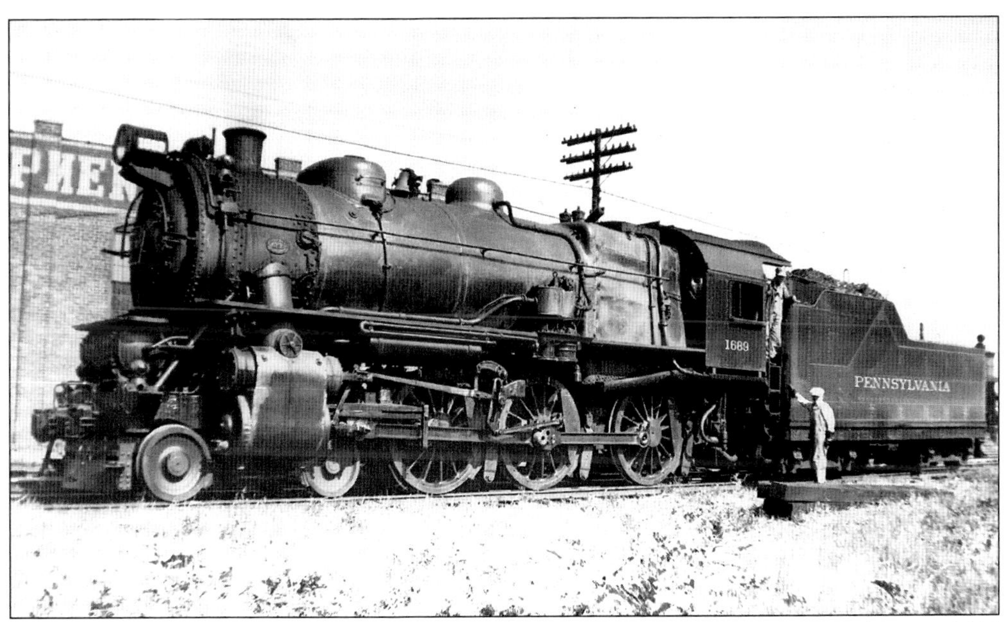

PENNSYLVANIA CLASSIC. With its driving wheels nearly as tall as a man, Pennsylvania #1689 and crew pose in this 1936 scene from Kalamazoo, Michigan. Kalamazoo was on a north-south PRR line that came up from Fort Wayne, Indiana, and continued as far as Mackinaw City. A carferry landing at Mackinaw City linked the rails of the Upper Peninsula with the Lower Peninsula, with boats operating across the Straits of Mackinac between Mackinaw City and St. Ignace. (Collection of Harold K. Vollrath.)

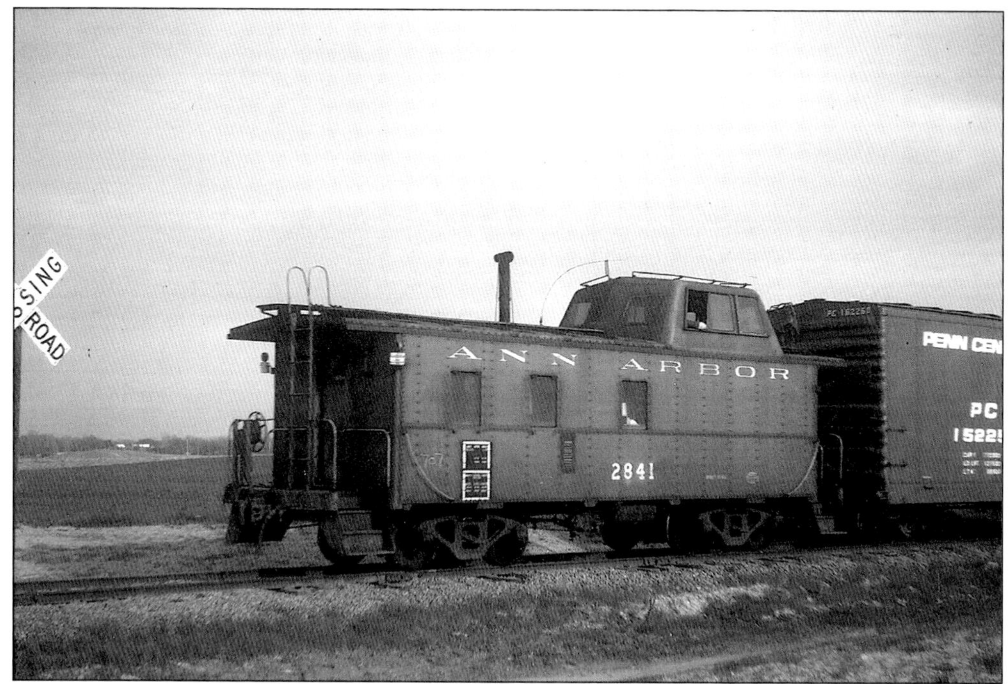

Links to the Penn Central. Ann Arbor caboose #2841 holds tight to Penn Central boxcar #152250 as it slips through Alma, Michigan, at dusk in May 1975. In this era, the Ann Arbor interchanged freight traffic with Penn Central at Toledo, Ann Arbor, Owosso, and Cadillac. Alma, the station this Frankfort-Toledo train is passing through, was an interchange point with the Chessie System. (Photo by Dennis Schmidt.)

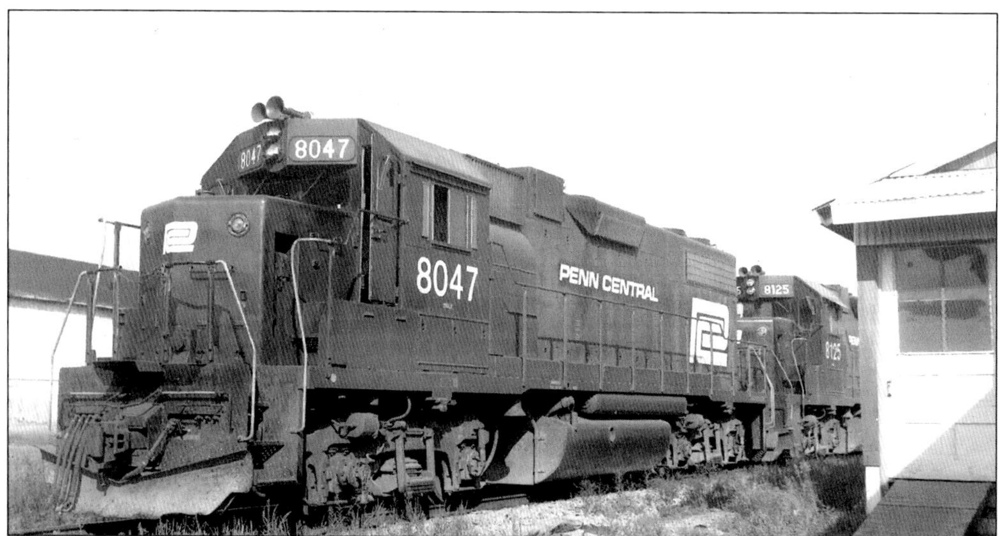

Dressed in Black. A westbound Penn Central freight arrives at Three Rivers, Michigan, in June 1974, behind EMD GP38s #8047 and #8125. Penn Central did not survive for long, but it kept the freight flowing at four vital connections with the Ann Arbor Railroad. The Penn Central, formed by the merger of the Pennsylvania and the New York Central (hence the name "Penn Central"), was in existence only from 1968 to 1976. (Collection of Harold K. Vollrath.)

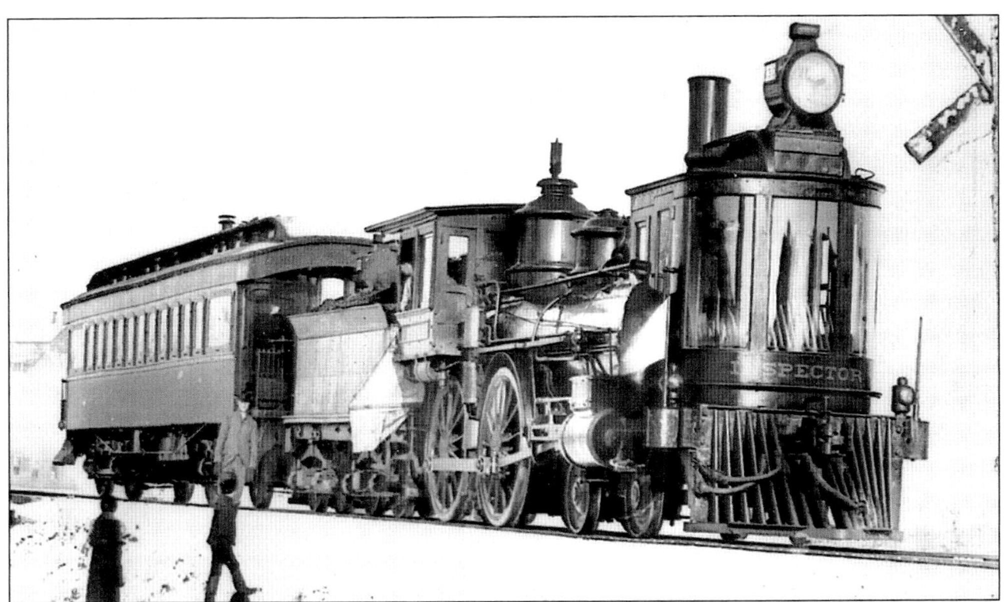

THE INSPECTOR. An inspection train on the Pere Marquette Railroad appears to have grabbed the interest of several youths along the snowy grade. This odd equipment was used to survey the railroad's physical plant, as its wide windows allowed an unobstructed view for those looking for defects in the tracks and roadbed. According to Fritz Milhaupt of the Pere Marquette Historical Society, this inspection engine, built from the former Chicago & West Michigan #130, was destroyed in a wreck in 1900. (Collection of the Benzie Area Historical Society.)

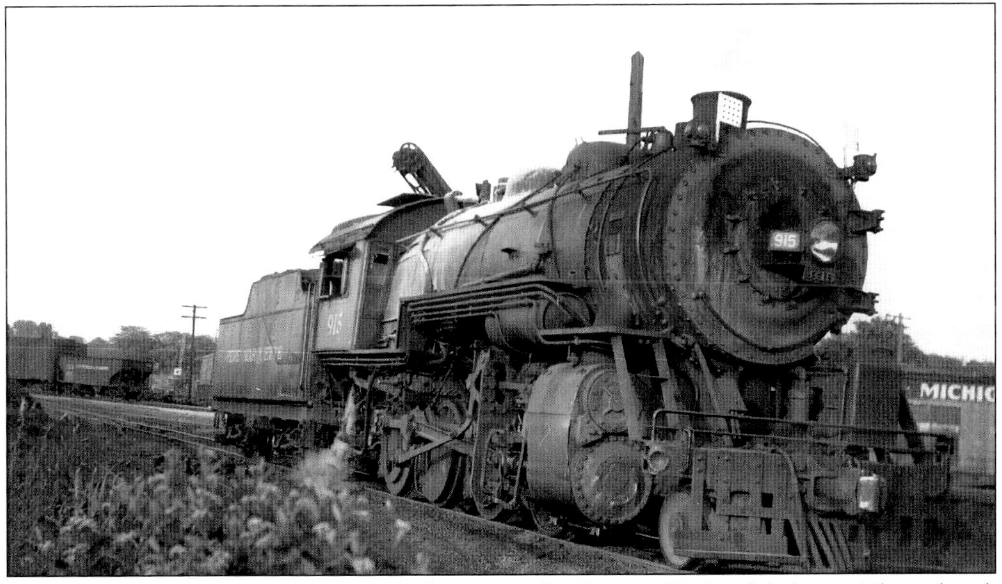

PERE MARQUETTE. Pere Marquette #915 is pictured at Benton Harbor, Michigan. The railroad, named for a French Jesuit missionary who explored Michigan in the late 1600s, was formed in 1900, and, like the AA, operated Lake Michigan carferries (the PM's boats sailed out of Ludington). The AA and the PM interchanged at several locations, including the fittingly named junction known as Ann Pere, south of Howell. The Pere Marquette merged into the Chesapeake & Ohio in 1947. (Collection of Harold K. Vollrath.)

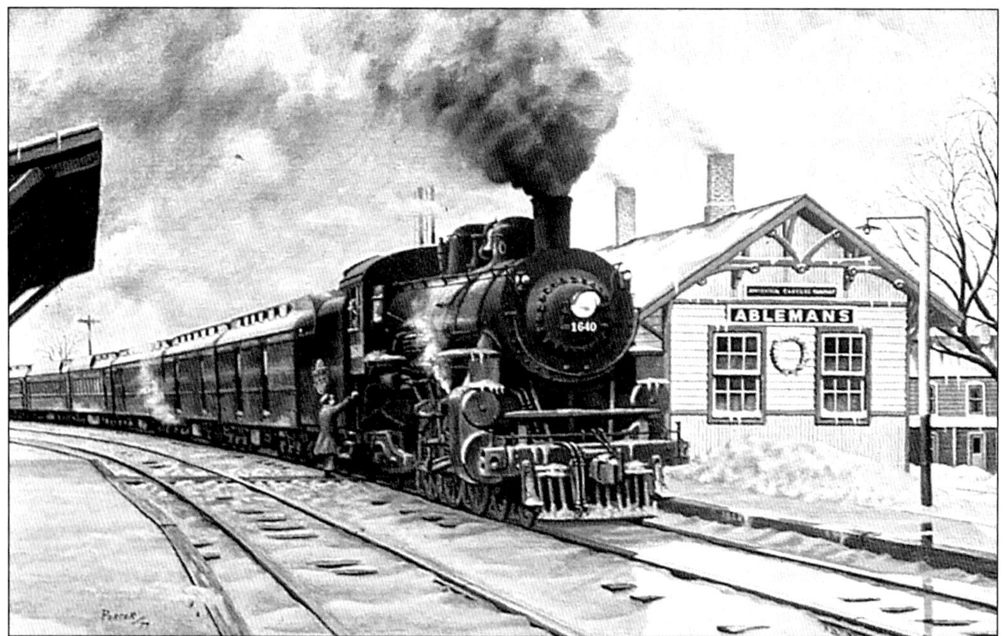

LET'S GET ROLLING. Chicago & North Western Train #501, the *Viking*, pulls out of Abelmans, Wisconsin, in 1946 in this postcard view from artist Russ Porter. This C&NW passenger train ran between Chicago and Minneapolis-St. Paul, via Madison, Wisconsin. The C&NW met with the Ann Arbor at Menominee, in Michigan's Upper Peninsula, and at Manitowoc, Wisconsin. In both cases, the C&NW-AA connections were via the carferries. (Collection of D. C. Jesse Burkhardt.)

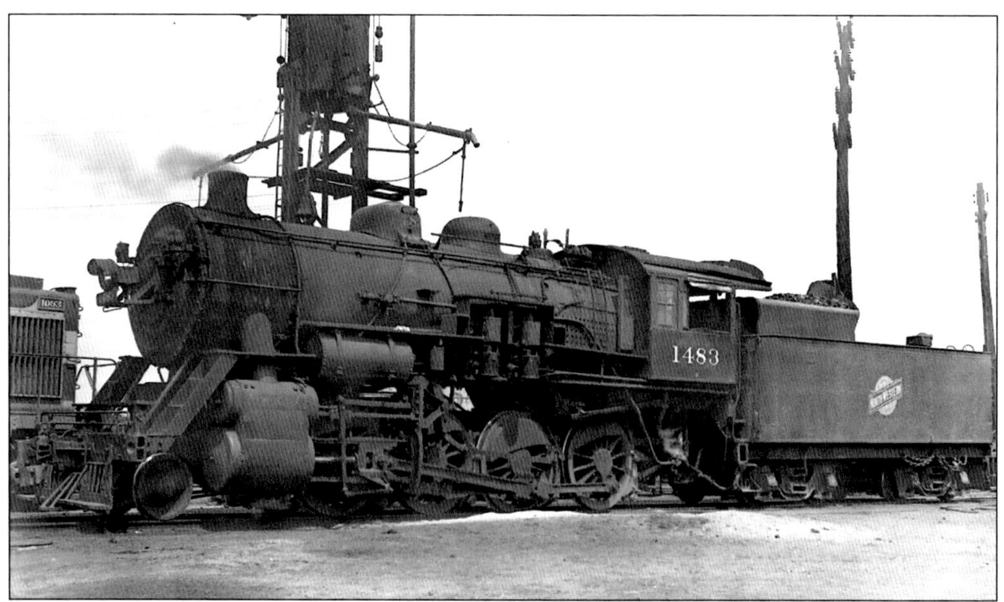

ERAS CHANGING. Chicago & North Western 2-8-0 #1483 shares the yard service track at Escanaba, Michigan, with one of the early diesels—Alco S2 #1083—in 1953. The structure behind the two C&NW locomotives is a sanding tower. The AA ferry dock at Menominee was about 65 miles south of Escanaba. (Collection of Harold K. Vollrath.)

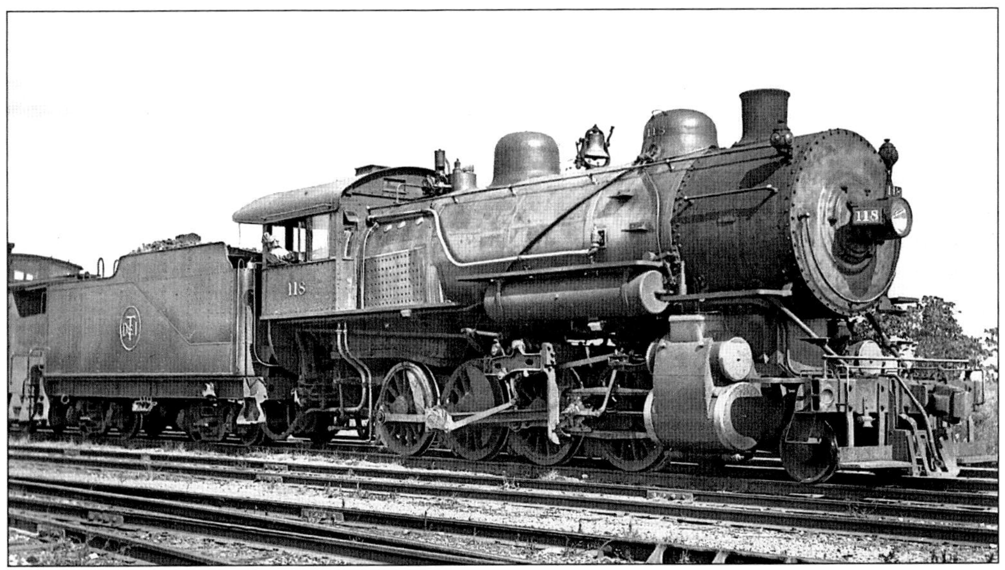

PAST AND FUTURE PARENT. Detroit, Toledo & Ironton #118 works at the DT&I's Temperance Yard in Toledo in October 1933. The DT&I first controlled the Ann Arbor Railroad from 1905 to 1910; decades later, in 1963, the DT&I again took over the AA, and remained its parent until 1973. The DT&I provided the Ann Arbor with its diesel-era slogan: *We Have the Connections*. Although the DT&I and the Ann Arbor both served Toledo, their rails did not physically connect there. (Collection of Harold K. Vollrath.)

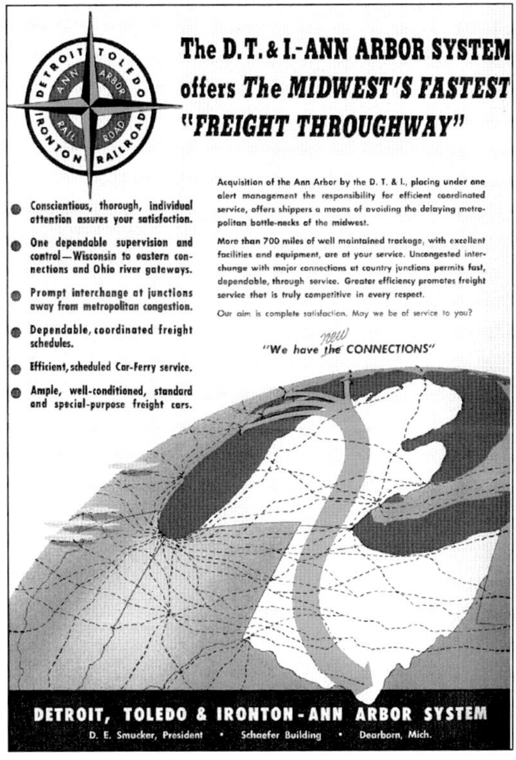

MIDWEST'S FASTEST FREIGHT. When the DT&I purchased the Ann Arbor Railroad in 1963, it launched an ad campaign to let the world know of the benefits of the combined system. This ad, from the September 14, 1963, issue of *Traffic World*, boasts that shippers on DT&I-AA can avoid freight bottlenecks: "Uncongested interchange with major connections at country junctions permits fast, dependable, through service," reads an excerpt. Note the subhead above the map, "We Have *New* Connections." (Collection of D. C. Jesse Burkhardt.)

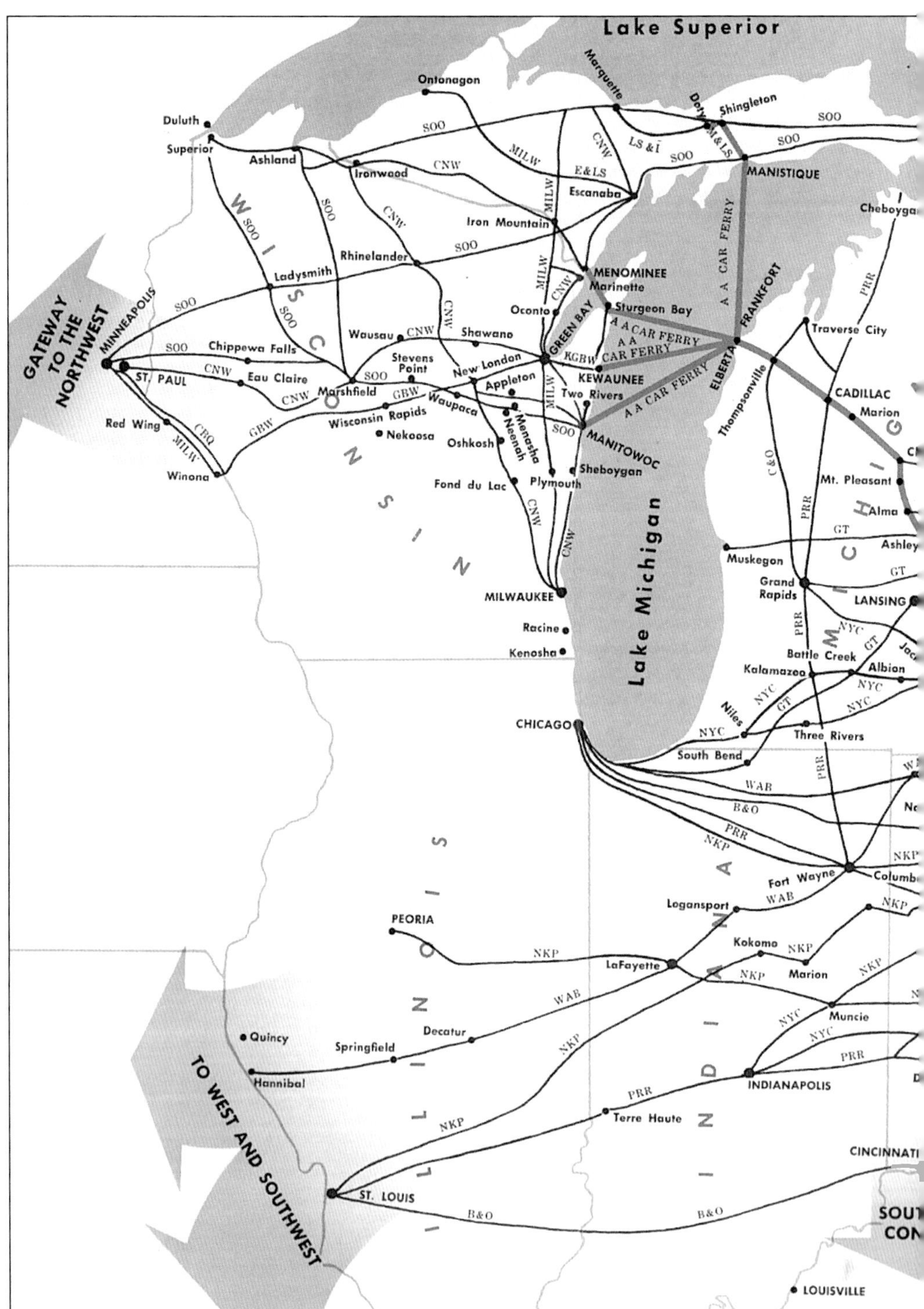

We Definitely Have the Connections. This 1960s-era map of the routes of the combined Detroit, Toledo & Ironton/Ann Arbor system displays the many connections the two carriers served. Not surprisingly, these connections were made a central part of the railroad's marketing

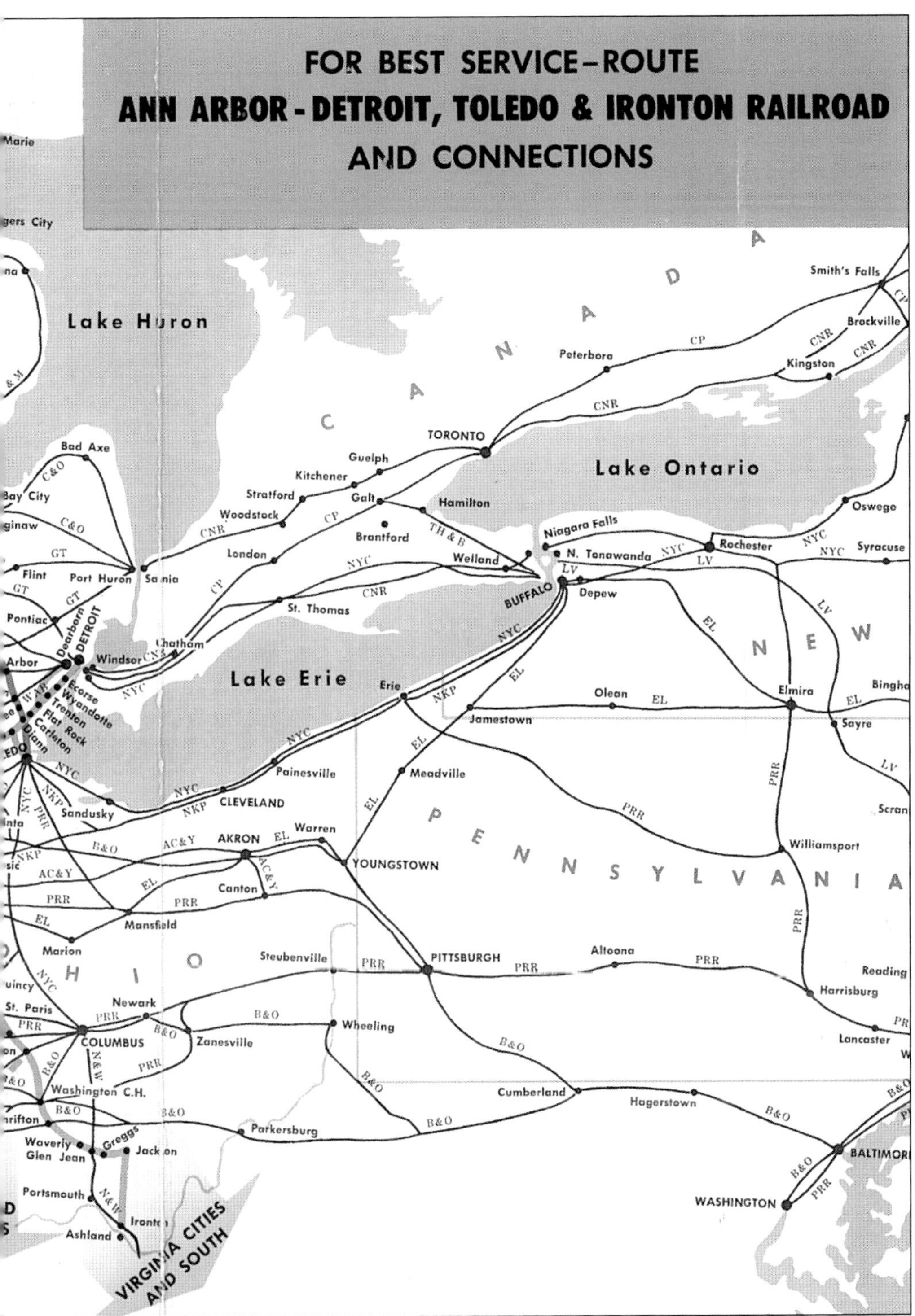

campaigns. Ann Arbor parent DT&I, a carrier that operated approximately 465 miles of track in Ohio and Michigan before consolidating with the Ann Arbor, was headquartered in Dearborn, Michigan. (Collection of D. C. Jesse Burkhardt.)

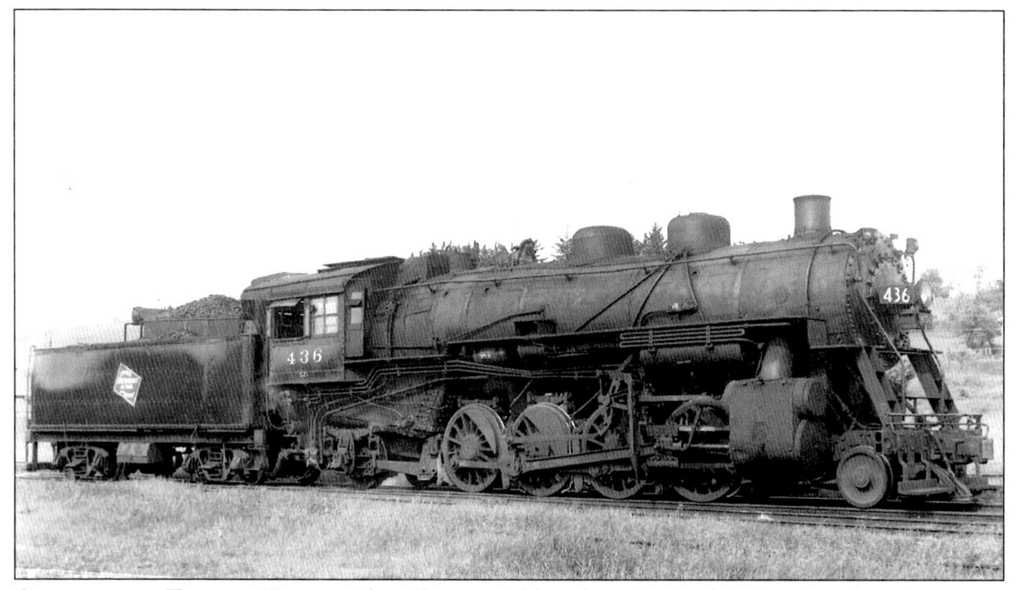

CONNECTION TO THE NORTH. The Chicago, Milwaukee, St. Paul & Pacific—later known as the Milwaukee Road—interchanged freight with the Ann Arbor at Menominee, in Michigan's Upper Peninsula. Milwaukee Road locomotive #436 was in Iron Mountain, Michigan, just 66 miles by rail from Menominee, when this scene was captured in May of 1955. (Collection of Harold K. Vollrath.)

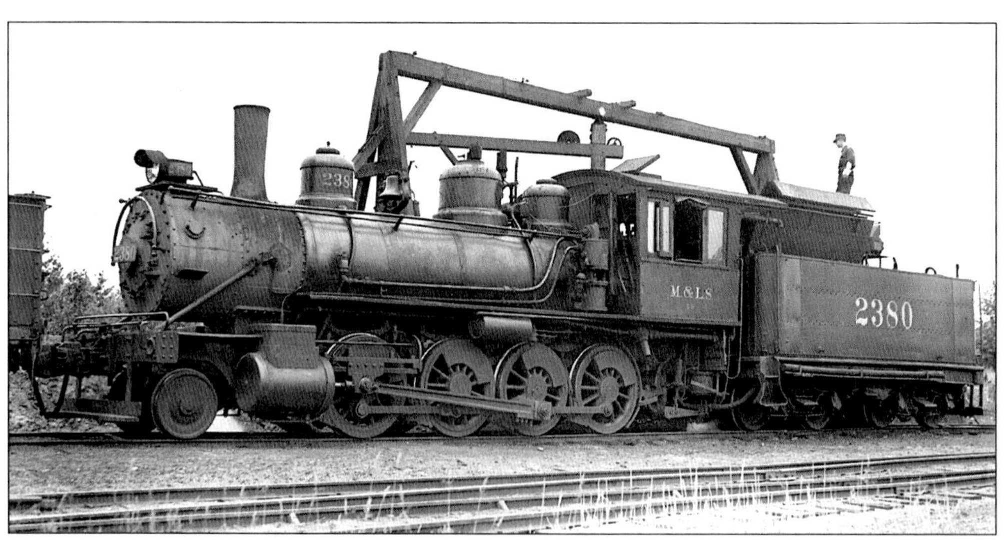

ANN ARBOR IN MANISTIQUE. For more than half a century, the Manistique & Lake Superior gave the Ann Arbor Railroad a direct rail link into Michigan's Upper Peninsula. In this look back to June 1937, Manistique & Lake Superior #2380, a Baldwin Locomotive Works 2-8-0, is seen at Manistique. The AA purchased the M&LS in 1911. (Collection of Harold K. Vollrath.)

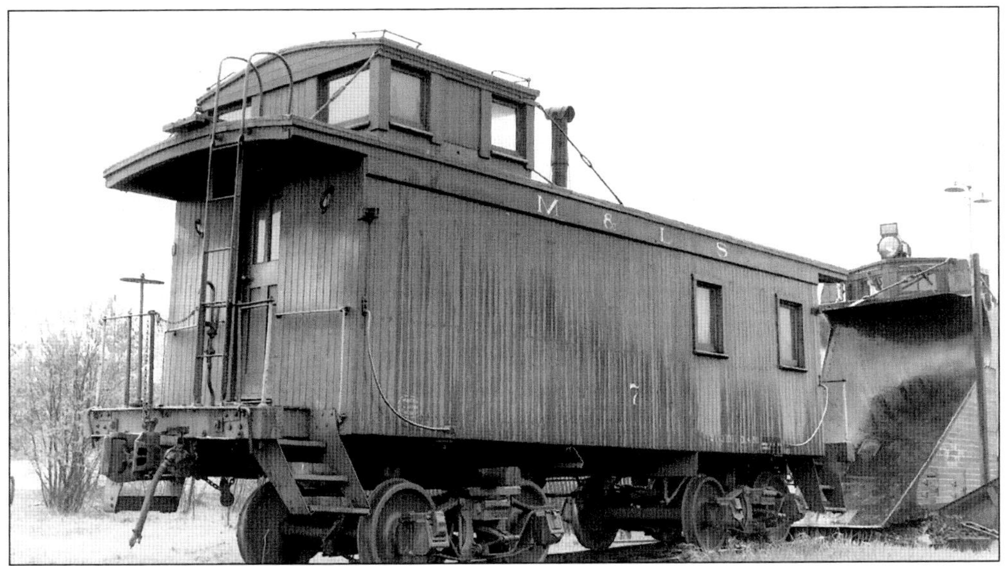

SEVEN. Manistique & Lake Superior caboose #7 rests alongside a snowplow at Manistique in June 1952. The snowplow would certainly see a lot of vital service, as the Upper Peninsula was famous for its severe winters, with snowstorms often blowing in off the Great Lakes. (Collection of Harold K. Vollrath.)

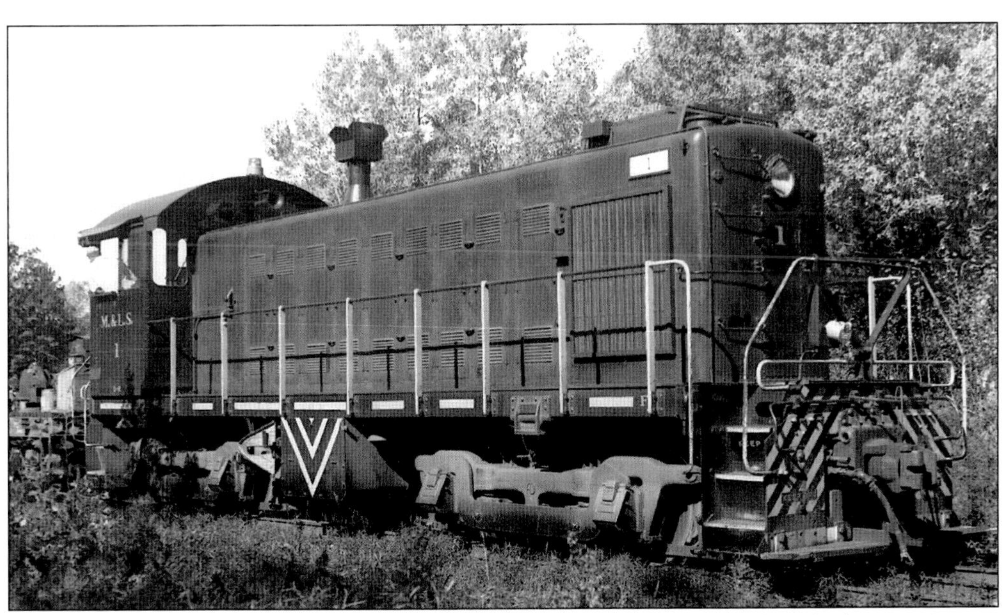

SOLD IN STEUBEN. When this photograph of M&LS #1, an Alco product built in 1952, was taken at Steuben, Michigan, in October 1968, the shortline had already ceased operations. The M&LS halted service in July 1968, and this locomotive was sold to the Ann Arbor in December of the same year. The AA renumbered it #10. (Collection of Harold K. Vollrath.)

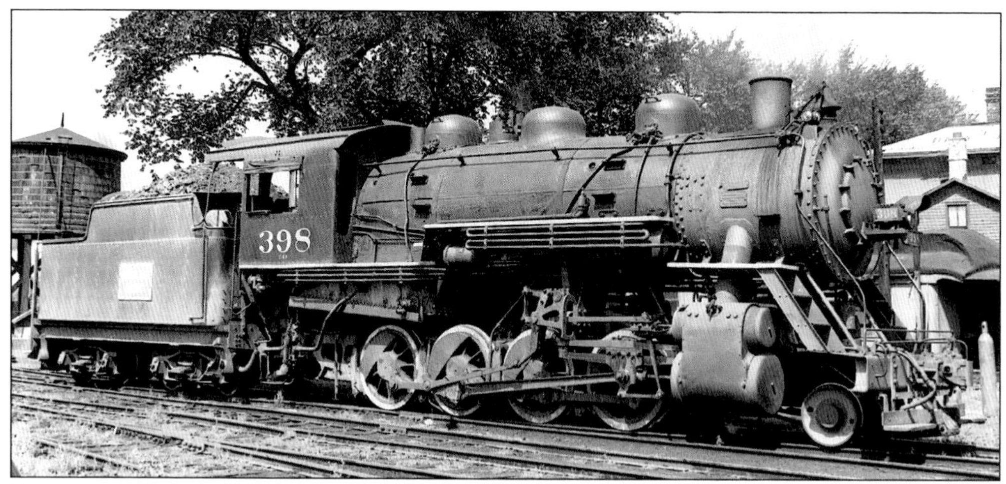

END OF THE GREEN BAY LINE. Green Bay & Western #398—previously Kewaunee, Green Bay & Western #45—rests at Winona, Minnesota, in 1947. Note the "Green Bay Route" slogan on the tender. The 255-mile GB&W operated from Winona to Kewaunee, Wisconsin, where a carferry terminal linked the GB&W with the Ann Arbor Railroad. It was the only direct connection the two railroads shared, but the case could certainly be made that it was the Ann Arbor's most important one. (Collection of Harold K. Vollrath.)

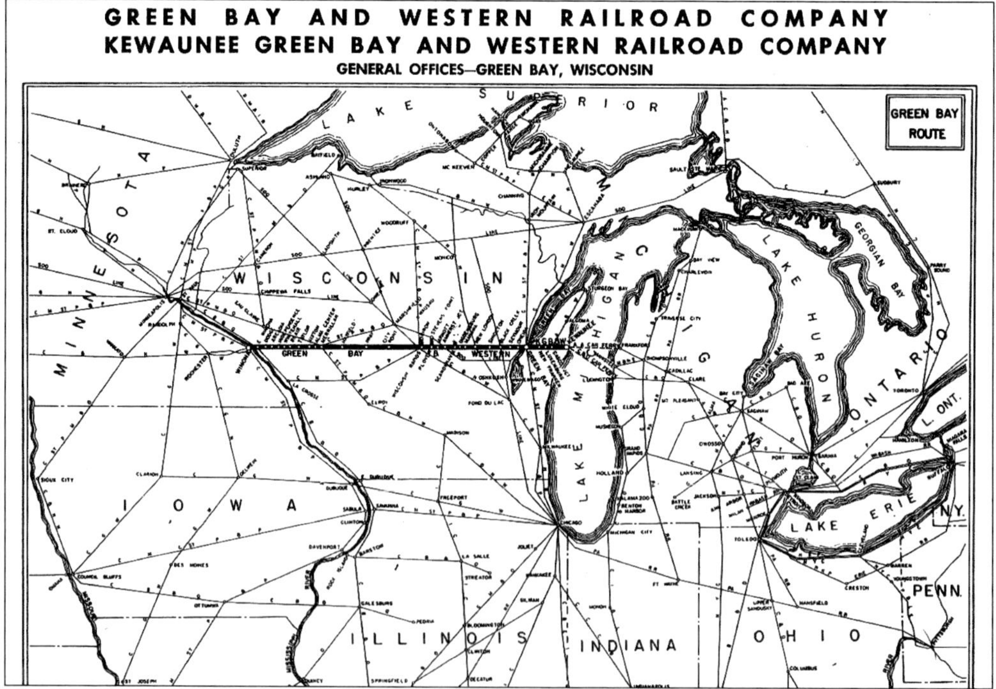

LIFELINES. The Green Bay & Western operated an east-west route that cut straight across the midsection of Wisconsin, and it all started with its Kewaunee carferry terminal. The GB&W (or Kewaunee, Green Bay & Western, as the eastern segment of the line was originally known) created two vital links for bridge traffic coming across Lake Michigan. As the map indicates, the GB&W connected to both the Ann Arbor and the Chesapeake & Ohio via the carferries. (Collection of D. C. Jesse Burkhardt.)

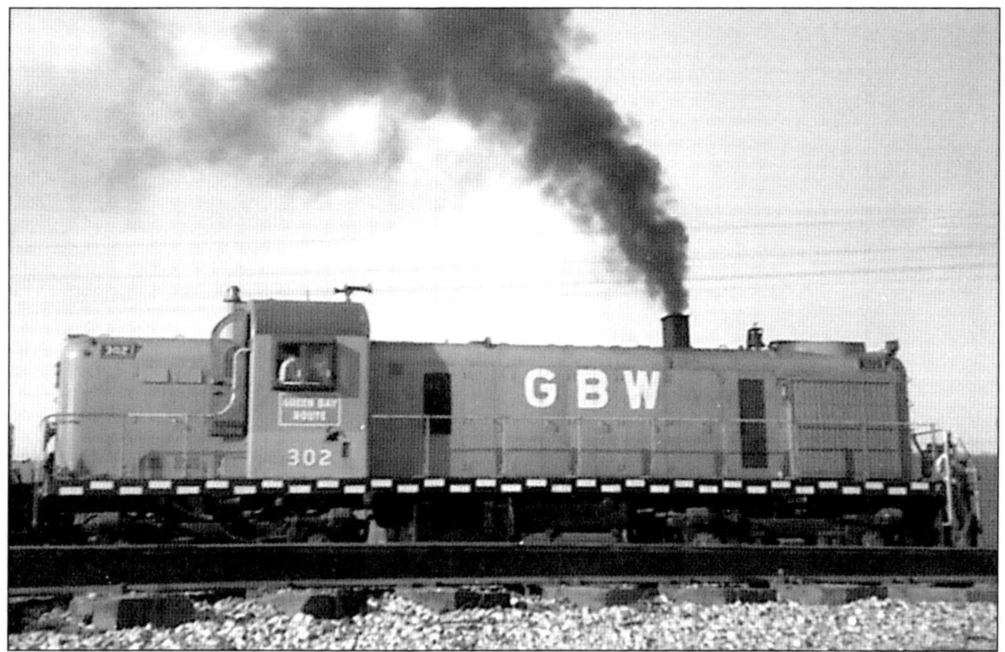

ALCO SMOKE AT GREEN BAY. GB&W Alco RS2 #302, in the carrier's distinctive red paint, pours out smoke as it switches freight cars in the railroad's yard in Green Bay in 1974. The GB&W's "boat trains," which served the carferry terminal at Kewaunee, originated here. (Photo by Larry Yaek.)

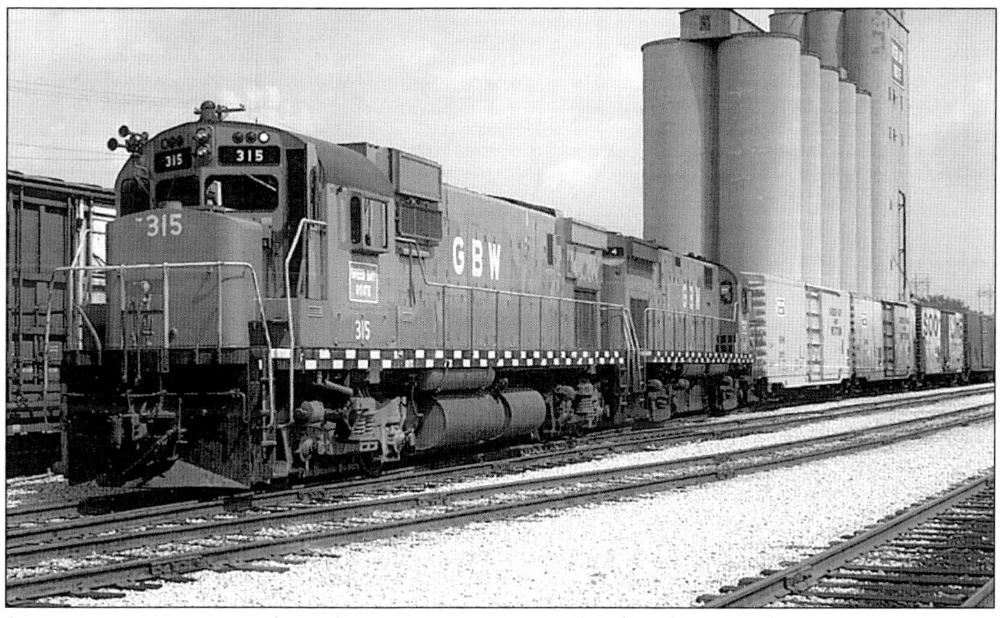

STEADY PARTNER. A westbound Green Bay & Western freight rolls out of the railroad's namesake Green Bay, Wisconsin, freight yard in this scene from August 1977. The GB&W served the Ann Arbor Railroad's carferry landing in Kewaunee. The Ann Arbor's Kewaunee-Frankfort route was financially its strongest, and it survived to be the AA's last remaining cross-lake operation. (Collection of D. C. Jesse Burkhardt.)

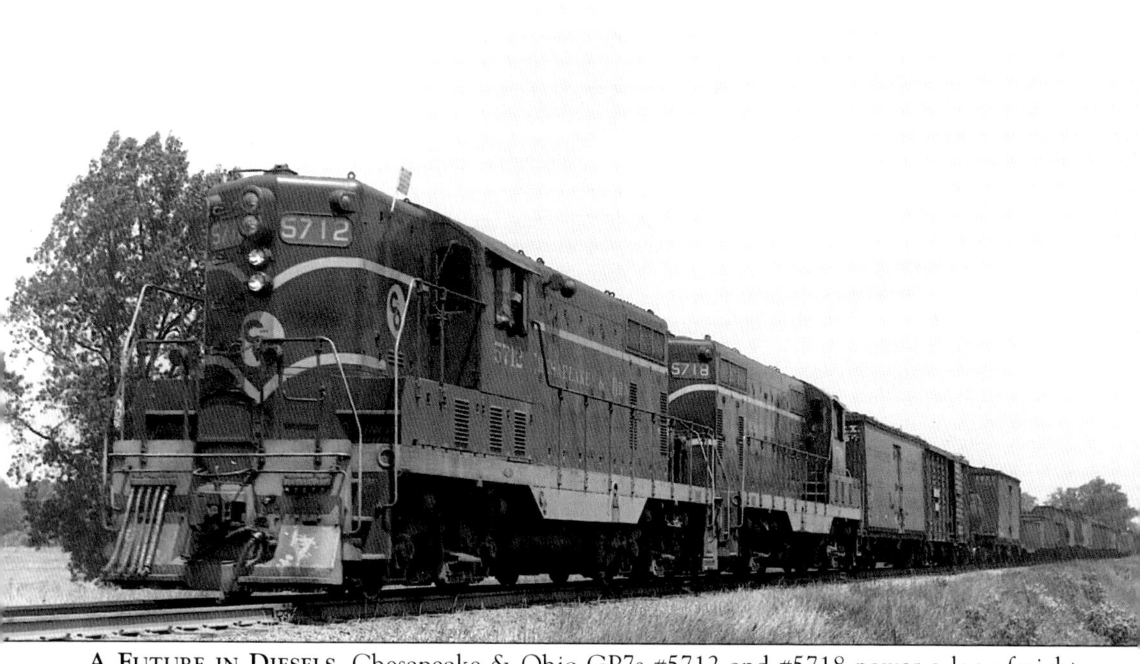

A Future in Diesels. Chesapeake & Ohio GP7s #5712 and #5718 power a long freight at Romulus, Michigan, in June 1951. No railroad connected with the Ann Arbor in more places than the C&O. The tracks of the two carriers crossed at no fewer than six stations: Toledo, Ann Pere, Alma, Mount Pleasant, Clare, and Thompsonville. (Collection of Harold K. Vollrath.)

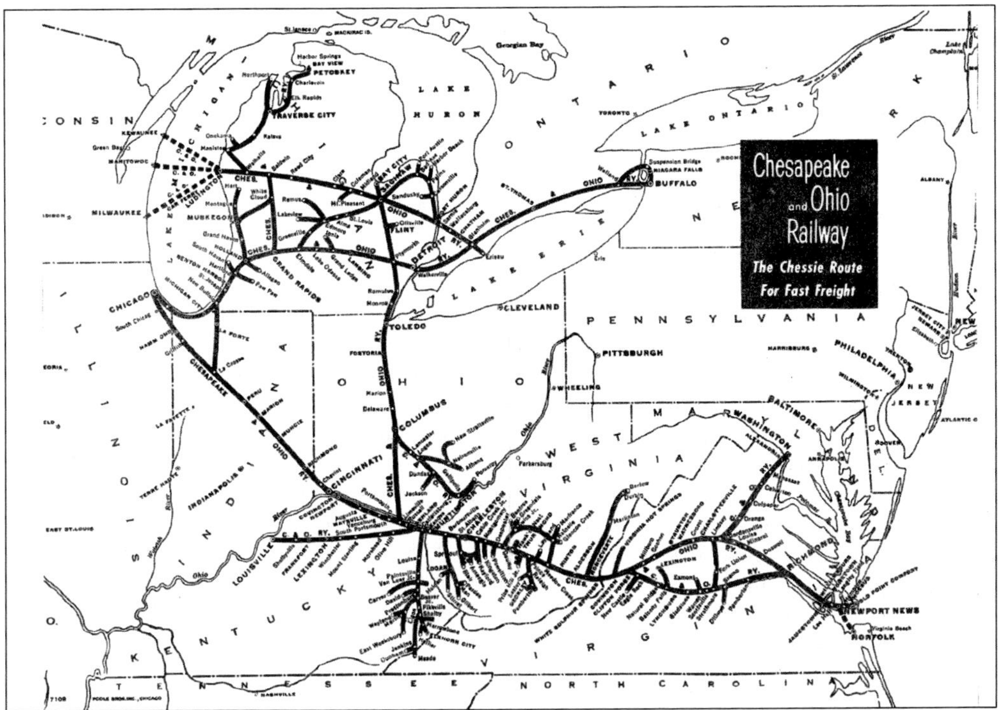

The Chessie Route. This map shows the trackage of the Chesapeake & Ohio Railway. The C&O was a major interchange partner with the Ann Arbor, and also a key competitor: The C&O operated three Lake Michigan carferry routes, with two of them going to Wisconsin ports also served by Ann Arbor Railroad carferries. Note the sweet slogan, "The Chessie Route For Fast Freight." (Collection of D. C. Jesse Burkhardt.)

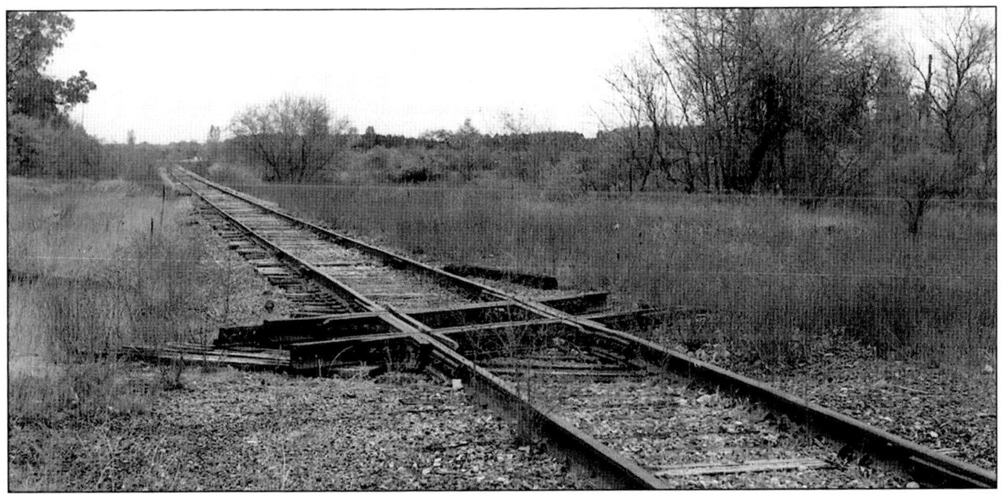

A Lost Connection. The Ann Arbor mainline is pictured at Thompsonville in October 1992. The AA and C&O crossed paths at this obscure junction, and until the 1980s, the station was relatively busy with daily freights rolling through on both lines. The Ann Arbor tracks here are no longer in service, and the crossing diamond is all that's left of the C&O's Petoskey-Manistee line. Only this fragment of steel—and a path across the fields—remains to mark the route. (Photo by D. C. Jesse Burkhardt.)

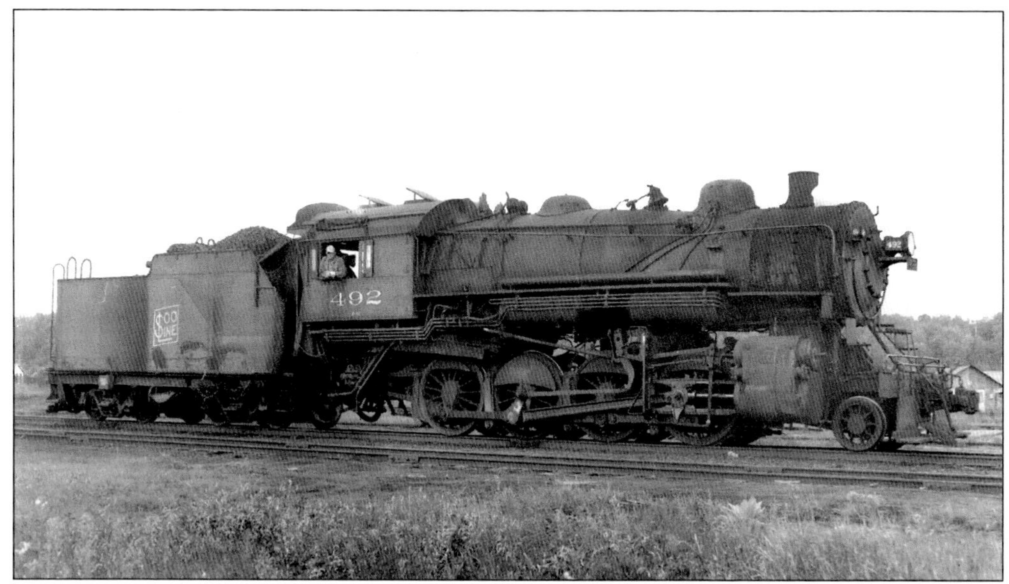

GLADSTONE. The Soo Line Railroad interchanged traffic with the Ann Arbor at Manitowoc and Manistique. This shot of Soo #492 was taken at Gladstone, Michigan, in August 1954, as the age of steam neared its end. Note the classic Soo Line "dollar" logo on the coal tender. The Soo Line's Gladstone terminal was only 44 miles from Manistique and the tracks of AA subsidiary Manistique & Lake Superior. (Collection of Harold K. Vollrath.)

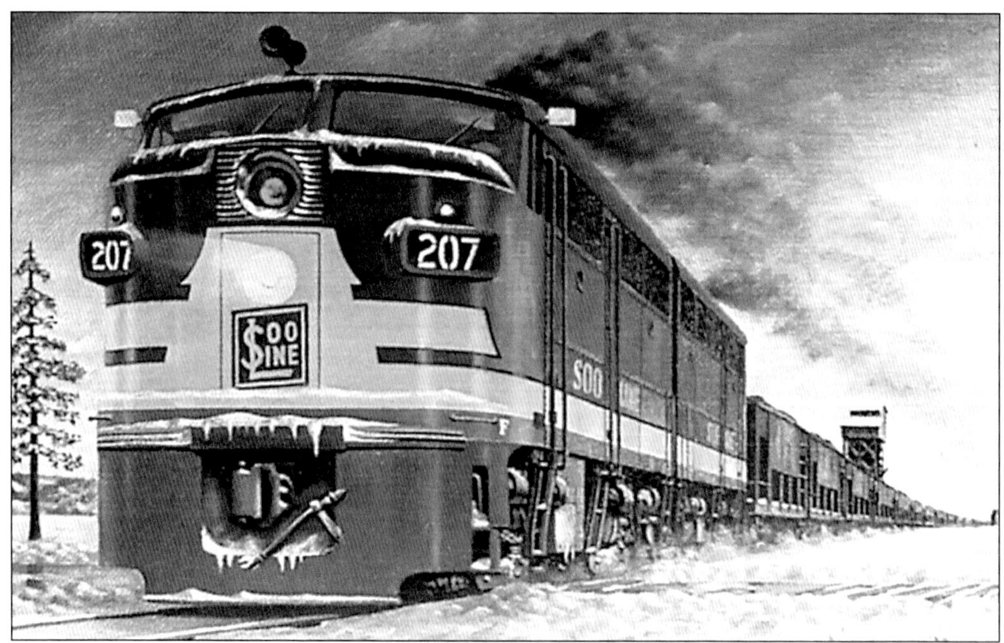

SNOW RUN. The Soo Line Railroad employed Alco FA locomotives in the 1950s, as did the Ann Arbor. In this postcard scene from an original painting by Russ Porter, a pair of Soo Line A and B units are shown hauling ore through a Midwestern snowscape in 1949. (Collection of D. C. Jesse Burkhardt.)

Seven

After the Carferries

Cross-lake business fell off in the 1960s and 1970s as rail traffic declined and the railroads directed more of the remaining freight through Chicago.
—Edward Hoogterp, "Finances May Keep Ferry Docked," *Jackson (Michigan) Citizen Patriot*, February 11, 1991

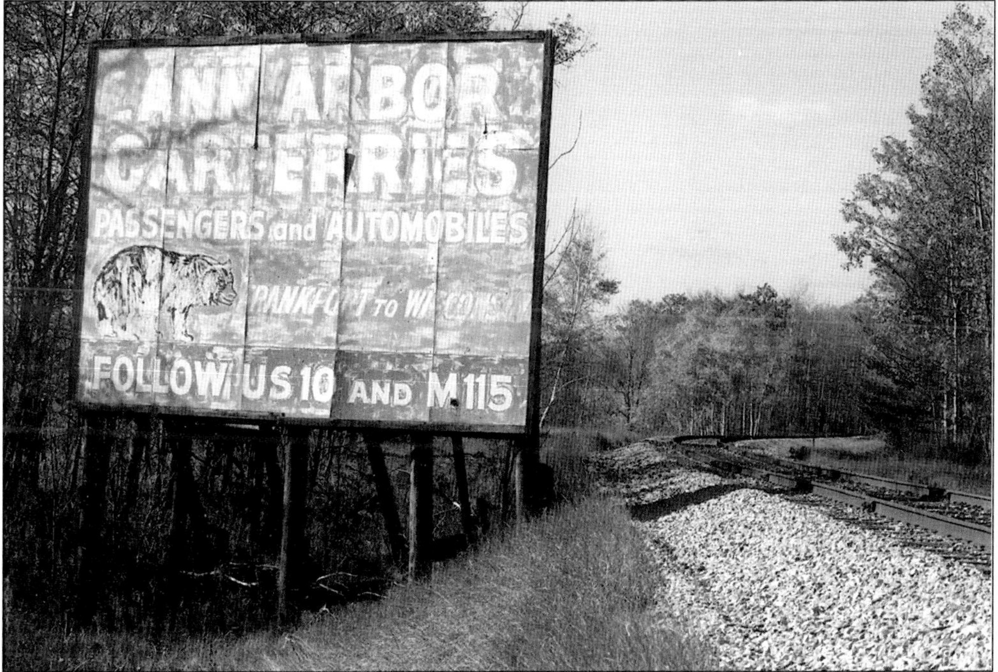

Only the Sign Remains. In October 1992, a full decade after the last boat ran, a weathered billboard along U.S. 10 west of Clare invites tourists to ride the Ann Arbor carferries across Lake Michigan. Behind the sign are the tracks of what once was the Ann Arbor Railroad's route to Frankfort, now operated by the Tuscola & Saginaw Bay Railway. (Photo by D. C. Jesse Burkhardt.)

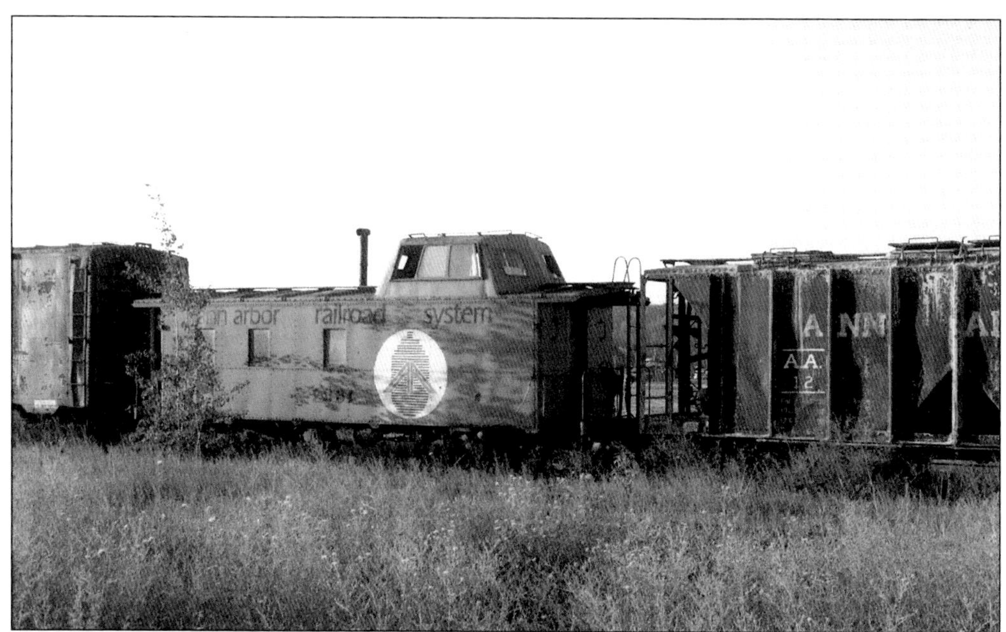

TWILIGHT IN ELBERTA. Ann Arbor caboose #2831, with the new "ferry in the fog" logo, rests amidst summer weeds, surrounded by other surplus freight cars, in this July 1988 scene from Elberta. At about this time, the cars pictured here were on the auction block, with the state of Michigan running newspaper ads offering all the Ann Arbor's unneeded rolling stock for sale for a minimum bid of just $100. (Photo by Scott Sparling.)

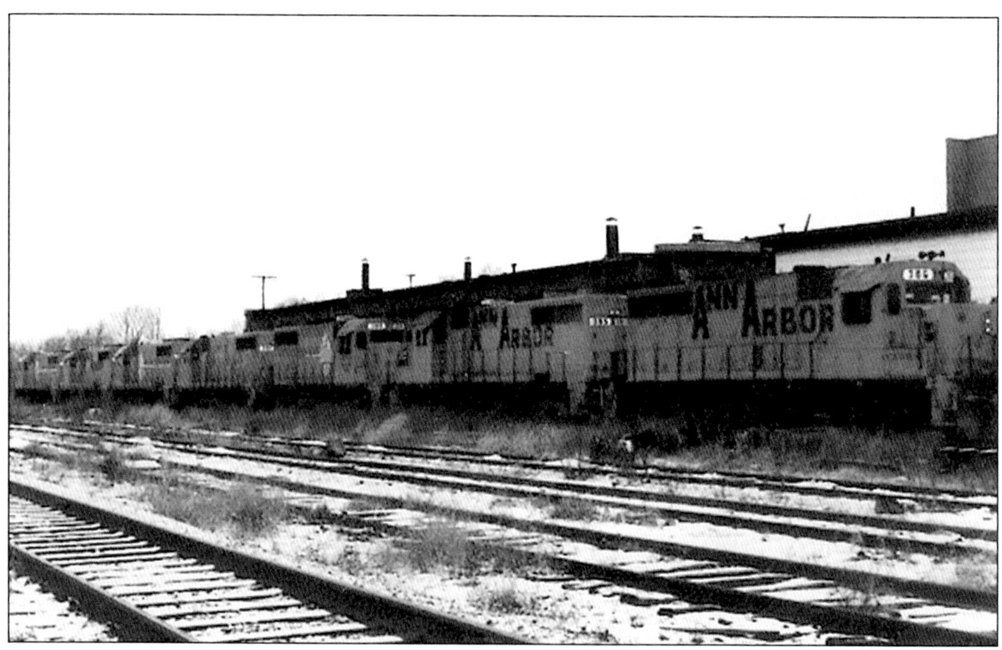

COLD STORAGE. Seven of the Ann Arbor Railroad's 10 GP35s stand inactive on a yard track in Owosso in the winter of 1982, out of service and awaiting dispensation following the demise of carferry traffic to and from Elberta earlier in the year. Without the ferry traffic, long-haul freights were no longer moving on the line, and the road power was excess. (Photo by Lee Hillier.)

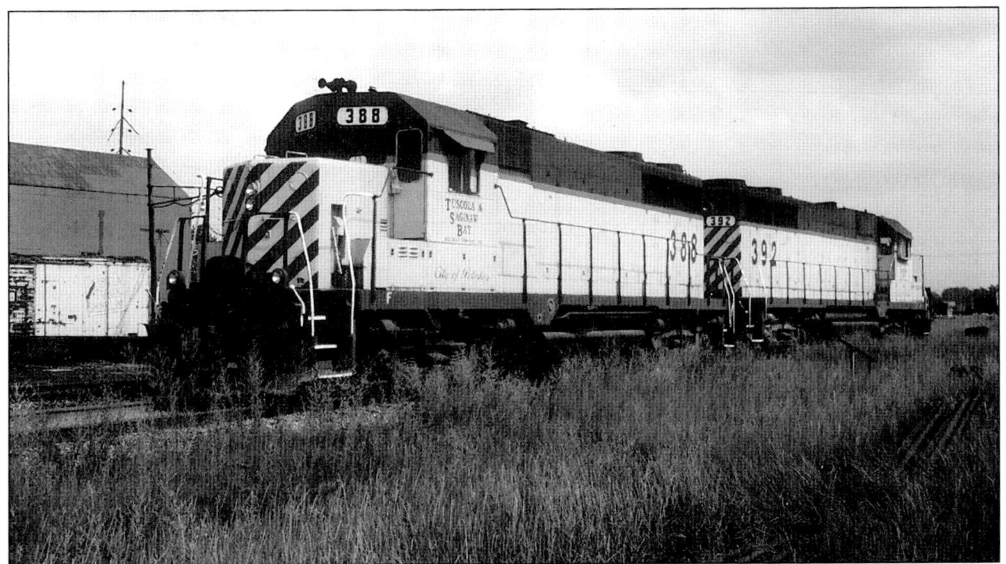

New Colors in Cadillac. On June 28, 1999, former Ann Arbor GP35s #388 and #392, in the yellow and blue of new owner Tuscola & Saginaw Bay Railway, take a break in Cadillac after handling switching duties. The T&SB inherited all 10 of the AA's GP35s (road numbers #385-#394), and at the beginning of 2005, 7 of them were still in use. The weathered Detroit & Toledo Shore Line boxcar in the background was serving as a tool and storage shed. (Photo by D. C. Jesse Burkhardt.)

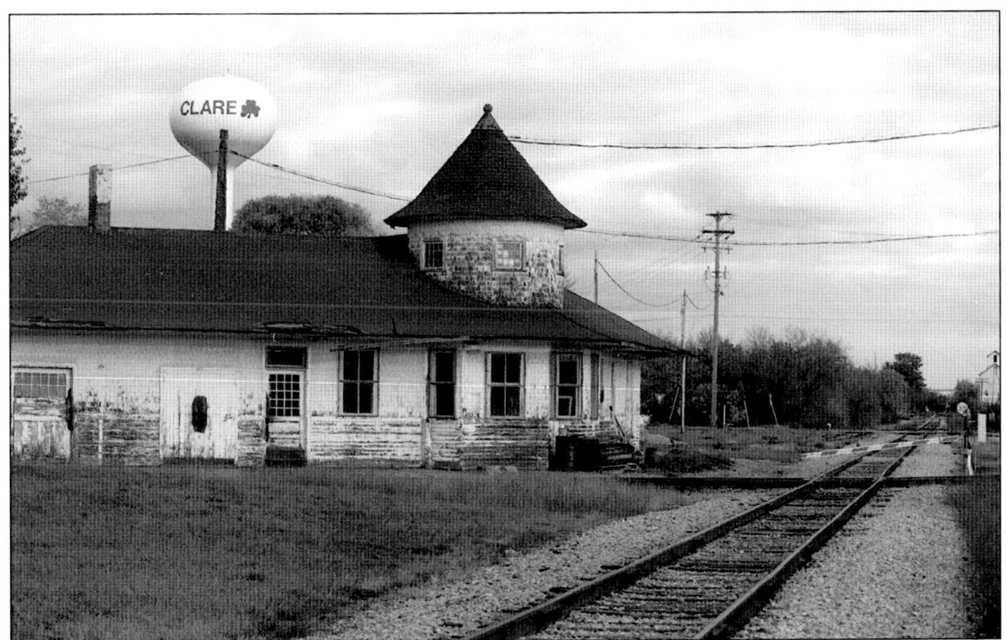

Clare Crossing. Looking east along the tracks of what was once the Ludington-Saginaw mainline of the Chesapeake & Ohio Railway, the intersection with the north-south line of the Ann Arbor is visible. Clare was once a major interchange point between these two carriers. Take a look at the classic but now dilapidated Ann Arbor station adjacent to the crossing, seen here in 1992. A shot of the Clare depot in its prime appears on page 22. (Photo by D. C. Jesse Burkhardt.)

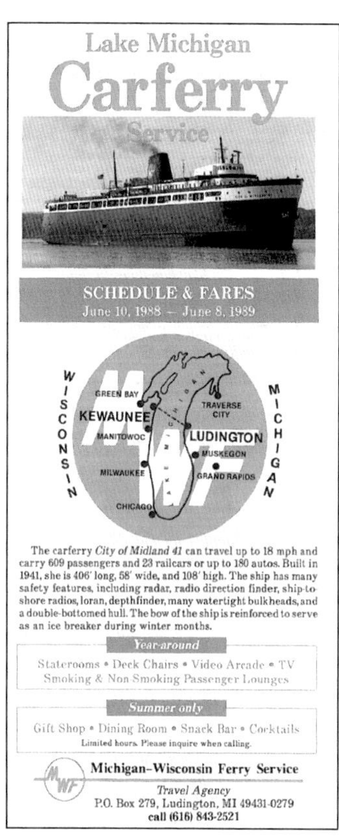

STILL MAKING WAVES. A Ludington-based company known as Michigan-Wisconsin Ferry Service kept trains making waves across Lake Michigan for eight years after the Ann Arbor Railroad's last carferry sailed from Frankfort. The MWF employed the *City of Midland 41* and later the *Badger* (both ex-C&O boats), to carry railroad cars between Ludington and Kewaunee. The MWF last moved freight cars across Lake Michigan on November 16, 1990. Not long after the final carferry left the harbor, rail service to Kewaunee was abandoned. The tracks to the ferry docks were pulled up in 1993; the tracks to Kewaunee itself were abandoned in 1998. (Collection of D. C. Jesse Burkhardt.)

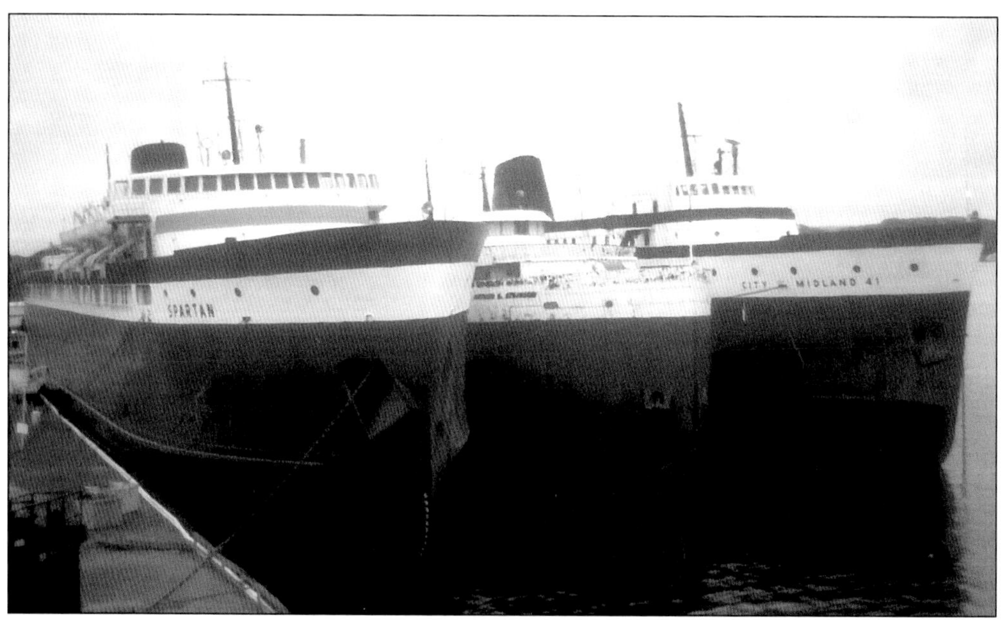

LOST TRIO. Three Lake Michigan carferries rest quietly alongside the dock in Ludington in this sad scene from September 1997. Retired and destined never to carry passengers again are the Ann Arbor Railroad's *Arthur K. Atkinson* (center) and ex-C&O carferries *Spartan* and *City of Midland 41*. (Photo by D. C. Jesse Burkhardt.)

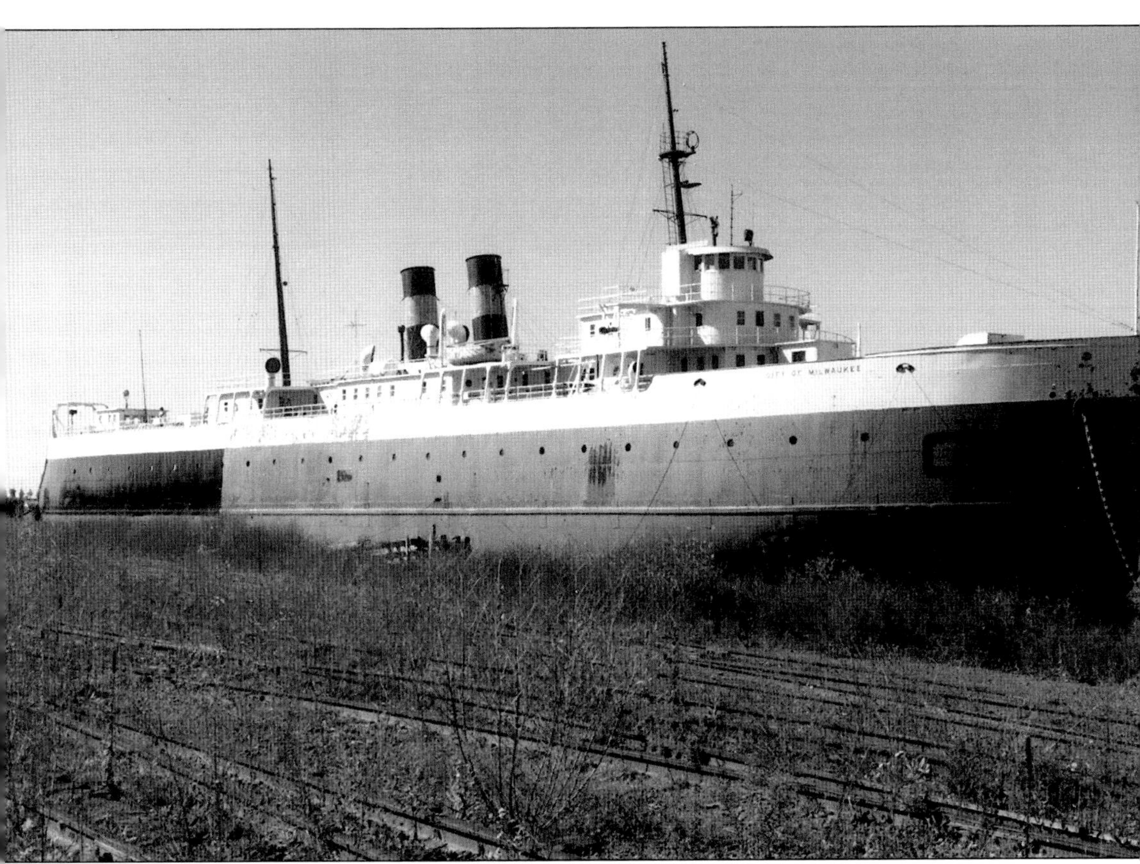

FLOATING MUSEUM. The *City of Milwaukee*, originally owned by the Grand Trunk Railway (witness the blacked out "GT" logo on the bow), floats beside the Ann Arbor's weed-choked classification yard in Elberta in 1989, years after daily trains called here. The boat was originally used by the Grand Trunk for service between Muskegon, Michigan, and Milwaukee, Wisconsin. When this photo was taken, the ferry was in the process of being renovated as a National Historical Landmark. In 2000, however, with some in the community expressing opposition to permanently siting the boat in Betsie Bay, the *City of Milwaukee* was towed to Manistee, Michigan, and turned into a museum. All of the yard tracks seen here were torn up a few months after this photo was taken. (Photo by Scott Sparling.)

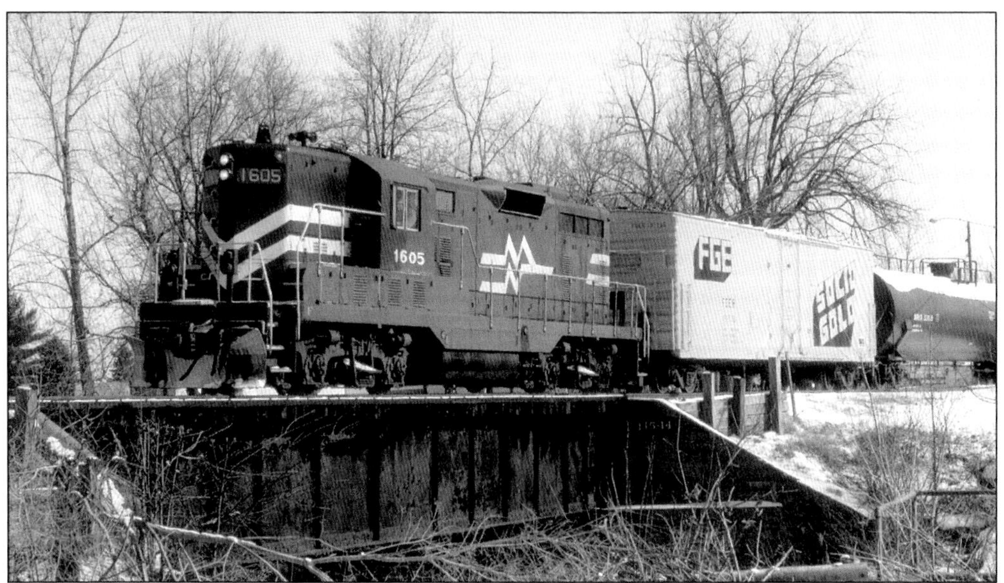

SHORT TOUR OF DUTY. Michigan Northern Railway GP7 #1605 hauls freight cars across the Pine River in Gratiot County on a snowy February 7, 1983. Through a lease agreement, Cadillac-based Michigan Northern operated the former Ann Arbor Railroad line from Alma to Frankfort for less than two years, October 1982–May 1984. After that, the Tuscola & Saginaw Bay—which was already operating on ex-Annie rails south of Alma to the city of Ann Arbor—took over responsibility for the Alma-Frankfort segment as well. (Photo by Dennis Schmidt.)

WARNING

THIS RAILROAD

All Sidings, Yards and Lands Connected Therewith are the Private Property of

TUSCOLA & SAGINAW BAY

RAILROAD COMPANY

And all Persons are Warned by this Printed Notice from Trespassing Thereon

UNDER PENALTY OF THE LAW

APPROVED—

P. J. De WOLF
Pres. TSBY RR

C. G. STEVENS
Chief of Police

WARNING. After the Tuscola & Saginaw Bay Railway took over operations on most of the former Ann Arbor trackage in Michigan, cardboard warning signs were placed around the road's terminals. This sign, posted in Cadillac, was typical of the T&SB's "no trespassing" signs of the 1980s. (Collection of D. C. Jesse Burkhardt.)

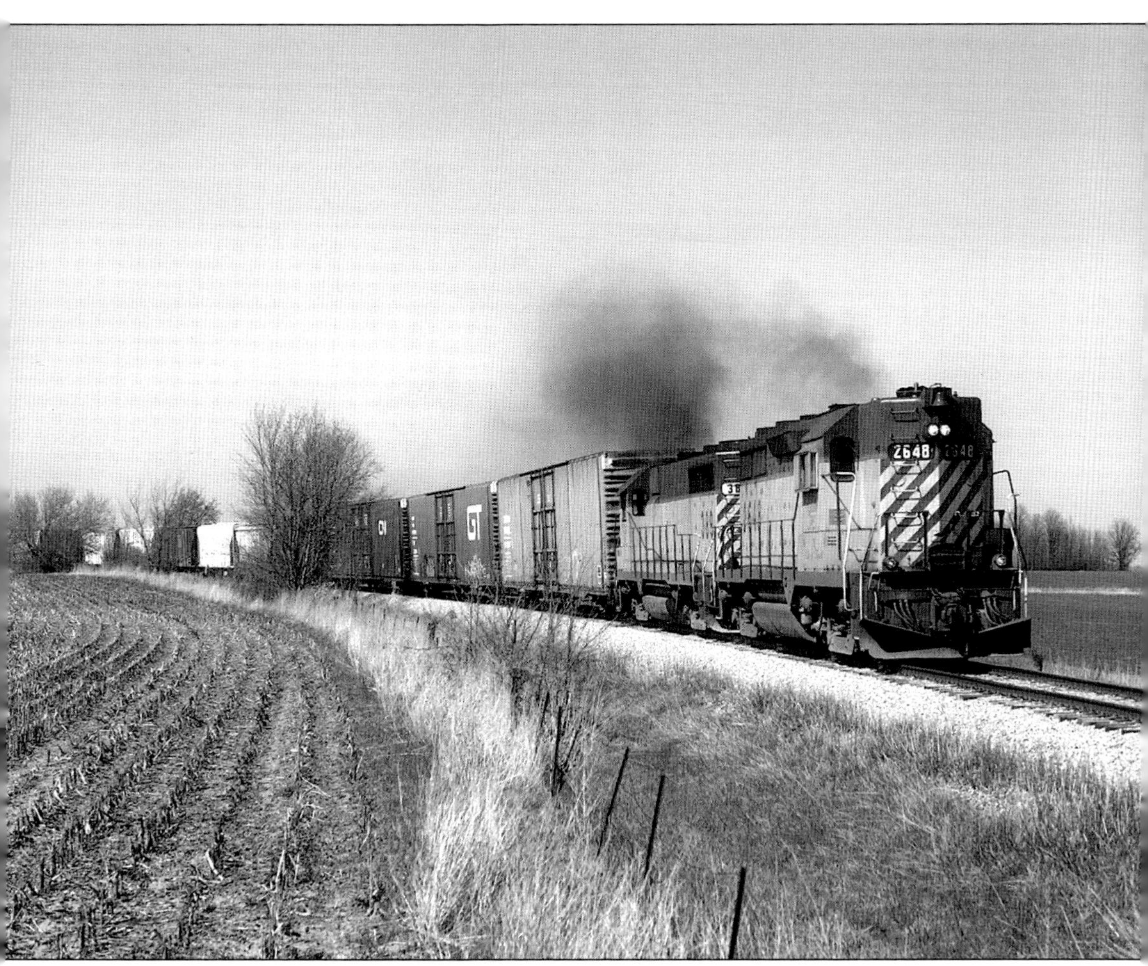

Past the Cornfields. In April 2002, two Tuscola & Saginaw Bay GP35 locomotives—#2648 and #389—make smoke as they pull a freight train through the farmlands of central Michigan on the rails of the former Ann Arbor Railroad. T&SB #2648, named *City of Howell*, is an ex-Southern Railway unit with a high hood, unlike the ex-Ann Arbor GP35s on the T&SB roster. A snowplow has been added to the front of #2648; it is designed to do battle with the snows sure to come again to Michigan within a few more months. (Photo by Dennis Schmidt.)

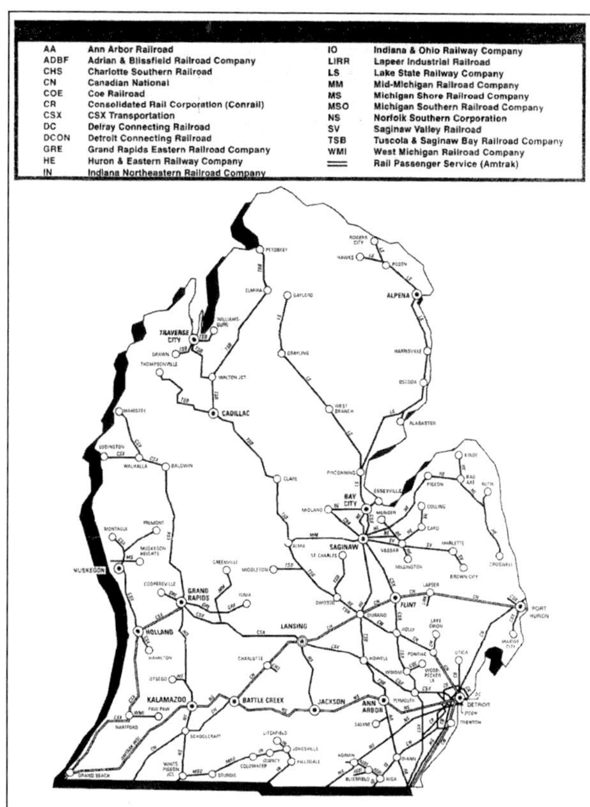

IN THE WAKE OF THE DOUBLE A. A map of the Lower Peninsula, showing the state's trackage as it existed c. 2002. Much of the Tuscola & Saginaw Bay is former Ann Arbor trackage, which the carrier began operating in 1982. The mainline heading southeast from Thompsonville to the Ohio line was all once part of the AA. South of the city of Ann Arbor is now the "new" Ann Arbor Railroad, which operates Ann Arbor-Toledo. (Courtesy of the Tuscola & Saginaw Bay Railway.)

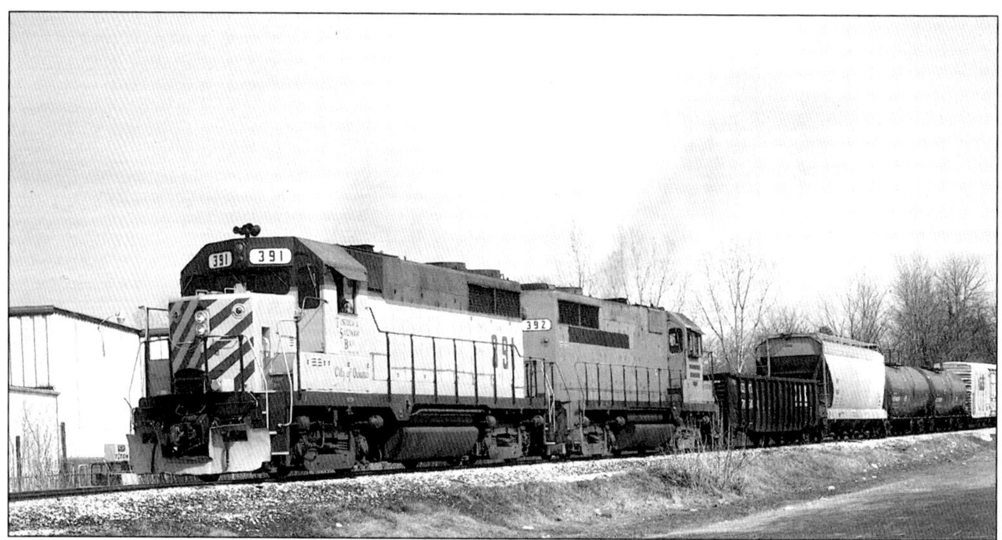

391 AND 392. Two former Ann Arbor GP35s, #391 and #392, pull a mixed freight through Alma on April 6, 1990. The second unit is still in the orange paint that instantly reveals its Ann Arbor Railroad heritage, although the words "Ann Arbor Railroad System" have been unceremoniously blacked out. GP35 #392 was soon to be painted into the same T&SB yellow and blue colors as displayed on its sister unit running in the lead here. (Photo by Dennis Schmidt.)

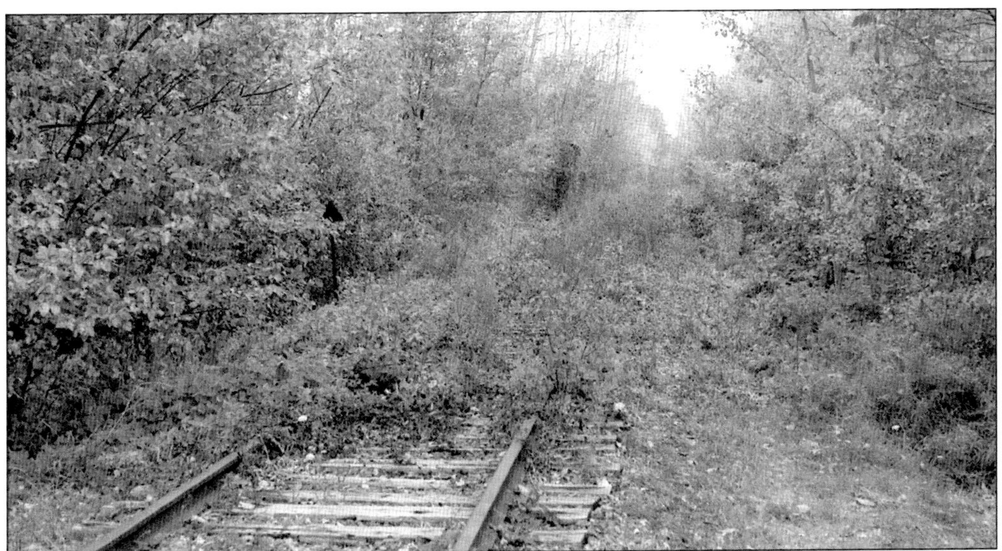

NEVERMORE. Until the early 1980s, the Ann Arbor Railroad's 292-mile line carried long, daily freight trains between Toledo and Elberta. After the trains stopped running here, however, weeds and trees begin taking over the unused mainline. Eventually, the AA's rails—seen here in 1992 adjacent to the Betsie Bay Campground, a few miles east of Elberta—vanished forever into the encroaching weeds. (Photo by D. C. Jesse Burkhardt.)

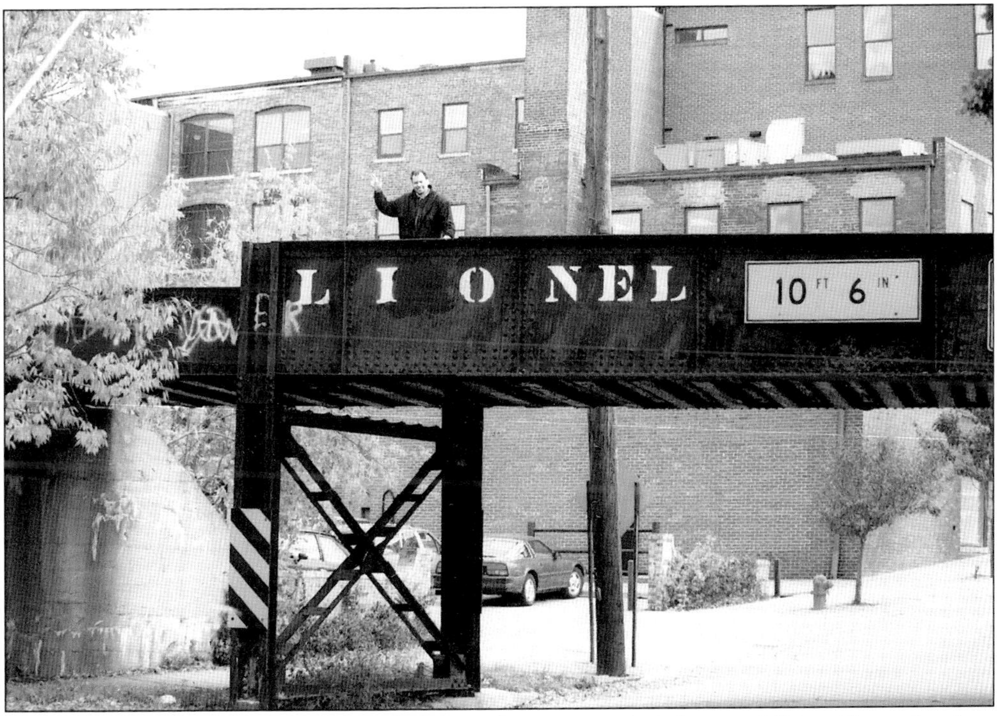

CAN'T YOU TAKE A JOKE? Some clever pranksters stenciled the word "Lionel" on the Ann Arbor Railroad's bridge over Washington Street in Ann Arbor in the early 1990s. The gag was probably good for the hobby businesses around town, although the railroad probably didn't appreciate the comparison. (Photo by D. C. Jesse Burkhardt.)

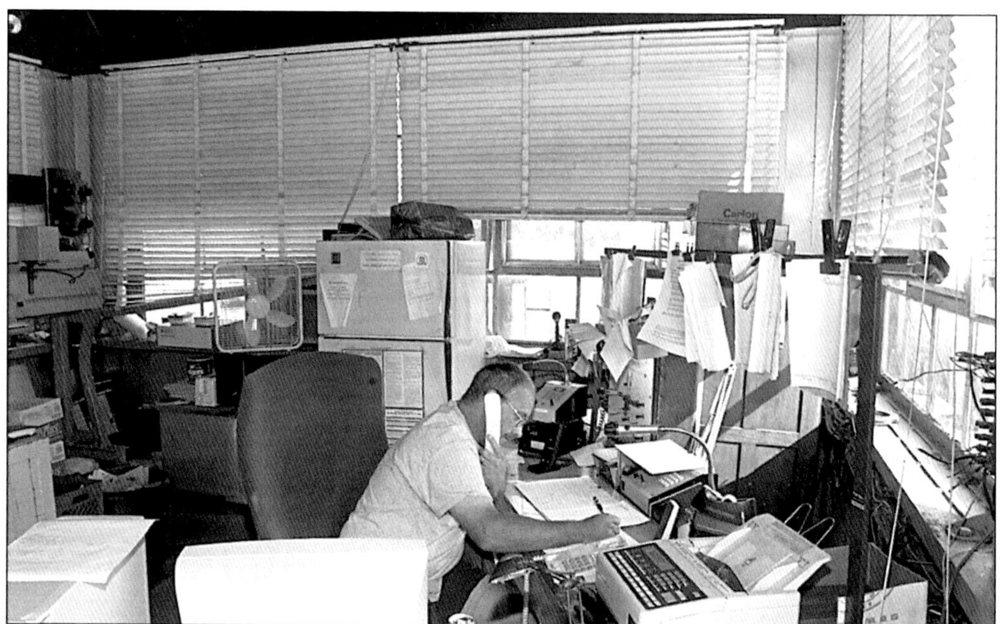

LOCAL NERVE CENTER. With bulletins and paperwork posted all around him, Sean Willis, the Ann Arbor Railroad's Hallett Tower operator in Toledo, talks with Norfolk Southern's Toledo dispatcher on July 16, 2002. Even in the "old" Ann Arbor Railroad days, Hallett was a key operations center. "All trains will register at Hallett and dispatcher's office, Owosso," reads one of the rules from the Ann Arbor Railroad's 1964 timetable. (Photo by Joseph Geronimo.)

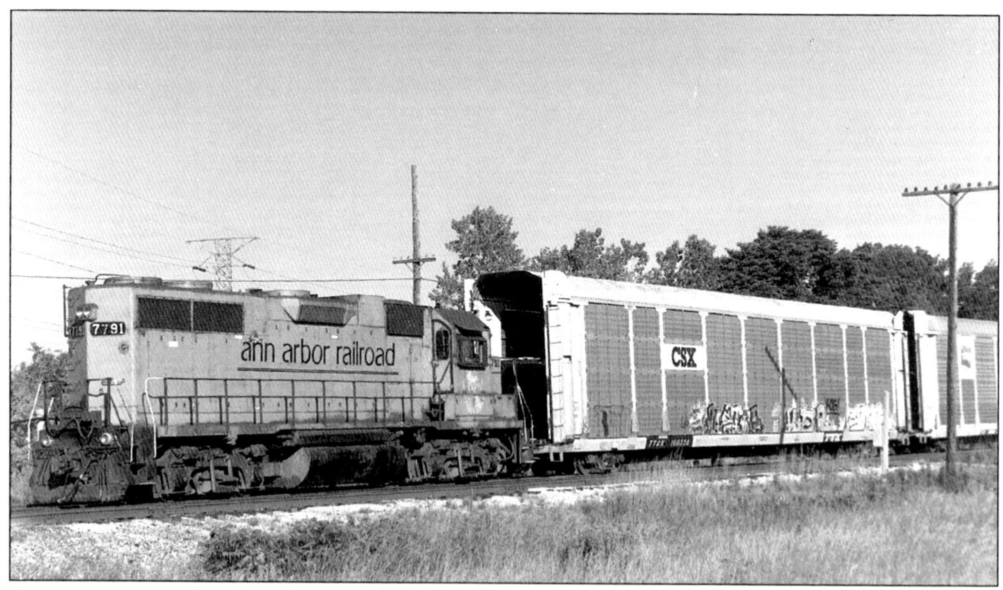

ON THE JOB IN OTTAWA YARD. The "new" Ann Arbor Railroad switches auto-racks in the AA's Ottawa Yard in Toledo in June 2000. The automobile industry is key to the shortline's success, with Ford, General Motors, and Daimler Chrysler all major shippers in Toledo. The Ann Arbor currently has three GP38s (#7771, #7791, and #7802; all ex-Conrail, same numbers) on its roster. All are in the AA's DT&I-era orange paint scheme —now minus the obsolete carferry logo. (Photo by Joseph Geronimo.)

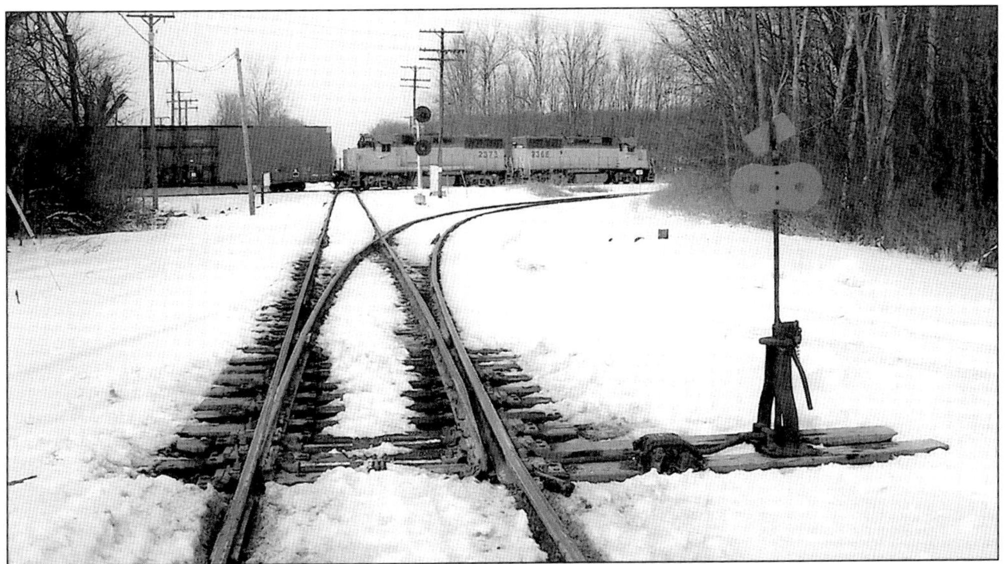

Back From Saline. Two Ann Arbor GP39-2s (ex-Union Pacific #2368 and #2373, purchased in August 2003) clatter across the Ann Arbor's main track at Pittsfield, Michigan, in this north-looking scene. The train is returning from the Visteon plant in Saline with a cut of nearly a dozen excess-height boxcars on a snowy March 4, 2005. The 86-foot boxcars carry vehicle parts. Visteon—the only active shipper on the 5.1-mile Saline Branch—sees trains twice a day, 5 days a week. (Photo by Kristian Foondle.)

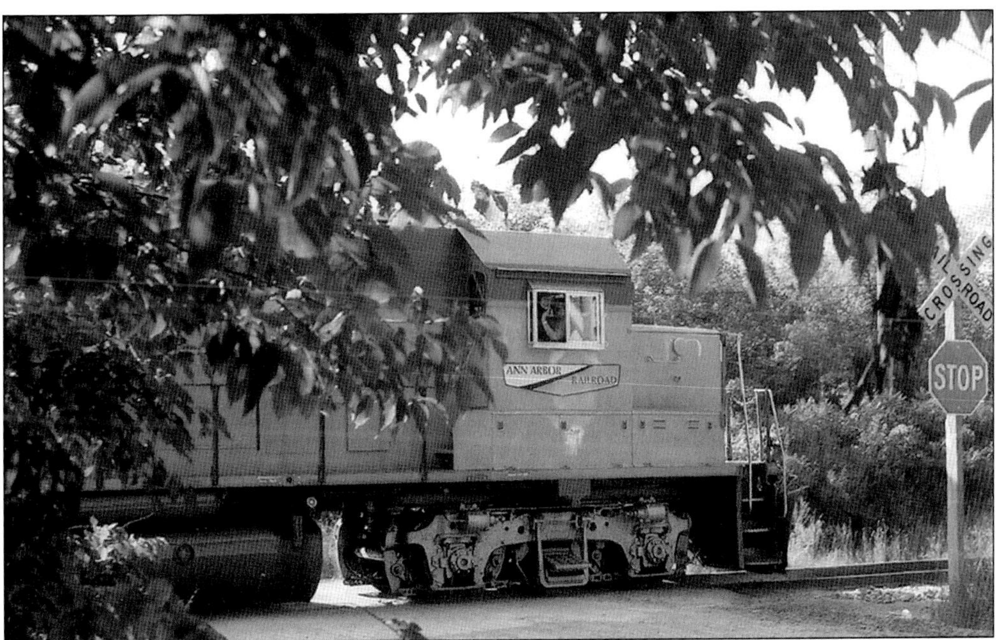

Still Rolling. The reconfigured, 50-mile shortline Ann Arbor Railroad still serves its namesake city from its base in Toledo. In this 2003 scene, one of the Ann Arbor's two GP39-2s emerges from the trees at the Traver Road crossing north of Ann Arbor with a friendly wave from a crew member. The train is headed to the Tuscola & Saginaw Bay interchange at Osmer, at Milepost 50.4. The shortline's new shield logo is plainly visible on the cab. (Photo by Chelsea White.)

The Ann Arbor Carferry Fleet
1892–1982

Ann Arbor #1: Launched in September 1892. Built by Craig Ship Building Company, Toledo, Ohio; 260 feet in length. Coal-fired. In service until 1910.

Ann Arbor #2: Launched in December 1892. Built by Craig Ship Building Company, Toledo, Ohio; 264 feet in length. Coal-fired. In service until 1912.

Ann Arbor #3: Launched in November 1898. Built by Globe Iron Works, Cleveland, Ohio; 258 feet in length. Coal-fired. In service until 1960.

Ann Arbor #4: Launched in November 1906. Built by Globe Iron Works, Cleveland, Ohio; 259 feet in length. Coal-fired. In service until 1937.

Ann Arbor #5: Launched in November 1910. Built by Toledo Shipbuilding Company, Toledo, Ohio; 360 feet in length. Coal-fired. In service until 1965.

Ann Arbor #6: Launched in January 1917. Built by Great Lakes Engineering Works, Ecorse, Michigan; 338 feet in length. Rebuilt and renamed *Arthur K. Atkinson* in 1959. Originally coal-fired; when rebuilt, converted to diesel. In service until 1982.

Ann Arbor #7: Launched in January 1925. Built by Manitowoc Shipbuilding Company, Manitowoc, Wisconsin; 347 feet in length. Rebuilt and renamed *Viking* in 1965. Originally coal-fired; when rebuilt, converted to diesel. In service until 1982.

Wabash: Launched in March 1927. Built by Toledo Shipbuilding Company, Toledo, Ohio; 366 feet in length. Rebuilt and renamed *City of Green Bay* in 1962. Originally coal-fired; when rebuilt, converted to oil-fired. In service until 1972.

City of Milwaukee: Launched in November 1930. Built by Manitowoc Shipbuilding Company, Manitowoc, Wisconsin, for the Grand Trunk Railway; 347 feet in length. For many years, the *City of Milwaukee* worked a Grand Trunk route between Muskegon, Michigan, and Milwaukee, Wisconsin. In 1978, this boat was leased (and later sold) to the state of Michigan for use by the Ann Arbor Railroad. Originally coal-fired; converted in 1947 to oil-fired. In service until 1981.

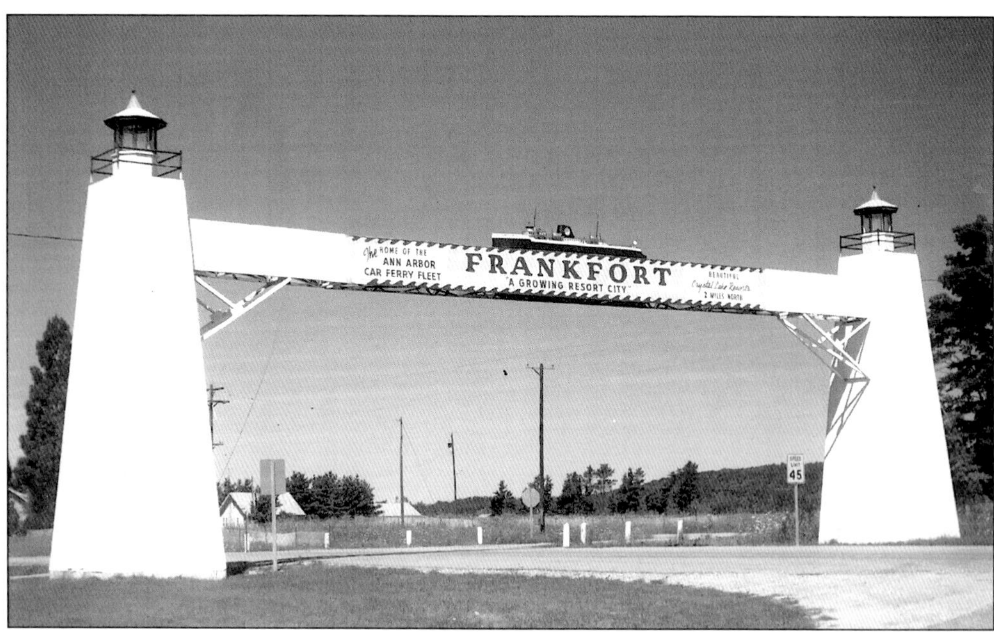

A COMMUNITY'S IDENTITY. Frankfort celebrated its carferries in many ways, but none were more touching than this impressive archway over M-115 at the Frankfort city limits. The arch proclaimed the city was "The Home of the Ann Arbor Carferry Fleet," and featured a scale model of one of the Ann Arbor's boats. (Photo by Dennis Schmidt.)